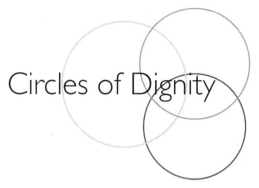

Circles of Dignity

Circles of Dignity

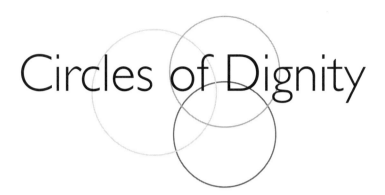

Community Wisdom and
Theological Reflection

James R. Cochrane

Fortress Press
Minneapolis

CIRCLES OF DIGNITY
Community Wisdom and Theological Reflection

Cover design by Marti Naughton
Cover illustration: *Amandla Ngawethu* by Jane Evershed, www.evershed.com. Used by permission.
Book design by Michelle L. Norstad

Library of Congress Cataloging-in-Publication Data

Cochrane, James R.
    Circles of dignity: community wisdom and theological reflection / James R. Cochrane.
        p.   cm.
    Includes bibliographical references.
    ISBN 0-8006-3182-X (pbk. : alk. paper)
    1. Theology, Doctrinal—South Africa. 2. Sociology, Christian—South Africa. I. Title.
BT30.S5C63 1999
230'.0968—dc21   99-36618
                                                                                    CIP

Manufactured in the U.S.A.   AF 1-3182

03   02   01   00   99   1   2   3   4   5   6   7   8   9   10

Contents

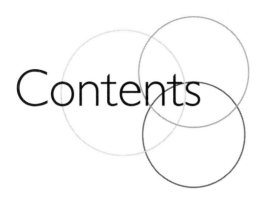

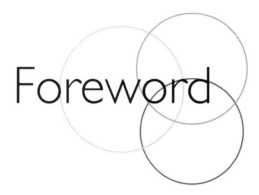

Foreword

The transition to democracy in South Africa during the final decade of the twentieth century captured the imagination of many throughout the world. Some of those who marveled at the remarkable turnaround in the fate of the nation were also aware of the role sections of the church played in enabling the transition to take place. President Nelson Mandela himself spoke of the church as a midwife of democratic change. Within the international ecumenical community there was also an awareness that a great deal of supporting theological reflection accompanied the church's participation in the struggle against apartheid. This was expressed in a significant number of confessing documents, liturgies of resistance, conference papers and resolutions, and the emergence of various contextual and liberation theologies, culminating in the Kairos Document. In many respects, South African theology came of age and began to make an impact elsewhere in the world.

The ending of statutory apartheid led to considerable soul searching among those Christians and churches that had shared in the struggle. What, they asked, is the mission of the church in a post-apartheid South Africa? By the same token, those engaged in critical theological reflection pondered whether or not they could do theology in a new key. How could theology help in the retrieval of a genuinely Christian faith and praxis in our new day of fresh opportunity? Was it possible, or even desirable, to break the mold of protest confessing theology with its strident "No" to oppression and begin to utter a positive, even if tentative, "Yes" to the attempt to procure reconciliation and achieve reconstruction?

Clearly, the awful legacy of apartheid still demands prophetic denunciation; equally clearly, the transition to democracy and the urgent task of transformation require affirmation and support. How, then, should the learnings of the struggle be taken up into the ongoing task of doing theology in a new historical epoch? This question is at the heart of James Cochrane's *Circles of Dignity,* a remarkably creative attempt to provide a model for theological endeavor in a "new South Africa" beyond apartheid, yet a country held to ransom by the destructive forces apartheid unleashed, underpinned by the ideological abuse of Christian dogma. Is it possible that this frightful legacy of colonial hegemony and apartheid legitimated by forms of Christian dogma can be overcome? If so, how?

By its very nature theology is a second-phase activity. It is, to use a traditional phrase, faith seeking understanding, or if you prefer, critical reflection on praxis. Christian faith expressing itself in love and justice, or communicative action, must always be primary. Doing theology is the attempt to explore, understand, and evaluate such praxis in dialogue with scripture, tradition, and with those disciplines that enable us to understand our present context. As such it is, or should be, an integral part of the universal endeavor to discern and articulate the truth that sets us and others free to live fully human lives. At the same time, participation in this universal project must be rooted in local experiences of reality, especially experiences of human suffering and the celebration of victories over oppression and despair.

Cochrane's project is, at one level, reflective of his own existential journey as a white South African male theologian. He has long since cast off the piety of evangelical adolescence and more recently the spiritual barrenness of so much political activism. But more significant in shaping the present direction of his theology has been the discovery of the wisdom and power of "popular religion" and what he refers to as "incipient theology" within an oppressed and marginalized black Christian community in violence-wracked KwaZulu-Natal. Led to them by one of his research students, Cochrane has, with due sensitivity, empathy as well as critical capacity, sought to rethink what it means to do theology both in the South African context and more generally.

Cochrane brings to this task all the skills he has accumulated as an academic theologian and a political activist over many years. A leading member of the Christian Institute in the 1970s, Cochrane was in part responsible for the establishment of the Institute for Contextual Theology (ICT), which made such a remarkable contribution to the theological struggle against apartheid. A signatory and advocate of the Kairos Document, published by ICT, Cochrane has subsequently made his mark as a leading professor of theology and pioneer of new initiatives in its teaching. *Circles of Dignity* is the fruit of his past reflection and engagement, the setting of an agenda, as well as the providing of a model for the task of theology in this time of transformation and reconstruction.

What is most remarkable about *Circles of Dignity* is Cochrane's ability to bring together in creative interaction the key loci of Christian tradition, contemporary hermeneutical debates, and the "incipient theology" of his reference community as it reads the Bible and ekes out an existence on the peripheries of society. There can be few texts that attempt, and even fewer that so successfully manage, to put all this together—and to do so in a way that is both lively and challenging. For my part, Cochrane has clearly signaled that theology, undertaken along such lines, remains of considerable importance for post-apartheid reconstruction and for enabling the church to discern its role and responsibility in that regard. But Cochrane has also done more. He has raised some searching, fundamental questions for all those engaged in the task of teaching and writing theology irrespective of their context, forcing us to take "incipient theologies" seriously if we are to do theology at all.

—*John W. de Gruchy*
Robert Selby Taylor Professor of Christian Studies
University of Cape Town

Preface

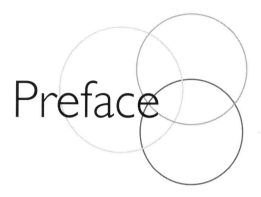

Much of the reflection I have carried out here depends upon encounters with a broad range of people whose lives have touched mine over many years, encounters that have shaped my interpretive interests. This was never a removed piece of research for me. It is a response to deeply felt concerns going back over three decades. Like many others, I have repeatedly had to face myself and my limited understanding of reality when confronted by the suffering of people who have lived the nightmare of apartheid. Equally, I have been repeatedly inspired by the spirit and the witness of those whom George Herbert Mead called "significant others," people who have struggled for a better life, for a just order, and for a meaningful peace on earth.

Long ago, I was told that the key to life was the love of Jesus and that the things of this world were transient and ultimately unimportant. As I grew older, the social and human reality around me made this claim questionable. So did one particular biblical text. Jesus is reported to say that the love of God, of our neighbor, and of ourselves is the sum of all commandments, the point of everything. What then does it mean to speak of love in a context of such profound suffering and social evil as was apartheid South Africa? Beginning from a purely personalist perspective and finding it inadequate to answer this question, I began a long search for an adequate theological response to this question. This book is merely a resting place along the way. Its antecedents thus lie deeply in the past even as they are explored in a new present.

That search has proved to be filled with ambiguity and doubt. During these many years I found myself becoming increasingly suspicious, despite my basic loyalty to both the church and my Christian beliefs. One great contradiction has run through it all. On the one hand, everywhere I turned I have encountered Christians who had "journeyed with Jesus" into the heart of the apartheid monster in order to join those who struggled to overcome the beast. On the other hand, to my dismay and confusion, I also found that great institutions of the church, many theological centers, and all too many Christians in positions of leadership, were openly hostile to those religiously inspired anti-apartheid activists with whom I now journeyed; or if not hostile, then not present. Indeed, even among those who presented themselves as part of the anti-apartheid struggle, all too often many acted and spoke with untoward timidity and unholy caution in the face of the pervasive evils that apartheid spawned.

For this reason I have learned to appreciate and value the lives and contributions of those people of faith who had the courage and the vision both to enter into the struggle against oppression and injustice, and to do so without being overcome by the sad contradictions, debilitating frustrations, and profound doubt they have had to endure.

This, however, is perhaps not the place to acknowledge the many "significant others" whose lives and witness never failed to call mine into question for its lack of courage or integrity, those who simultaneously offered living examples of courage and integrity. I do not know when or if I shall ever be able to name them all publicly, but it has been a privilege to feel their indelible imprint on my life. In this respect I acknowledge my debt to them, my conviction that the history of the labor and struggle of such people must be taken as a sine qua non of the efforts of any one of us in our attempts to build or define a new future. In calling to mind this history, I also wish to recognize those upon whom this work depends more directly.

First, and above all, I owe an enormous debt to members of the local community with whom I had contact in Amawoti, in particular the Ilimo Primary Health Care Project, its management committee, and their resident Bible study facilitator, Graham Philpott. Their lives and reflections, as expressed in their Bible studies, are the prime inspiration for this book. Philpott's facilitation of the Bible study sessions of the Amawoti base ecclesial community produced most of the texts that are the foundation of my own interpretive efforts in this work. In fact, he was the one who made them available to me, with the agreement of the local controlling committee. Through my attempt to listen to these people—to understand what is going on among them—I have had to question many of my long-standing presuppositions, prejudices, and purposes as a theologian and a Christian. In the final analysis, that is what this book is about.

In addition, Martin Mandew provided substantial help as my research assistant, as well as through his own research in 1993 in Amawoti, "Power and Empowerment: Religious Imagination and the Life of a Local Base Ecclesial Community." He was more than willing to give his time and energy to the community in Amawoti, and he went far beyond what I could have expected of him. This undoubtedly made a great difference to the quality of the research material he helped me gather. More importantly, his style of participatory research exemplifies a strong accountability to the lives of his subjects, a style that has long extended his personal relationship with the community. For this I honor him.

Other students and colleagues have added considerably to what I have learned. In this sense, they shape the book even if they are not responsible for its content. Key among them are Megan Walker, whose supervised study on Mariology with women in the community of Mpophomeni, Natal, is full of helpful insights. Gerald West, friend and frequent coresearcher, whose enthusiasm for hermeneutics and for life in general is contagious, pushed me to undertake this book in the first place and made valuable contributions along the way.

Other friends and colleagues have read chapters of the manuscript or commented on parts of the work leading up to this book. They have helped me develop my thoughts beyond what I could have done alone. They have guided me in ways large and small, helping to improve many aspects of the book. Among them: Denise Ackermann, Tony Balcomb, Renate Cochrane, Philippe Denis, Volker Drehsen, Juan Garcés, John de Gruchy, Albrecht Hieber, Ted Jennings, Chris Langefelt, Tim Long, Douglas McGaughey, Klaus Nürnberger, Robin Petersen, Herman Waetjen, and Vitor Westhelle. I am grateful too for the willingness of others who would like to have read the manuscript but could not find the time within my time frame. I thank them all for their interest and support, while acknowledging that they can neither guarantee the end product nor be held responsible for whatever weaknesses it exhibits.

Two postgraduate classes at the University of Natal have also had to bear the brunt of my often frustrating efforts to work out my thoughts in class. For their comments, criticisms, and participation, I owe a special debt of gratitude.

For the opportunity to share these ideas and have them criticized, I would like to thank the following institutions: Chicago Theological Seminary, San Francisco Theological Seminary, Graduate Theological Union in Berkeley, Willamette University in Oregon, Tübingen University in Germany, and the universities of Zürich and Berne in Switzerland. In respect of the latter two, my particular thanks to Leni Altwegg and Albrecht Hieber for making possible the running of two block seminars on this research, as well as Professors Werner Kramer and Wolfgang Lienemann, respectively, for hosting these seminars.

For financial support, I wish to thank the University of Natal, which gave me the opportunity to take sabbatical leave and contributed to the research costs during this time; the Center for Science Development, Pretoria, for the grant that paid for much of my work overseas; and the Human Sciences Research Council, which supported initial empirical research. Thanks also go to my colleagues at the School of Theology, Pietermaritzburg, who had to bear the administrative and teaching burden in my absence.

The work presented here is my responsibility alone. No institution listed above is responsible—nor should they be held accountable—for the ideas or arguments put forth.

Finally, my family and friends helped me believe that this work was worth doing, though they were not always sure that I was giving them equitable time and attention in return. I hope that they will enjoy the fact that it is over, and rejoice with me that its publication means, in Ricoeur's terms, that the author is now dead (no longer able to influence the outcome) and that the reader must do the work. And in that grace, I dedicate this book to my youngest child, Tebo, whose name means joy and who is just that.

Introduction
A Journey within Boundaries

It was a small journey in April 1994. A woman in her early eighties, determination on her face, eyes wrinkled in the harsh midlands sun, marched to cast her vote in South Africa's first democratic elections. Methodically she trekked for five hours across the mountainous hills of KwaZulu-Natal, her feet shuffling along in the dirt, occasionally resting her arched back by leaning on a crooked stick. She arrived at the polling station on the wrong day. It was the day for special votes only; she was one day too early. Tired and disappointed, she meandered down the dusty road on her long journey back home again.

The next day the old woman made the journey once more, this time successfully. For the first time in her life, she cast a vote for her own government. Satisfied with her efforts, she declared, "At last I am a human being."

Hers was a Lilliputian voice, one among countless more like it. Her journey was only one step in what will be a much longer journey for the country as a whole. So long set aside, her voice now counted.

African history is filled with stories of small but great journeys that have become legend. Some are as long ago as Moses' journey out of Egypt with the Hapiru slaves, some as recent as David Livingstone's journey into the Zimbabwean and Zambian interior. Many have been the purposes of African journeys: to trade and explore, to war and enslave, to settle and flee.

Whether people have journeyed out of or into Africa, across from east to west or from north to south, this vast and variable continent has been romanticized and admired, demonized and denigrated. For some it is the original source and an ongoing experience of humanity. For others it is the basket case of the

world and a place of savagery. However one looks at it, Africa is unquestionably in deep pain. The suffering of its people is manifest, often searing in its intensity and frightening in its scope.

Africa, it must be said, has its own responsibility to bear in this respect. Yet the slave trade and the scramble for Africa by colonial powers wreaked havoc with the peoples and places of Africa. Decolonization and the rise of new, independent African nations promised some health to the African body. But the patterns of conquest and the effects of direct and indirect imperial rule were not easily washed away, and secondary infections—dictatorships, religious and ethnic wars, and corruption on a grand scale—have made the task all the more difficult.

The story of South Africa is similar, in many respects the generic example of what has been experienced across Africa.[1] It is by now a well-known story that requires no summary here. My story takes place in South Africa, and it is both a personal journey as well as a reflection of the journey of a local base ecclesial community. To be confronted with the faith of black South Africans in the face of oppression, poverty, and discrimination is, in the provocative Christological imagery of Takatso Mofekeng, to recognize "the crucified among the cross-bearers."[2]

It is a Christian claim that there is no path to the resurrection of life except by way of the cross, through a confrontation with the forces of death. These forces are manifest in Africa. Here religious experience forms a vital center to life, where the seen and the unseen are not treated as separate or incompatible realities, where ancestors who have gone before are honored and made part of the present for the sake of the future.

A religious milieu of this kind may seem captive to the past or subject to the hegemonies of the present. Yet religion often is to African people themselves a source of life and practical hope—perhaps even a victory in myriad small spheres of daily life and activity over would-be conquerors and rescuers. There is much more here than the opium of the oppressed, whether we mean a state of drugged confusion or, as Karl Marx did, a soothing medication applied to a festering wound.

The importance of local religious experience among the suffering and the marginalized shapes key questions in this book, which seeks to understand the significance of religious insights drawn from daily struggles in a local community. It does so by examining their interpretative activity in local Bible studies carried out over several years, readings that formed the reflexive basis of much communicative action and practical involvement in the suffering of their own people.

An Act of Listening

In this work I have attempted to listen to the members of a base ecclesial community (BEC),[3] or at least their voices as recorded in transcriptions of their Bible study meetings. It is a poor community where resources are few and daily life a burden for most.

My act of listening, of course, inevitably changes what was originally expressed, casting it in a different key and with a different purpose. What I report is therefore no longer the pristine voice of this community. This raises many questions about my relation to the originating voices, and it directs us to a vital dynamic lying beneath the surface of all conversations bedeviled by unequal relations of power, and to the dichotomy of the self and the other. We are forced, I argue, to come to terms in our theological reflection and practices with the fundamental instability of dialogue between unequal or unfamiliar partners. We must face many questionable claims about such dialogues, whether these claims are made in research processes or not. How we do so is another part of the book.

Still, despite the inherently unstable nature of this act of listening, it remains important. Precisely because it is neglected, the subjugated voice, suppressed for a while, bursts forth again in dissonant and dissident ways, sometimes with deep effects on the health of society as a whole. The "insurrection of subjugated knowledges" (Michel Foucault) points to a phenomenon we seldom grasp adequately, that of the social significance of the suppressed presence (perhaps analogous to the surreptitious work of the unconscious on the conscious). This issue must also be considered in its implications for the theological enterprise.

The strategic point of this book is to challenge, from a particular location, the dominant discourses in global theology. In this sense, it is a deeply ecumenical venture in theological thinking, not a study of a local community pleading their case. Voice rather than context predominates. The voice here, often regarded as unsophisticated, is usually seen as a minor consumer or contributor of theological ideas, the voice of an outsider.

Ordinary believers, in their original experiences of faith and their practical reflection on daily life, however unsophisticated or flawed their theology, confront us with issues and challenges too seldom incorporated into the formal theological work of the Christian community. Listening to this voice (which may be found in every context, and for which Amawoti is a cipher rather than an exception) drives us to consider more than ethical questions. It affects our understanding of the church and its theological foundations, and thus the way we practice and teach theology, practice ministry, and exercise leadership.

Ambiguities and Contradictions

Who are the so-called ordinary believers? The empirical work, done in collaboration with colleagues and students, was conducted in and with a local BEC in the informal settlement called Amawoti. Amawoti is part of a much larger conglomeration of similar settlements in Inanda near the subtropical coastal city of Durban. Poverty, unemployment, lack of infrastructure and services, violence, and political marginalization characterize the conditions that govern the lives of this community—a familiar litany in South Africa as in many other parts of the "Third (or two-thirds) World."

Suffice it to note for the moment that the members of that community have shaped much more than this text. They have significantly altered my ways of thinking and being in the world, as they have those of my colleagues and our students. They have refashioned our vision of the church and its gospel. What was altered and why? That question may be seen as the core of this book. Partly it has to do with what it means to develop a credible interface between theologically trained Christians and ordinary believers, between clergy who represent authority and laity who do not, between the academy and marginalized local communities. Clearly, this is uncomfortable territory, but one that is vital and of wide significance.

Less visible in this book is an internal struggle to grasp in writing some surer vision of life in the midst of the realities of death. In the last years of living in Pietermaritzburg and the province of KwaZulu-Natal, the reality of death has been horribly present: The machinations of Bantustan politics and the last violent spasms of apartheid killed many people and wrought great harm, leaving a legacy not yet overcome of hate, revenge, distrust, and fear. Yet, in the midst of daily atrocities and waves of hate, there are powerful signs of whole, healing life. This has been evident in Amawoti.

The dichotomy between the sources of life and the forces of death, between hope and fate, and between agency and impotence is present in this work. Dealing with these dichotomies in a manner sensitive to our own implication in hurting, failing, or disempowering ordinary people is thus a framing issue for the conclusions I draw.

Defining the Journey

In an earlier work, I wrote of the church as a "site of struggle."[4] Where I then focused on the structural location of churches in the contradictions of a colonial, capitalist economy, I now turn, with rather different tools, toward the contradictions in the church itself, in its institutional patterns, processes, and theological constructs. The move is from macro-analytical categories, which deal with large social aggregates and systems, to local contexts and micro-symbolic worlds and life practices.

My concern is with the church as it is understood and experienced at the local level. There are two major reasons for this concern: First, contextual theologians, like other theologians and trained intellectuals generally, are not free of the ambiguities of knowledge and power, of affluence and status. Their interactions with each other, dominant representatives of the churches to which they belong, and other intellectuals easily leave them in control of theological discourse, and untrained believers on its margins. This is so even when such theologians can demonstrate strong connections to a local community. Second, the work that contextual theologians do may well be important in the public contestation of dominant, oppressive hegemonies, but what is done well at these "higher" public levels needs to be rooted in and redirected toward the less-visible local level. An ecumenically engaged theology requires this, as does a theology genuinely related to the faith and experience of local communities.

Key theological and important tactical questions are at stake in realizing this double agenda. These have to do with the difficulties and complexities of overcoming the huge gaps between thoughts and practices of those represented in the public by others and those who represent them. Multiple hermeneutical, ethical, and dogmatic questions accompany the attempt to find a resolution to these questions. A response is necessary, but I have become convinced that no particular response ends the questioning. Indeed, as virtually all the great theologians of our century have demonstrated, question marks remain a decisive part of an adequate theology for our time. What I have written here, then, is necessarily a discourse about processes and possibilities rather than a fixed solution to anything.

Key Themes

The first and most important theme is that of voice. I begin my reflections with a simple question: Given the search for a people's theology in the last few decades, at least among Christians in the struggle against apartheid, who are the people? How are they construed? Whence comes their voice? And, how do we know what their voice is?

The various theologies of liberation, whether self-designated as black, African, prophetic, feminist, or contextual, all assume such a voice. All make various claims based upon the authenticity of this voice. Yet it is not often clear whose voice is meant. Nor is it clear who really speaks when a theology supposedly represents the voice of others. There are, for example, a number of voices in South Africa, but in almost all cases the true voices of most Christians gathered in one or another African-initiated church remain severely reduced, if not simply absent.

This kind of contradiction contains further conundrums. For example, if there is in fact a multiplicity of voices, does one privilege any particular voice, and if so, on what basis? All of the theologies I have named preferentially privilege one or another voice, according to the particular commitment and framework of the theology concerned. Whether this preference is described in terms of blackness, Africanness, poorness, womanness, or any other analogues by which oppression is identified and challenged, the question remains.

Besides a need to understand why this should be so, and on what theological or other grounds, we face also the problem of a plurality of voices as a fact of the Christian community. How are these connected to each other, and what is the nature of the connection? Is there an edification of the Body of Christ at work with each particular contribution part of an organic whole; or is there merely a confusing and finally unresolvable conflict of interpretations, as many external critics of Christianity would suggest? Here one may discern the underlying question of power. Voices are not disembodied sounds reaching us through an empty ether. Bodies speak, persons speak, and these persons are located socially and economically in multiple matrices of power, each of which constrains and affects their speech. For this reason, even silence may be a communicative act.

Each and every communicative act has its particular material context. Two elements of this situation cause concern. First, in the dialogue between Amawoti BEC members and the group's facilitator, who has authority and a measure of control, what constrains either party's speech? What is not said? What changes in the act of communication so that nothing heard is quite what was meant? How do different social locales, and sources and forms of power (or lack thereof) affect this speech? What of the dialogue result can be trusted?

Second, because I write as a Christian and a trained theologian, my text necessarily engages with texts of the past. While the Christian tradition begins with Scripture, other aspects of our common identity are rarely agreed upon. Sometimes disagreement reaches the fundamental level. Our tradition evolved well beyond Scripture, thereby forming a deposit of further identity claims. To these competing claims we normally attach names, such as Catholic, Lutheran, Methodist, and so on. Some carry more weight than others, but it is not always clear to an independent observer why they should.

What does tradition mean for those theologically untrained, marginalized Christians who make up the Bible study group whose texts I interpret? Even more pertinently, what does their reflection on faith mean for the heavy weight of Christian tradition that surrounds them, much of that, if they are aware of it, may be unattractive or lacking meaning? Can they contribute to the formation of these traditions? If so, on what grounds and under what conditions? How will they be taken seriously?

These questions come back to voice, locale, and power. Between me and the community whose dialogues I seek to reflect upon, between them and their trained Bible study facilitator, there are boundaries. There are boundaries between the BEC's reflection on faith, or their incipient theology, and the theologies deposited as dogmas in one or another tradition they encounter or I represent for them. And, between church powers and those who live outside these circles of power, there are boundaries. These boundaries, sometimes murky and often strong, separate us from each other, create distance, and establish difference.

Boundaries: Uncovering Difference, Overcoming Distance

Differences created by boundaries inevitably raise questions about the involved parties' respective identities. Identity can in turn be related to questions of space, place, and location. Postmodernist feminist hermeneutics has taken the question up with special force, using metaphors of cartography, geography, and architecture to explore the identity of the self. In this context, the notion of boundaries, how they are constructed and changed, and how they define us or destabilize us, is a metaphor particularly fruitful for this discussion.

All around us, boundaries are established, maintained, shifted, transgressed, ruptured, and, occasionally, overcome. Sometimes visible and conscious, very often hidden and semiconscious, these boundaries and the struggles over them need to be discerned and understood if we are to treat seriously the human and divine imperatives to seek reconciliation and act in love.

Differences in beliefs and practices also enter into the distance across boundaries, and these differences are not always easily reconciled. Let us take, for example, the kind of community whose daily life and religious faith constitute the starting point of the questions with which this book deals. Its members frequently experience the teachings and the discipline of denominational churches as boundaries that separate them, marginalize them, diminish their voice for a means to an end defined by others, and reduce their needs to an occasion for charity. Orthodoxies might well be, and often are in such contexts, sufficiently different from local experiences and expressions of faith as to become alienating, building barriers rather than understanding. The formal, institutional presence of the Church, as denominations primarily, is then easily experienced as oppressive or, at the least, repressive.

The judgment of the church as yet another dominating institution alongside the many others that determine so much of the lives of poor and marginalized groups of people may be contested, but its validity may be found in the vast number of Christians who choose to belong to African-initiated Churches (AICs). These are churches whose origin lies outside the missionary churches from the North who played such a key role in establishing Christianity in southern Africa. They began as breakaway movements from "mainline" denominations toward the end of the nineteenth century (in the so-called "Ethiopian" movement), but now include a vast array of Pentecostal churches (often referred to as

"Zionist" or "Zionist-Apostolic" churches). The latter have arisen almost entirely within African communities around charismatic leaders who have encountered Christian teachings or texts in some way or another. For most of this century, except in the early years when the Ethiopian movement was seen as a potential threat to white rule, AICs have been ignored by denominational churches and even, to some extent, by ecumenical groups.

The relative marginalization of AICs within the broad range of denominational ecumenical bodies is an uncontested fact, though the reasons for this state of affairs may be attributed differently by diverse analysts. Their very existence, however shaped by class and cultural factors, expresses a judgment about boundaries, the identities they circumscribe, the protection they may offer, and the pain they may constitute.

It seems to me clear that one must look more closely at the kind of religious experience involved in popular expressions of faith in relation to the boundaries that exist there: their nature, their rationale, their limits, and their liberating character. Why do ordinary believers think in certain ways and how do they relate their thinking and their daily life through patterns of belief and conviction? What may people like myself learn from this?

A community such as the one I interrogate here stands on one side of the boundary created by the denominational churches, whose history and traditions I most clearly represent in my own experience and training. Distinct spheres of life and experience between us are discernible as different practices and understandings of Christian faith. This difference is defined on the side of the denominational churches in fixed confessions, creeds, and dogmas against which those on the other side are measured or, as often happens, measure themselves.

We may—and do—describe this boundary in terms of the difference between experienced faith (*fides qua creditur* or *Glaube*) and the ecclesially authorized teachings of the correct or "true" faith (*fides quae creditur* or *Glaubenslehre*). The relationship of *Glaube* to *Glaubenslehre*, sometimes complicated by suspicions among ecclesial authorities of *Aberglaube* (superstition) amongst those who appear to challenge or ignore "right teaching," has frequently been addressed in the history of Christian thought. We revisit it here in the recognition, in Africa, as elsewhere no doubt, that authorized teachings are to many people a constraint, a parentally stern voice which sets up boundaries that become fixed, opaque, and ultimately destructive of the church.

Constraint may work by pummeling a person's conscience, judging him or her deficient. It may also work through a closed understanding of tradition, exorcizing or expelling those who step outside the circle of "true believers." Control over a particular identity is often the reason for this, as are the maintenance of authority and the survival of an institution. There may therefore be both positive and negative reasons for the inflexibility of particular religious traditions. Equally, however, one finds again and again a contrasting experience of faith that brings its own insights and wisdom without bondage to a particular doctrine. The powerful appeal of charismatic and Pentecostal churches evidences this impulse. It also points to faith as the source of doctrine and not the other way around.

Doctrine, or teaching expressed as particular readings of Christian tradition, has another side to it, however. It reflects the attempt to understand and learn from experience. In Christianity perhaps more than anywhere else, the human mind as a gift of God with its own cocreative potentiality drives the believer to translate the experience of faith into forms of thought, into understandable formulations and concepts that communicate the significance of belief for the world in its history. This universal, communicative impulse is the source of texts and written traditions that, again and again, break the immediacy of experience to make specific claims about the world and about human beings. These claims are not confined to the Christian community but are intended to be significant for and are embedded in practices that attempt to reach all human beings.

This intention elicits an encounter with otherness, interaction with those people who do not necessarily accept the claims that are made, or the form in which they are made. Christians, therefore, feel compelled not only to make their claims but to protect their identity. Authorized teachings and fixed texts (particularly Scripture, but also particular doctrines or liturgical formulae) become the primary means for protecting that identity. Yet, authorized teachings, relying on the past and on a partial history, cannot adequately cover the experience of faith in the present, including the altered understandings that arise in the new experience of faith. The tension between the experience of faith and the teachings by which that faith finds its identity is thus ineluctable, irreducible, unending. It is that which forces the believer again and again to reinterpret the tradition. In fact, it is the creative wellspring of Christian theology and the dynamic that drives it forward.

This particular theme is of special importance to my consideration of the incipient theology of the Amawoti BEC. The boundaries generated by confessions and denominational identities tend to marginalize a community such as this in respect of the social whole, parallel to other forms of marginalization in the economic and political spheres. In turn, it engages in a wide range of "arts of resistance"[5] to the imposed boundaries, some more conscious than others. As James C. Scott suggests, these arts of resistance often remain hidden from those who exercise powers of domination, or they might be disguised so as to avoid or minimize the negative consequences of an open challenge to domination. Yet until that which is hidden or disguised enters more consciously and overtly into the public sphere, the boundaries will remain relatively stable and their negative effects relatively unchanged.

The accounting I give here of the interpretative activity of the Amawoti BEC exposes the problems and uncovers the weaknesses of what appears to be a dialogue between equals where boundaries to understanding and mutuality are assumed in principle to be absent or minimal. Ironically, this accounting exposes the fragility of my own interpretation. What is in it for the Amawoti BEC? Why should they allow anyone to breach the boundaries they have erected to protect themselves? What control, if any, did I have over the breaching of their boundaries?

In order to minimize the effects of this problem, it was necessary to make clear my own intellectual, academic, and strategic interests in reading the texts of the BEC, and to have permission to undertake this work with those interests declared and accepted, even if provisionally. Permission was given, but this is less the point.

The BEC representatives with whom these negotiations took place were suspicious about my role (researcher), specific location (a university), status (a trained academic and, in some sense, a church authority), power (control over the way in which knowledge is produced and reproduced), and integrity (whose interests would dominate in the end?). They decided in the end to entrust themselves to the process after sufficient discussion and clarification. Over time, they came to learn that my research assistants could be trusted, yet their suspicion remained.

And so it should. The truth is that specific factors that give rise to suspicion (role, location, status, power, and integrity) have not changed—and normally do not change—very much. They form a permanent complex of characteristics which, if they are to be managed openly and constructively rather than be allowed to function covertly and subversively, must also be addressed methodologically, that is, as a determinative part of the communicative process and its unfolding. This, too, is an important theme in the book.

Sensitive and Sensible Engagement

The incipient theology—a concept still to be defined—of a local BEC is my starting point. In the viewpoints that follow the incipient theology is examined from differing analytical perspectives. Systematization has not been my primary goal. Instead I have sought to probe the problems of contextual theology by exploring the same phenomenon with different lenses—incipient theology, tradition, power, speaking with the other, and a *Gestalt* of theology—each lens cohering around a particular emphasis. This method fulfills another intrinsic role, namely, destabilizing the systematizing rationality formal theology is so fond of and that so easily becomes a means of control over the wisdom of local communities and ordinary believers.

For whom is this book written then? The audience uppermost in my mind are who have a reasonably solid training in theology; who enter into dialogue with or at least take an interest in other disciplines; who have a responsibility for training, forming, leading, or influencing future generations of Christian leadership; and who share a commitment to theology as a transformative process of faithful reflection on praxis in the world. My experience is that many such people ask questions similar to mine, and for similar reasons: It matters to the way they, the churches, and Christians generally deal with the material, human, and spiritual contradictions of a broken world.

Contextual theologians constitute a second part of the audience. Here my questions aim at shifting gear from a context in which much was learned during struggles against oppression and for liberation to one where the construction of a new society has become possible and necessary. The blind spots and impasses of the past have left us with many unanswered questions about commitment, engagement, identity, representation, voice, popular religion, tradition, and power.

Yet another segment of the audience are academics, skilled theologians, shapers of sophisticated theological arguments—those whose influence is most profound in determining what is researched, which questions count, and why. These are the intellectual leaders of the church, and though popular mythology often sees them as disembodied minds in an ivory tower, they have a considerable significance in shaping the discourses that determine doctrine and ecclesial practice.

This audience is important to me because the case I make for taking incipient theologies seriously can be argued on grounds that leave suspect foundations of the theological enterprise untouched. One could easily provide ethical grounds for listening to the Amawoti BEC on the basis of a moral responsibility to local communities, particularly those who are marginalized or suffer oppression. Equally, doctrinal arguments can easily be brought to bear through the strong warrants in the Christian tradition which support a strong and positive view of the *sensus fidei*, the faith of ordinary people. I wish to go further, to suggest philosophical or foundational arguments for the question of the intellectual significance, the human value, and the social importance of the wisdom and experiences of ordinary people.

The importance of the voices and reflections on the margins, precisely because they are marginalized, requires, I believe, a strategic intervention in those hegemonic ("taken for granted") discourses that frame "right" or "correct" interpretations of faith, and that judge other discourses accordingly. Such intervention needs to be sound enough to break open some space that was not there, to force respect and attention; and it needs to be strong enough to provide encouragement to those who are otherwise intimated by dominant discourse

practices. The point of the work, then, is to draw from an interpretation of the readings of this one local community a set of theoretical perspectives that may be meaningfully placed before the church at large. It seeks to spell out the parameters for our time and for many places of a sensitive and sensible engagement with the practical faith and local wisdom of ordinary believers, against any new colonization—material or spiritual—of their life worlds.

1. Salt Stops Ghosts
Context and Scope of Local Wisdom

In matters of religion, as of art, there are no "simpler" people. . . . [The human being's] "imaginative" and "emotional" life is always and everywhere rich and complex. . . . It is not a matter of different cognitive structures, but of an identical cognitive structure articulating wide diversities of cultural experience.
—Victor Turner[1]

Victor Turner suggests that human beings all share an identical cognitive structure, the diversity of our thought patterns being simply the result of different histories, different linguistic and cultural contexts. If Turner is correct, then we have no *a priori* grounds by which to privilege a particular stream of history or a specific cultural framework above another. Certainly we cannot lay claim, as has often been done on the part of those who brought European traditions, customs, and epistemologies to Africa, to its greater wisdom on the grounds of the alleged primitive, undeveloped, or simple perspectives of indigenous Africans.

We can make instructive distinctions in the kinds of technology used to manipulate and control our world, and between methods of analyzing the reality of our world. It is not misleading, therefore, to speak of a more adequate technology, say, a channeling method for distributing water across farmland. It is also reasonable to claim that analytical methods which enable us to understand and harness electricity are desirable and beneficial, even preferable to the wholesale eradication of combustible vegetation for fuel to cook our foods and heat ourselves.

Yet, manipulation, control, and particular methods of analysis are not the sum of wisdom or knowledge. As we well know, much of what was taken for granted in the force of progress has now become questionable. Traditional sources of wisdom and knowledge outside the Western scientific paradigm once overlooked are now being revisited. In contemporary physics, medicine, philosophy, psychology, anthropology, and sociology, fundamental questions, doubts, and uncertainties destabilize the confidence that characterized the mind-set of modernists. I take this to be the situation of modern theology too.

In part, therefore, this book deliberately sets aside some of the dominant patterns of theological thought and practice in order to seek out other sources of wisdom. It draws upon insights from other disciplines (especially sociology, anthropology, hermeneutical philosophy, and literary theory) and other theological trajectories (especially liberation, black, and feminist theologies) that have begun the task of questioning and contesting the dominant modernist paradigm.[2]

The Question of Hegemony

To the extent that dominant theological paradigms function to preside over what constitutes the theological enterprise and what does not, the task is to challenge and undermine their hegemonic influences. Behind the notion of a theological hegemony lies the question of whether any theological tradition can actually succeed in naturalizing all knowledge and wisdom within its frameworks and categories.

Often particular confessional bodies function as if their presuppositions and terms are accepted by all who claim their confession. They imagine that everyone abides by their claims and they avoid the possibility that what is claimed and proclaimed formally may have little relationship to what is held to be true and valid informally. Confessional authorities of one kind or another are inclined to believe that popular religion or local theology is inherently flawed, or that it is incapable of contributing to an emancipatory transformation of the world, being largely a form of false consciousness.[3]

A fundamental conviction behind this work is that local wisdom, expressed here mainly through theological categories, is not overwhelmed by dominant intellectual paradigms. It attempts to reclaim local wisdom as it appears in religious language, and to challenge certain dominant positions concerning the nature of the theological task and the doctrinal claims embodied in its results. It grounds and vindicates a particular kind of voice, not so much against other voices, but against their silencing effects wherever they overwhelm or simply ignore the marginalized or subjugated voice.

The widespread need to counter a culture that silences is not confined to the particular community of my interest, as African theologian Teresa Okure eloquently notes: "We have depended either on expatriates . . . or on African men to speak for us theologically and otherwise. Has the time now come to speak for ourselves?"[4]

A relevant illustration of the South African context lies in the way in which the Christianity of African-initiated Churches (AICs) is viewed by outsiders.[5] Their discourses are seen either as passive responses to hegemonic missionary traditions made victorious through colonial conquest, or as illusory expressions of an escapist religion, or as sites of minimal freedom in the interstices of society, or as a composite result of an uneven struggle between hegemonic and counter-hegemonic forces. They thus offer a helpful route into understanding the nature of hegemony as played out in South Africa. More pertinent, their reshaping of Christianity[6] bears resemblance to the processes at work in Bible studies of the Amawoti BEC, several of whose members belong to Zionist churches.

AICs, who now make up the bulk of the Christian population in South Africa, originally disturbed representatives of settler-originated churches.[7] They saw in them a threat that was more than theological. AICs, deemed intrinsically subversive, were often blamed for political hostility toward settlers. This was particularly true of the earlier "Ethiopian movement" whose various constituents usually began as overt breakaways from colonial churches which were experienced as oppressive. Only in the latter part of the 1920s did fears of this movement subside, partly because its political and theological challenges had waned to the point that they were no longer threatening. Since then, this large body of Christians—their experiences, their perspectives, and their theologies—has been ignored or submerged, set on the margins, by the rest of the Christian church in South Africa, with one exception.[8]

Black Theology has also raised the question of the submerged African voice,[9] and Black theologians have been particularly interested in the marginalization of the AICs and their religious experience. Yet even here matters are not simple. Not infrequently, AICs have been regarded by Black theologians as religious expressions of false consciousness. The dilemma can be seen in the view that, on the one hand, AICs (and, in general, popular religion among blacks) should be taken seriously as the significant starting point for an indigenous theology. On the other hand, these same forms of popular religion are simultaneously described as caught up in ideological (traditional) production that is no longer relevant[10] or as reactionary (apolitical), and thus of little help in constructing a contemporary liberation theology.[11]

Bonganjalo Goba illustrates the point nicely in *Agenda for Black Theology*.[12] Discussing some of the recent literature on what he calls the Black Independent Church Movement, he notes:

> Any theology within the black South African context which does not deal with this phenomenon of the Black Independent Church Movement will, at best, be

extremely narrow, at worst, completely irrelevant. The Black Independent Church Movement represents the future of the black Christian community in South Africa out of which a relevant theology should emerge.

This remarkably strong statement seems virtually programmatic for Black Theology. Yet how is this program to be met? For Goba simultaneously judges the Black Independent Church Movement to be utterly unreliable in respect of either social or theological reconstruction. The movement "has become apolitical," he says, and the leadership and power conflicts that characterize the movement make it "impossible for them to offer any significant political contribution." More pertinent for my purposes here, Goba adds, "This would also be true of their theology."

Perhaps the political value lying within the history and experience of the Black Independent Church Movement can only be realized by others. But then it acts as little more than a storage silo for African cultural idioms and practices. At most, under the tutelage of the avant-garde who have the necessary analytical tools, ideological weapons, and strategic resources, some elements of the movement may be sufficiently "politicized" to begin to play a significant role. But the avant-garde would have to fit those elements into a new program.

This inevitably disfranchises the Black Independent Church Movement. Agency—effective, intentional human action—is implicitly attributed to the political and intellectual avant-garde, and not to those who lead churches within the AICs. It thus becomes easier to sideline the AICs, to treat them as demographically important but ecclesially and theologically problematic, if not irrelevant.

Black theologians have a point in their negative analysis of the political significance of the AICs. It would be romantic idealism to imagine that the faith and reflection of local Christian communities, because they may be black, poor, or oppressed, is free of distortion, of entrapment in increasingly dysfunctional paradigms, or of contradictions not yet experientially significant. Ordinary believers may well hamper the emancipatory goals for which Black Theology strives, and even act as counterrevolutionary agents against freedom.[13]

At the same time, one cannot help but be suspicious of theories purporting to function in favor of people whose own thoughts and symbolic systems are regarded from the outset as highly suspect or even false. If transformative human agency is already denied them at the level of reflection and imagination, whence arises the possibility that such a community can ever challenge, let alone escape, their conditions of oppression or marginalization?

The intellectual or activist elite, may view their role as delivering those who are unable to deliver themselves. The sense of the interpretative activity of the Amawoti BEC suggests that this is too strong a view of the importance of the avant-garde role, and too weak a view of the multifarious activities through which ordinary people survive or resist even the most severe oppression. The role played by intellectuals and activists should not be underestimated, but neither should it be overestimated. The trap of romanticizing the capacities and effects of popular struggle in daily life has to be avoided, but so does the tendency of grand theories of domination and revolution to falsify or neglect the ordinary.

The ordinary is what intrigues me. Like many others, I have wondered at the seeming imperviousness to change or transformation by so many people who are deemed to need and want it. Perhaps this is an illusion fostered by a reliance on macro-historical and structural theoretical frameworks that undercut the notion of human agency (as emancipatory action) at the local level. Perhaps in adopting a critical distance from local phenomena in order to disclose the unconscious, nonpersonal, and ideological character of reality we have also distanced ourselves from those perspectives that will enable us to grasp what is going on at the semiconscious, interpersonal, and cultural level. I find myself suspecting the claims of intellectuals and activists in general—an ironic twist, since suspicion must then be directed at my own enterprise as well.

This suspicion is strengthened by the experiences I have had of a gritty, potent wisdom and practice among marginalized people which seems to belie the thesis of false consciousness. The Amawoti BEC is not an independent church as such but a composite gathering of people from various churches and none. Yet it functions readily as a test case of the issues raised, and of the meaning and significance of local religious discourse amidst externally derived hegemonic discourses that have become naturalized. My investigation of the readings of the Amawoti BEC serves to explore this concern, and to provide clues to possible answers.

What emerges is not a system of theological thinking or reflection on faith, but a growing sense of a complex process of communicative action which leaves in doubt unstable histories, even as it clarifies faith in the construction of a new history. Out of this process arises what I now call an incipient theology. What I seek to uncover, therefore, is the nature, constraints, and possibilities for reshaping dominant theological discourses, of incipient theology.

The Amawoti BEC, therefore, as it concerns this study, is a particular case I take to be far more widespread. In order to establish the point, nevertheless, some description of the context of the Amawoti BEC texts is required. Equally, the location of those texts emphasizes a key methodological point—that the interpretative activity of the church and its theologians needs the wisdom of specific local Christian communities if it is to be both ecumenically and pastorally valid.

Context of Reading:
The Community at Amawoti

The BEC is made up of a group of people who live in the area known as Amawoti,[14] part of a huge settlement of Inanda some nineteen miles from Durban in the province of KwaZulu-Natal. Officially designated Released Area 33 during the last years of apartheid, Amawoti was intended for incorporation into what was then the *bantustan* (homeland) of KwaZulu. It may be described as an "urban-fringe shack community," and is classified by sociologists as consisting largely of "the marginal or emergent working class, the lower working class, and a socioeconomic underclass or lumpenproletariat."[15]

The bulk of the population in this rapidly growing peri-urban context consists of a mix of rural and inner-city people. Some are immigrants pulled from rural areas to the city through personal and familial aspiration, and the desire for greater access to urban infrastructures and job opportunities. Others emigrated from the city of Durban for lack of accommodation or because of life cycle needs (family bonds with longer term residents in the shack settlements).

Amawoti is an urban shack community in one of the fastest growing cities in the world where it is estimated that more than 50 percent of the population now live in shack communities. The people are distinguished by certain features that have become common in South Africa, and elsewhere. These features describe to some extent, according to statistical projections, the situation of more than half of the South African population. Most important among these are poverty, unemployment, rapid informal settlement, and minimal or no infrastructure. State resources, transportation, health care and educational facilities, employment possibilities, water and sewerage services, fuel, building materials, among others, are either entirely absent or severely lacking. The material reality of poverty shapes daily life. So do violence and structural injustice.

Martin Mandew analyzes the specific socioeconomic characteristics of the Amawoti community in terms of three general categories, each describing a particular set of forces or interests at work in the community.[16] The first may be described as external. These are the effects of interventions by agents outside the interests of controlling the community. This includes the apartheid state which acted against those they felt to be an actual or potential threat to the ruling regime. Its actions were given effect through police and military activity, and under the rubric of what national intelligence services described as a "total strategy" against a "total onslaught" on apartheid.

State control was also rooted in a far-reaching bureaucracy (controlling migratory labor and pass laws, for example) whose regulations were backed by policing apparatuses and a widespread network of military structures, known as

Joint Management Committees. This meant that even the most isolated community was not immune from the daily impact of the apartheid system. Amawoti was no exception as the state laid siege to the efforts of the community to escape its material and social conditions.

The second of Mandew's categories may be described as internal. Based on the ownership of domestic property, these divisions fractured the community. The two primary divisions consisted of tenants and landowners. Tenants, who make up 70 percent of the population and live on African freehold land, were classified in three categories: those who site-rent, those who room-rent, and those who sub-rent. Landlords, who make up the rest of the population, were divided into legal landlords (title-deed owners who collect rent) and illegal landlords (rent collectors who do not legally own the land but who exercise authority over tenants). Some of the debates in the Bible studies refer to tensions generated by these economically based divisions.

The third of Mandew's categories has to do with authority, in this context, claims for local and regional political authority. Organized groups—on one side, mainly the Inkatha Freedom Party, on the other, the African National Congress or United Democratic Front[17]—have fought battles over who controls whom. These larger political struggles are not the only sources of violence. For example, strife arose between tenants and landlords because of "the explosion of [the] normally dormant stress of competition for scarce urban resources between individuals or communities" occasioned by severe structural inequalities.[18]

This besieged, fractured, and contested settlement is the context of the BEC whose Bible studies I consider.[19] On average, fifteen people came to each Bible study, with up to sixty people attending two workshops whose content is also included in this study. BEC members, comprising Ilimo Primary Health Care Project staff and members, as well as several people not directly linked with the project, constituted the group, which as a whole might be described as ecumenical. Many were members of AICs, most of one church or another, and one or two claimed no clear Christian commitment.

Three major areas of activity empowered the members of the BEC and those with whom they worked in Amawoti. The first was the Ilimo Primary Health Care Project,[20] which expanded beyond its original intentions to include work in the fields of environmental health, personal health, leadership development, income supplement (garden farming, sewing), and resource utilization (assistance for pensioners and disabled persons).

The second area of activity was the BEC's Bible study program, which they called *Funda IBhayibheli Wenze*, meaning "read the Bible and do/act." Similarly, the group described itself as the *iqembu likaFunda Wenze*, meaning "The Read and Do/Implement Group." Mandew describes the communicative activity of the group as "expropriating the means of symbolic reproduction" in the creation of a "counter-hegemony" to the readings of "oppressors, wrongdoers, and those who seek fame," an analysis supported by my own readings.[21]

The third major activity of the BEC revolved around two special events, which acquired almost legendary significance. These were two Good Friday Easter marches, the first held in 1991 under the rubric "In the cross there is suffering and hope," and the second held the next year under a theme reflecting their interpretation of Jesus Christ: "Died for the struggle, lives for freedom."[22]

All three sets of activities are reflected in weekly Bible studies over approximately four years. These study groups, and the specific context out of which they arose, are the source of my own reflections. The argument I develop begins with a reading of particular pericopes from Scripture discussed by the BEC. As I have indicated at the outset, I make no claims to speak for the local community. Nevertheless, it is important to my overall argument that significant congruity can be found between my speech and their speech.

There is some integrity to the positions I work out in relation to the context, experience, and understanding of the local community with whom I am implicitly in dialogue.[23] The importance of integrity has to do with the act of listening, out of which respect for the wisdom of ordinary believers may grow. This was in fact my experience. During their long interaction, the confidence of the members of the Bible study group grew. They came more strongly to believe that they had something to say about their own lives, and more convinced that what they had to say has a significance beyond the boundaries of their own experience.

But how are they to consolidate this empowering experience? How are they to reach beyond their own particularity when their context is defined precisely by its marginality to the wider audience and by its lack of infrastructure and resources by which to reach further? In the words of Teresa Okure once again: "Having arisen from the sleep of silence, will we now let others determine how we should speak and do theology? Or will we find our own way of doing theology?"

There is a larger ecclesial context behind my interest in listening to the interpretations of the Amawoti BEC. One of the failings of the great activist campaigns for which the prophetic or liberation church was known in the last decades has been to anchor its learnings at a local level. This can only really be done by local people, precisely those people who would normally have a relatively small sphere of influence. In these local practices, effectively linked with other local practices, lies the possibility of overcoming marginalization. In the words of one of the members of the Amawoti BEC, "We still have a small chance to do the right thing. Now is the time to change. There is no time to sit down. It is useless just to talk, to discuss the Bible like this every week if we don't change."[24]

The Interpretative World of Amawoti

The material upon which the following analyses are based derives exclusively from the Gospels of Luke and Matthew, and focuses almost entirely on the ministry and teaching of Jesus as represented in these Gospels. The "canon within the canon" these texts represent is small; both Gospels share common original oral and textual (Q) traditions; Jesus is the primary enduring focus, not the Holy Spirit, the disciples, Yahweh, or the church.

These constraints limit the interpretation we may legitimately make of the religious universe of the BEC. Nevertheless, the data offers an impressive and useful point of departure for a discussion of the nature, the reach, and the significance of local, incipient theologies. Present in the Bible studies is duration and, consequently, a developmental dynamic. Also present is a consistent exploration of the meaning of Christian core narratives for life in Amawoti. Of course, the biblical texts are already a written deposit of tradition whose materiality implies an authority of its own, an authority lacking in oral tradition, which is the dominant mode of communication for the BEC members. As Catherine Bell notes, "In general, such textual codification involves a shift from the authority of memory, seniority, and practical expertise . . . to the authority of those who control access to and interpretation of the texts."[25]

Thus there is a tension between the religious worldview that the base Christian community of Amawoti builds up in its prolonged dialogue with the gospels, and the already deposited worldview represented by these texts. The deposit is at work before the BEC begins its own interpretations. While this cautions against the complete originality of anything arising from Amawoti,[26] it also points to the more positive feature of the power relationship: the power of interpretation in the hands of the base Christian community.

This hermeneutical struggle is not hidden, but becomes conscious to the members of the base Christian community themselves:

> [Xolile comments on a verse very broadly, in a manner that goes well beyond the literal text. This causes unease among the group:]
>
> Lungi: Where does Jesus say that?
>
> Xolile: Between the lines.
>
> Thabo: The Bible is not very straightforward.
>
> Phumzile: Yes, you have to work to get what you want from the Bible.[27]

Working at the text to read what lies between the lines brings us directly to the question of interpretation. What hermeneutical strategies are in fact adopted by the base Christian community in Amawoti? What is the nature of the encounter between their reality and the projected world of the text? What are the consequences for the authority of the text vis-à-vis the authority of the group's experiences or context?

One exemplary piece of dialogue helps us explore this question. The text of Matt. 5:13-16, following on the Beatitudes, calls for disciples to be the salt of the earth, the light of the world. The BEC begins with the symbol of salt.

Facilitator: What are your uses for salt?

Thabo: To make food tasty, to stop ghosts, to kill ants, snakes, and snails, to scare frogs, to stop blood, and to stop thieves. You can also put it on the chicken's mouth before you slaughter it.

Lungi: If you throw it on top of the roof it will chase ghosts away. The ghosts start counting the salt and soon the time is finished and they must go back to the graveyard.

Xolile: Salt can also be used to preserve things, like biltong. Salt also helps a dead person not become swollen because salt absorbs water. Too much salt can cause diabetes and high blood pressure.

Group: We take the frogs and snails as the Pharisees. If you put too much salt in your food you can't eat it.

[The reading of the text takes place.]

Thabo: God sent us into the world to be like him; he wants us to represent him. We must help others to become salt. Those people who have lost their conscience can be changed, like salt in water.

Nomtheto: Salt is a ghost buster! In our belief, we believe that a Christian can chase a ghost away.

Phumzile: Does a Christian need to risk his life?

Facilitator: Why do you ask?

Phumzile: You said a Christian must stop bad things. For example, if you see someone pickpocketing, what do you do? But, please, don't answer like Jesus Christ.

Thabo: Remember, light can be a warning, you can warn the person.

Phumzile: What if the thief will kill you for warning his victim?

Thabo: I will be taking a risk. It's reality.

[The facilitator then offers another example: A participant is asked to give something he values and another needs. What would it mean to be salt or light in this context?]

Phumzile: That's easy to do. Why do we run away from the word killing? It's said that everyone wants to go to heaven, but they don't want to die. People are afraid of dying. It's useless to go to church and put on a good show when I know I'm not prepared to stop the pickpocketer. And I'm afraid that when I get to heaven, Jesus says I was foolish to do that![28]

This text brings to the fore a number of pertinent hermeneutical issues: the role of the facilitator in the interpretative act, the link to a cultural tradition, the interest in a contemporary interpretative context, the role of the ordinary reader in constructing meaning, the polysemy of symbolic language, and the capacity of readers to challenge interpretative authorities (in this instance, the facilitator).

The Role of the Facilitator in the Interpretative Act

The Bible study begins with an open-ended question about the significance of salt. The facilitator preempts any preconceived meaning of the symbol of salt by leaving the text reading until this first question has been explored. Moreover, by presenting open-ended questions, the facilitator undermines any idea that he will provide the correct or most appropriate interpretation.

This tactic is strongly present in the dynamics of the BEC meetings, though the facilitator does dominate the interpretative act more strongly in the early stages of the group's life. After a year of weekly meetings, his initial fear that the group will read the text heretically subsides; he begins to trust the group's interpretative activity. Indeed, heretical readings (readings that go tangentially beyond the facilitator's inherited range of meanings) are increasingly allowed, while the facilitator's occasional attempts to constrain the possible meanings of a text become increasingly infrequent.

This particular facilitator lived with the community for six years, during which he actively pursued a participatory research paradigm.[29] But he was well trained, holding a postgraduate degree in theology. Inherent in these Bible studies, therefore, is the troubling issue of the tension between the trained reader and the untrained believer.[30]

The tension must be maintained if the interpretative acts of a base Christian community are not to succumb to two common problems of interactive interpretation. If the trained reader dominates (by far the most common occurrence, and the one to be most wary of), then the wisdom of the base Christian community is replaced by the dominating knowledge of the trained reader. Knowledge is power, Michel Foucault reminds us, and that is just what marks such a relationship. If, on the other hand, the untrained readers are left unchallenged by the knowledge of the trained reader, the world of the text is often reduced to a particular experience or context. The text becomes an instrument in another game, and the interpretative relationship is deprived of the critical wisdom of the global Christian community, past and present, which the trained reader should represent.

This suggests one important role of the trained interpreter, whether facilitating the group or merely a member of it: to represent critically and constructively the wisdom and accumulated experience of the Christian community (synchronic and diachronic). But my reference to Foucault's connection between power and knowledge suggests a further implication. No theology, past or present, is free of power relations. Suspicion thus accompanies the inherently reconstructive hermeneutics I am proposing.

What the Amawoti Bible studies demonstrate is (1) the importance of the distinct roles of what we might call the "organic intellectuals" (Antonio Gramsci) and the vital organs of the people, and (2) the need to develop strategies of interaction which promote the tension between the two parties and which embrace the permanent ambiguities of this interaction.

Interpretation and Cultural Traditions

What is the role of culture in shaping interpretation? Is it a conserving, perhaps reactionary, factor or one vital to effective transformation? South African theologies have been strongly influenced by the idea of liberation, while many theologians in other African countries regard a theology of inculturation to be their primary goal. Yet cultural factors powerfully shape Christian experience and thought in South Africa, and questions of liberation—from poverty, ecological disaster, dictatorships, and dysfunctional social structures—are relevant to most of Africa. The tension between inculturation and liberation[31] is thus necessarily part of our exploration. To what extent is this tension present in Amawoti? We find an ambiguous picture.

Contemporary cultural practices are indeed an important part of making the Bible come alive. The uses of salt depicted in the dialogue above exemplify this. They are simultaneously mundane, rich in African lore (Christians as "ghost busters" suggest traditional practices of overcoming evil spirits), and in some cases the source of new interpretations of the biblical narrative. The new interpretations are instructive: Pharisees, like frogs and snails, are damaged or destroyed by salt; alternatively, they have too much salt (religion) and thus have made the faith inedible.

The hermeneutics visible here includes a simultaneous reinterpretation of the text and of traditional culture. In either case, the link between text and context is clearly complex and transparent. But, that BEC members show that their readiness to incorporate African idioms, grammars, and symbols into a reconstructed dogmatic field is both theologically appropriate and ecclesially enriching.

Another layer of complexity may also be discerned. There is no one single African tradition, and none of the multiple African traditions is static or unaffected by complex historical forces. Like any tradition, African traditions are constructed and contested terrains of human activity. We thus find no pure reading of African tradition in Amawoti. The BEC on occasion draws on the notion of traditional (African) thinking, but what members talk about reflects an altered and altering economic and political landscape. This includes the context of struggle for liberation since the 1950s, worker militancy since the 1970s, earlier wars against conquest, and most commonly, the conditions of a peri-urban settlement that creates a hybrid of rural life and urban industry and commerce.

Cultural tradition in this case is a mix of the past and present. The ingredients cannot be easily separated from each other. Ambiguity remains, particularly in the desire to return to a past imagined as still valid:[32]

> Nomtheto: Jesus is getting more strict than before. We need to feel free. We are a different nation. We need to follow our cultures.
>
> Thabo: But culture has changed.
>
> Xolile: Most blacks would like to go back to the old days.

The yearning for something experienced as lost but vital is there. Yet in the ensuing dialogues over four years, no one is able to define with any consensus or clarity what "the old days" were or how to recover them. The Amawoti Bible studies demonstrate that it is not past culture that influences the interpretative process, but present conditions of life. Accordingly, the religious worldview that emerges is an attempt at interpreting life as it is and as it is desired. Past cultural inheritances are drawn into this picture as appropriate, and reinterpreted in the process, but they do not dominate, nor is there evidence in the BEC of a desire to have it any other way.

Expressed sociologically, the material conditions of life in a squatter area establish the primary parameters for the construction of the religious symbolic universe considered real. This suggests that the incipient theology of a local base Christian community will not distinguish between material and spiritual realities, but will be "incarnational."[33]

The Contemporary Context of Interpretation

In the first dialogue reproduced above, pickpockets rate a special mention. Stealing—thievery of all kinds—is a common theme in the Bible studies of Amawoti. Not only are members of the group and their relatives and friends often depicted as victims, questions are also raised about the effects of severe poverty in driving one to theft, as the following comment suggests:[34]

> If a rich person understands it, they will share what they have and support others. If someone pickpockets every day, what makes him do that? It's because of basic needs not met. It means he doesn't have the power to get a job.

Once again, the interpretative activity of the base Christian community is able to accommodate ambiguity. This is most apparent in discussions concerning violence, one of the most depressing and seemingly intractable aspects of daily experience in Amawoti and its surrounding areas. About Luke 4:16-22 the comment is made that "Jesus says he will release prisoners, but he cannot release prisoners who have attacked people, like Inkatha vigilantes."[35] This can hardly be called a clear ethical statement. Perhaps the search for clarity is what drives the group back to this issue again and again. A growing sense of what is and is not appropriate thus includes a developing capacity to see long-term consequences, as is evident in the following dialogue on Matt. 5:38-42:

> Thabo: In Amawoti, it's "an eye for an eye and a tooth for a tooth." But would the faction fight stop? The followers might carry on, organizing fighting, and their relatives too if they were killed.
>
> Phumzile: The warlords must be killed.
>
> Bonginkosi: Then what is freedom of speech?
>
> Phumzile: Fighting doesn't solve the problem always, but sometimes. In Amawoti it does.
>
> Lungi: It may in the short term, but not in the long term. It never does. Violence is disastrous because it multiplies.[36]

The attempt to develop a rich interpretation continues by drawing on another context of violence (domestic) to make a different point:

> Phumzile: What if a wife is being beaten by her husband? Must she come back for more?
>
> Thabo: Doesn't it say something else than this? This is practically impossible. Maybe he [Jesus] is trying to say that if we want to live in harmony, we don't have to take revenge. It's actually about an enlightened way of acting.

This "enlightened way of acting" includes a broad vision of society, a vision that overcomes the divisions and hatreds of the past, though not without a critical assessment of contemporary realities. Not surprisingly, there are moments in which questions of providence also raise their head, as in the following dialogue:

> Lungi: They say Jesus is everywhere.
>
> Facilitator: But what is he doing here?
>
> Bonginkosi: Crying to God to stop this.

Phumzile: But somehow the violence was good,[37] and people dying helped a lot. I wouldn't like it to happen to me, but somehow it was good. There was a balance. Control used to be with the councillors, indunas, etcetera; now the community has control.[38]

Though several Bible studies over the years provide a similar picture, one further example, a reflection on the story of the Good Samaritan, makes this point nicely:

A Zulu person has been injured on the road. Gatsha [Chief Mangosuthu Buthelezi, then head of the apartheid instituted KwaZulu "homeland" government] goes past, and so does the induna [headman]. So does a councillor. Then it is a Pondo [traditional enemy of the Zulu] who comes and helps the man and gives him what he needs. The neighbor is the one who does a favor.[39]

An analysis of the interpretative dynamics underlying these interchanges shows us that the contemporary context functions hermeneutically in several ways. First, it enables understanding of an ancient text, though the nature of this understanding still needs to be explored. Second, it locates the text in relation to a known life situation and thereby allows the projected world of the text to speak to the reader or contemporary interpreter. Third, it allows the members of the base Christian community to appropriate the text for themselves, that is, to establish power over it. Fourth, and central for my purposes, this means that the base Christian community is less inclined to cede their right to interpret their world to some external authority.

Importance of the Ordinary Reader in Constructing Meaning

Understanding the biblical texts is important to the base Christian community: "By studying the Bible we come to understand, like taking away our blindness."[40] One of the remarkable aspects of the story of this base Christian community is the manner in which the weekly Bible studies, over time, provided members the leverage for a growing self-understanding and a measure of conscientization about their context.

Paulo Freire developed his notion of conscientization in Brazil, where fatalism and a relatively low level of political awareness were evident.[41] The Amawoti BEC members, however, are by and large steeped in anti-apartheid politics, directly or indirectly. "Conscientization" in this context means the gathering of a range of otherwise disparate discourses and actions into a coherent, complex, and communicatively established perspective on the common struggles and legitimate aspirations of the community.

What the Bible studies did is encourage the development of an overall framework by which the members of the BEC could reflect on their multiple levels and spheres of decision making and experience. As one follows the four-year history of the group and their ongoing discourses, one readily discerns a growing capacity to incorporate the complexities and ambiguities of life into an overall picture of reality.

Mystery, magic, and rationality merge; paradoxes are dealt with by holding their elements in dialectical tension; contradictions are argued through and the ambiguities that remain are accepted as descriptive of reality; personal and public realms of activity and ethical judgment are brought together into a larger framework; a set of symbols and images begins to emerge as constitutive of the picture of reality the group holds to be "true."[42] For BEC members, the Christian tradition as they interpret it offers the necessary "rhetorical strategies"[43] by which the Christian tradition is able to provide a discourse capable of undergirding a way of life adequate to the intellectual, existential, and material conditions of the contemporary world.

Yet the biblical text does not simply offer a worldview for the group to adopt. The evidence of the Bible studies points in the direction mapped by the hermeneutical philosophy of Paul Ricoeur: While the text reflects its own world (the focus of historical-critical studies) and constrains the range of possible meanings through its semantic structure on the other, it also opens up worlds to the reader. It offers indeterminate ways of interpreting the present.

In Ricoeur's terms, the text is polysemic (having multiple meanings). Any one meaning is the result of an interaction between the text and the reader who, in the act of interpretation, momentarily reduces the polysemy to monosemy (one meaning). Thus interpretative activity becomes a creative agency in the cycle which reduces the text from polysemy to monosemy, and then incorporates the resultant interpretation into the range of meanings of the text. As Croatto puts it:

> When . . . the Bible is read from out of socio-cultural reality—political, economic, cultural, religious and the like—it reveals dimensions not previously seen, helped by beams of light not captured in earlier readings. What is unsaid in what a text "says" is said in a contextualized interpretation.[44]

In part, this entire essay is an argument to allow this process its freedom in the local context. The members of a base Christian community such as the one in Amawoti must be allowed to speak, freely. The simplest and first criterion of speaking freely is that other interpretative interests are placed in the background until such time as the dialogue of the community has become rich enough and confident enough to overcome the tendency of all authorized interpretations (and interpreters) to foreclose new readings.

Critical Challenges from the Ordinary Reader

Where this happens, it is clear that authorized readings are challenged by the members of the BEC, and that these challenges are not only legitimate contextually (they arise from genuine needs and experiences) but also dogmatically (they are often matched by similar, acknowledged challenges appearing throughout the history of the Christian tradition). Some examples will indicate the way in which this happens.

I have already referred to the tendency of Western theology to psychologize faith, a tendency that easily leads, in a liberal capitalist society with its strong individualism and secularism, to a spiritualizing of the gospel. The Amawoti base Christian community finds spiritualized approaches to faith alien. A reading of Matt. 13:44-52, containing the three linked parables of the hidden treasure, the pearl, and the net, gives us an insight into this dynamic:

> Bonginkosi: It's about development. It tells about something you find and develop, something very important.
>
> Lungi: It means we must give up everything worldly. Can you triumph spiritually if you continue with these worldly things?
>
> Thabo: I don't know what you mean by spiritual things. I'm in this world—that's where I am living, that's where I am. How can I reject it? The parable is talking about preparing our lives and being prepared to do something. But heaven is something we don't know about. We're not sure of it and it's not in this world.[45]

Similar sentiments are repeatedly expressed, perhaps most poignantly by one person who argued that Matt. 6:11 ("give us this day our daily bread") refers to basic needs. He wants us to have them: pray for basic needs, then we can go to church and praise him because our stomach will be full and we can concentrate."[46]

The hope for the fulfillment of basic needs and for social needs such as justice, evidenced in many of the Bible studies, is not simply a forlorn cry. It is accompanied by a recognition of the demand to act in accordance with desired goals. Jürgen Moltmann's claim that hope becomes concrete in anticipatory planning for the future[47] finds ready support in the concern of the base Christian community for the material conditions of their lives:

> Phumzile: Wisdom means knowing and thinking about other people, because we know God, and it means planning ahead, like an ant who works hard in summer to collect its food, then in winter it doesn't have to go out.
>
> Thabo: To be wise, you need to have a foundation. Otherwise you can sink. But it also depends on how you build onto that foundation. As the house goes

up, the builders may lose their start, so the structure is poor. The inspector will see that the foundation is okay, but the building is not.

Xolile: I think this is very relevant. After we've made the foundation—that is God—planning is part of wisdom. We need to plan continuously, each part of wisdom, or we will go astray.

[laughter from someone] I'm laughing because this office doesn't even have a foundation.[48]

The critical capacities of the base Christian community, born of their context and strengthened by their dialogue with the texts of the Bible, are substantial. Given the freedom to interpret, ordinary people will threaten so-called authorized interpreters or facilitators, particularly those trained theologically, if they are insecure or determined to limit such critical activity.

The members of the BEC themselves are acutely aware of this. They acknowledge that they are engaged in interpretative activity with which local clergy would not be able to cope. What they experience instead, from the side of clergy, is a retreat into precisely the kind of dominating practice they will no longer accept. Note the metaphor they use to express their critique and concern: the Pharisees.

The Pharisees today are those who have high positions, like Mbubi and Mandlaza.[49]

It's the way church ministry is carried out. They concentrate on the Bible and not on the community. They only preach in a church hall. Most ministers drive around in cars—they never walk, so they never get to know the people. They hide away from them. They should be involved in the community. It's wrong! To intimidate people with the Bible is not treating it as the word of God.[50]

They don't touch people, they point with their sticks![51]

That the base Christian community is capable of self-criticism, particularly in applying the same principles to themselves by which they assess others, is also evident in the same semantic context:

What makes God happy? I think we need to search ourselves about the work we do in the community. Do[es] the community see us as the Pharisee or the tax-collector? Are we disrespected, like the Pharisee?[52]

Or, in another context, reflecting on Matt. 7:24-29 (build on rock, not sand):

Thabo: Jesus has been explaining how to live. Now this is a summary: We know what to do, building a strong house. The whole community knows about peace, protests about police and warlords. People are united in looking for a new South Africa. We are all the same in the end.

Xolile: We need to take the plank out of our own eye, we can't judge Inkatha.[53]

Lungi: Only God can.[54]

Conclusion

The Amawoti base Christian community has been involved in a long, painstaking process of dialogue and interpretation, a journey of discovery and a test of the intellectual and emotional integrity of each of its members. As one of them put it, "[We] treat this as if Jesus has been running a workshop about our lives."[55] It has been an essentially communal activity, and its life has depended upon this fact as much as anything else.

The Amawoti BEC has shown that it possesses a complex religious symbolic universe that derives from and prompts important reflexive practices. They evidence a powerful, if scholastically unsophisticated, capacity to incorporate into their own world the world projected by biblical text. They show that they can do so self-critically.

A provisional judgment may be made here, a judgment I hope to substantiate in the chapters that follow: The approach evidenced here encourages the much wider adoption within churches of methods and strategies that cede a significant part of the power of interpretation, and thereby the production of (theological) knowledge, to base Christian communities. The benefits well outweigh the dangers. There are risks, but they appear to be within the range of a long and venerable thread within the core traditions of Christianity, which in theory gives considerable status to the faith of the ordinary believer. What is emphasized here is the significance of the ordinary believer's own reflections on her or his faith in relation to daily life and practice. This is one aspect of the recovery of incipient theologies.

2. Incipient Theologies
Marginal Reflections on Faith

All the same you do believe all that nonsense. God, the Trinity, the
Immaculate Conception . . ."
"I want to believe. And I want others to believe.'"
"Why?"
"I want them to be happy."
"Let them drink a little vodka then. That's better than a make-believe."
"The vodka wears off. It's wearing off even now."
"So does belief."
—Graham Greene, Monsignor Quixote

incipient \in-si-pe-ent\ adj. *Beginning to exist or appear.*

W e know that belief in God, when focused on the internal life or away from the
world, easily conceals the material or social contradictions under which people suffer and are broken. Such belief cannot withstand the critical questions of the person
who demands an end to suffering, nor the painful gaze—the face—of the other
who suffers. It fails the reality test. An adequate foundation for belief must find an
intelligible approach to human brokenness. Where does one begin? The wise beginning, from a religious, social, or human point of view, lies in taking those who experience brokenness as our primary interlocutors, our first point of reference.

In what follows, I argue that local communities—particularly those on the
margins of the centers of power in a society—possess a theologically and socially
relevant wisdom about their situation and context. When this is drawn into the
hegemonic centers of theological discourse, it questions prevailing assumptions

and offers important new insights, introducing "contrast experiences" into those dominant discourses.[1]

In this sense I agree with Per Frostin that local wisdom, as subjugated knowledge, may be grasped as epistemologically privileged: It gives us insight into what otherwise remains unseen about ourselves, our theories, power relations, and society. Because local wisdom is systematically marginalized, it provides a particularly sensitive measure of the nature of a system's boundaries and effects.

Those, then, who stand outside the situation and context of such local communities have the task of understanding the meaning and the wider validity of this knowledge. This means according such local communities a certain kind of respect in regard to what they know, not normally given by those closer to the centers of power. It means recognizing that what they know is not simply a matter of ideas, or of our judgment on those ideas, but a reflection on hard-won experience. It means grasping the relationship of their ideas to contexts that make these particular ideas practically relevant, and to those specific actions with transformative potential.

We will pursue these points in relation to specifically Christian theological knowledge.[2] More than familiarity with biblical narratives, homilies, creeds, and liturgical habits, this knowledge refers to a conscious reflection of Christians on their specific faith in order to transform it.[3] Faith here signifies that set of beliefs and associated practices which express for the believer their encounter with the sacred, which represent to them the fundamental nature of reality, and to which they give allegiance in their conduct of life.

Archbishop Anselm's simple definition of *faith in search of understanding* helps make clear that anyone of faith who consciously seeks to understand the practical, intellectual, and moral implications of their faith does theology. Such a person engages in constructing theological knowledge. Of course, the knowledge one constructs is not necessarily profound, original, or enduring. This would still have to be tested, and that test can only be carried out in relation to what others have experienced, learned, and thought.

I argue that when ordinary believers, believers untrained in the formal canons or history of theological method, reflect upon their faith, they engage in the task of theology in a provisional way, gathering an as yet untested wisdom about the meaning of their faith. This theology I call incipient, a concept to which we will return.

I assume that the faith upon which one reflects, at least if it is Christian (though most faiths would fit), aims at some vision of the comprehensive well-being of all reality, aware that present reality fails that vision. It seems obvious, therefore, that theology based on a faith concerned with transforming social reality is vital, and theology lacking such a view untenable. Yet it would be theoretically deficient not to incorporate a concern for personal transformation.

The social and the personal are bound together at the outset by the way in which theological knowledge orients one to reality.[4] Orientation is necessarily personal, and a new orientation is what we mean when we speak of conversion. Conversion implies a personal viewpoint on the world. This includes interpersonal relationships, for no person is without other relationships. Conversion implies a changed set of practices or behaviors as well as a consciousness of the broader location of the self in relation to the world, including society.

These elements of a foundational theology, beginning with that personal orientation we call faith,[5] may be observed in the Amawoti BEC and similar local communities. For them the personal, the interpersonal, and the social are one. To understand the broader meaning of theological knowledge among such communities, we will focus on their knowledge of our common world—theirs, mine, and yours.

Listening to another perspective that may be both foreign and difficult to decode is a formidable task. It requires open-ended self-criticism. In the struggle to learn, it is not enough to digest information, record it, and then call it forth when needed. Learning occurs more profoundly in the practical attempt to find solutions to problems, responses to needs. I believe this is also true of theological knowledge.

The idea that learning is a struggle implies that the construction of theological knowledge has something to do with seriousness. Theology is not in principle trivial, though it may be treated as a frivolous game or used to convey sterile formulations. It concerns life in the face of death—life in its multiplicity, complexity, and totality; death as an experience of a wide range of forces that threaten the quality or existence of life.

The notion of struggle also points to the link between knowledge and the conditions under which life is lived and death is faced. Life is not only a matter of struggle, but it certainly depends upon meeting basic needs, and this requires effort and produces pain, no matter how sophisticated the tools or institutions available for the task.

My argument throughout this book therefore privileges struggle as a locus of knowledge of considerable importance for theology, as well as other fields of knowledge.[6] The interpretative activity involved in accessing the relevant knowledge or engaging with the incipient theology of a local community is complex and complicated, however. We will attempt to demonstrate both the difficulty and the promise of carrying out the task by turning to the religious images and symbolic language of the BEC, noting that their encounter with the world projected by biblical texts draws on their own world as well.

God and the World:
Empirical Experiences of Faith Reflected

It could not be expected, and it is not the case, that a fully articulated, systematically reflected theology should emerge from a base ecclesial community such as that at Amawoti. Its members do not draw together their disparate insights and experiences into a defensible, coherent whole. What I will try to do is construct a picture of God and the world as seen in the Amawoti Bible studies. My purpose is simply that of uncovering a whole that points to the integrity of the parts in relation to the conditions of life out of which they arise.

The community's theological reflections have two dominant foci: an understanding of the specific nature and purpose of Jesus Christ, and a view on redemption. A concept of God is also occasionally present in what is said about Jesus Christ. Other traditional dogmatic loci do not feature strongly, though an early decision to focus on texts about the reign of God, parables in particular,[7] does introduce eschatology. The texts from this particular community have little to do with pneumatology.

The Bible studies used, which extend from 1989 to 1992, cover selections drawn from several parts of the New and Old Testaments.[8] Wherever fruitful, I have used the translated words and Zulu phrases of the group itself to convey the sensibility of the relevant discussion. The ensuing analysis of the content is mine, though in some cases I build directly on perspectives expressed by the group members as they reflected on their own interpretations of the texts.

Who Is Jesus Christ?

Most of the ninety or so Bible studies were not about Jesus Christ as such, though many dealt with teachings about the reign of God. Christology does not govern the BEC's understanding of Scripture. Their African context and cultural-linguistic framework, however, allowed a ready identification with many ancient Jewish traditions. Overall, however, there is enough said about Jesus Christ to allow us a fairly good picture of the local Christology of the BEC.

We begin with one of the most startling statements to emerge from the Amawoti community: "Jesus is tricky!" At the outset we realize we are dealing with something other than an inherited Christian tradition. A "tricky Jesus" does not refer to the jester or clown image found within their tradition. Rather, it signals caution, even distrust, about the way in which Jesus operates or speaks. The underdog trickster represented by "Brer Rabbit" in J. C. Harris's popular fables in *Tales of Uncle Remus* is the more appropriate analogy.

The statement that Jesus is tricky arises from a reading of Matt. 6:25ff, in which Jesus is depicted as telling the disciples not to worry about their lives, about what they are to eat, about their bodies and how they are to clothe them. The Amawoti group associates this advice, specifically its apparent caution against concern for material needs, with people who take advantage of their poverty: a used car salesman who offers a car but asks if a buyer wants the front *or* the back wheels, a crook who goes after others' property, or someone who wants to drive them into poverty through woefully (or no) education (as under the Apartheid system). In the Amawoti culture, there are sound material reasons to be cautious about this Jesus and his tricky teaching about material things.

The group concluded, therefore, that only rich people could make any sense of what Jesus says, because they would be challenged to give up a dependency on material goods, to forego their love of possessions—a love which also produces a proud arrogance over those less fortunate. This makes sense in Amawoti.

The group did not, however, simply discard the text as irrelevant. They wondered what this passage could mean for those who are poor.[9] First, Mbuso suggests that, if they have God's love, the rich "won't continue to have their bacon while the poor have three-day-old bread" because they will be willing to share their wealth, and "the poor won't be scared to ask the rich for what they need." Second, it means that Jesus understands the predicament of the poor and will join in their struggle to find what they need. Third, it means working in a different way, as a servant of the people, seeking first the justice of God, struggling for the prize like a runner. "Don't worry about the warlords," the text says to the Amawoti group, "worry about apartheid. Deal with the cause and not just the symptoms." Fourth, it means resisting the great temptations money brings in a context of poverty. Fifth, it is a teaching of hope, a depiction of God's justice for which one must struggle. Finally, it means sharing whatever one does have, however poverty stricken, in solidarity with others.

These understandings of the person of Jesus and the significance of his teaching take us into the kind of Christology and attendant soteriology that makes sense to the people of Amawoti. Let us expand the picture by turning to some of the traditional christological categories: the titles and works of Jesus.

Identifying Jesus

What use is made in Amawoti of traditional titles for Jesus? Not much; few of them appear. We find others instead: street kid, imitation of God, liberator, fighter for justice, fellow sufferer, transforming presence, comrade, an activist helping make the country (Palestine) ungovernable. These titles reflect a particular interpretive emphasis, one that turns away from the being or nature of Jesus Christ to one that focuses on the work and actions of Jesus. At the same time, they convey something of the classical tradition's interest in binding promise and fulfillment in identifying the person of Jesus.

Central to the BEC's discussions of the significance of Jesus is his active presence in the Amawoti community. Verb forms rather than noun forms predominate. Jesus "breaks the yoke of oppression," "frees and educates the poor," "burns (or "confiscates") the weapons," "supports the community," "brings good news to the poor because he was poor," "releases political prisoners" (but not vigilantes who attack people!), "tells people what their situation is like," "tells the rich to forgive the debts of the poor," "suffers for the people in Amawoti," "tells the community to differentiate between the truth and the lie," "puts forgiveness and healing in the hands of the community."[10]

The active presence of Jesus in the Amawoti community calls forth an analogous activity from those who accept him, as further statements made by the group affirm: "Jesus dies for our freedom, now *we* need to be active." "What does it mean for *me*? It means I will work for the liberation of the community."

Certain provisional conclusions can be drawn from these images. First, though sometimes the name *Christ* is used rather than *Jesus,* it is usually the human figure of Jesus that predominates. More importantly, the figure of Jesus is of one who is intensively active in the struggles and experiences of the community. At almost every point, Jesus relates directly to those things that shape daily life at a political or economic level, specifically those things experienced as lacking, negative, or threatening: oppression, "Bantu" (Apartheid) education, violence, poverty, and political imprisonment.

What is significant about Jesus is that in some sense he is present in addressing these matters: He is where the people are; he is "down below" on their piece of earth. In a poignant image, one BEC group member describes Jesus using a picture of an open hand drawn by another of the group: "This hand does not come down like a fist from on top, but the hands come underneath, to support, and not to oppress."

In the Bible studies I have analyzed, the theme of hope predicated upon the divine presence of God in the world is thus the prime meaning of the term *Christ.* The risen Christ sitting "up above" on the right hand of the Father is barely visible, except in rare statements about the importance of knowing that what Jesus does is what God does. This is what guarantees ultimate victory.

That God is present in Jesus is of extraordinary importance, because of the way Jesus is read from the biblical text: "Jesus goes through suffering as he is born, but he brings hope in that. He wasn't born in a fancy place, like a church; he was born in the community." Strengthened by making it general, this theme continues: "God is where the people are, and [he] loves not only Christians and believers." Such statements are made all the more powerful when one discovers that the name *Nkosinathi* ("God with us," Emmanuel) permeates the discussions of the group both in and outside the Bible studies. By contrast, the general tone of comments on all language that speaks of "God up there," language most often attributed negatively to clergy, is that such a God "plays games with us," is undemocratic, or is not to be trusted.

Jesus as Active

We have noted that the christological emphasis in Amawoti lies on the work of Jesus. But the actions of Jesus appear more important than his teachings. The group began its studies on the parables by trying to understand what *the reign of God* might mean. The parables are primarily pedagogical literary forms, ways of teaching, even if they signify new ways of being. The Amawoti group found that questions generated in their studies could not satisfactorily be resolved by dealing primarily with the teachings of Jesus. Frustration grew about their inability to relate the teachings per se to practical problems they faced in Amawoti. The deductive approach did not seem sufficiently fruitful, despite insights into the values of the rule of God.

At the facilitator's suggestion, the group turned to the actions of Jesus portrayed in Mark's Gospel. Immediately the tone and the content of the Bible studies changed. Various activities of Jesus suggested present actions and brought the entire tradition alive. It enabled an integration of the teachings, but also a questioning of their validity, as in the view that Jesus is tricky.

This shift in the mode of interpretation from a focus on ideas (teachings) to a focus on practice (the acts of Jesus) was decisive in motivating the Amawoti group to a thorough, contextualized reinterpretation of Jesus Christ. It encouraged group members to generate interpretations from their own wisdom rather than the wisdom contained in the teachings of Jesus, although these were not neglected.

The shift in mood made it possible to encounter the teachings in the form of a dialogue rather than in the form of dogma. It was a turning point in the empowerment of the Bible study group itself, leaving the facilitator more free to speak with the group on the basis of his wider training and exposure to the discourse of the church at large without the fear of dominating them or of failing to listen properly.[11]

Redeeming the Broken Body

The question of redemption is the second major theme present in the BEC texts. It is clear throughout the Bible studies that belief in Jesus Christ for the BEC members is not separated from the desire for an end to their pain or a resolution of the conditions of their suffering. Redemption and liberation were for them virtually synonymous, if one understands liberation in broader terms than the political.

In Christian theology generally, soteriology is indissolubly linked to experiences of suffering, of need, and of liberation. Soteriology may even be regarded as *the* foundational theme of Christian faith. Because each human situation must be dealt with anew, the repeated search for redemption necessarily gives rise to new understandings of faith, theology, and ecclesial practice.[12] What I ask here is whether, and in what way, those who are the epitome of suffering and need, the poor and oppressed, offer a perspective on redemption capable of challenging dominant views in church and society. In what way might their perspectives contribute to the welfare of the community as a whole, and to the reconstruction of society?

I compare the interpretations of the BEC to the views of Takatso Mofokeng, an influential Black theologian in South Africa who would argue that his experience as a black South African is in many respects akin to that of the Amawoti community. Such a comparison opens up space for marking the difference between his experience and that of the BEC. It will be hermeneutically fruitful in understanding incipient theologies to compare a trained theologian's work on redemption with that of the untrained members of the local community, especially if both share common elements as victims of, and strugglers against, the racism of apartheid.

A Particular Locus of Redemption

Mofokeng's interest is in grasping the concrete conditions of an adequate notion of redemption for black South Africans. For him, one's christological starting point in the narratives of the Gospels has a direct bearing on soteriology. He rejects Jon Sobrino's depiction of Christology as beginning in the crises of Jesus' Galilean ministry, and Karl Barth's emphasis on the baptism of Jesus in the Jordan. Mofokeng claims that "Black Christology starts in the stable and the manger in Bethlehem."[13] Jesus was not merely a Jew, but a despised Jew. Particularity of person, time, and place is pertinent. And the soteriological consequences? Salvation has to do with redemption in the context of particular, despised, poor, and afflicted people.

Mofokeng's specific concern for particularity is not his focus on black people as the poor, but his concern for the redemption of black subjectivity in the face of racist doctrines of white superiority. *Negativity* has too long been the meaning of blackness, both existentially and ontologically. Black culture, religion, and history have been assaulted. In the process, "the black man [sic] disappeared or perished as a subject." Redemption or liberation for the black person must therefore include "the birth of the new black subject." This can only occur by way of embracing negativity, celebrating blackness.[14]

A counterculture, a counterreligion, and a counterhistory are affirmed. These become the data for theological reflection, neither abstractly nor simply politically, but in the practical reconstruction of black subjectivity. A new consciousness and a new material situation go hand in hand. They constitute a dialectical history whose goal is the overcoming of a systematically imposed attempt to alienate black South Africans from black history, black culture, and the land.[15]

The movement of the dialectic is between creation and salvation. Jesus' suffering on the cross and the rise of a new subject in his victory over the cross redeem the suffering of the black person whose created subjectivity has been broken. Christ is God in us, re-creating the new subject who would otherwise remain broken.

For Mofokeng, this claim is not merely symbolic but concretely ontological. Wherever there emerges a black community whose subjectivity in the face of suffering (the cross) has been redeemed (the victory), this is the work of the resurrected Jesus. The liberating practice of this community is in turn the verification of the resurrection of Jesus. Resurrection, like the cross, must be understood as history, as event or movement within black history.[16] Accordingly, for Mofokeng, specific people, movements, and communities "are the visible, recognizable and identifiable trail of the Spirit of God in the long Good Friday existence of black people in South Africa."[17] We may take the Amawoti BEC as a potential expression of such a spirit.

To test its actual soteriology, Mofokeng provides us with an evocative range of categories. His analysis produces six points of reference: a particular identity, creative power, solidarity with others, a struggle for and suffering in the cause of justice, a recovery of land taken, and a bond between the living and the dead who provoke the recovery of lost memories.

First, Mofokeng reaffirms the anthropological question as primary: "Who does Jesus Christ say that we are and how shall we become ourselves, our liberated selves?"[18] It is a question of particularity and identity. Second, the theme of creation implies the idea of power: Power *for* rather than *over* the other is a sine qua non for redemptive experience. Third, community implies solidarity, living and sharing communally in the establishment of mutual love and dignity—"or as an old African saying goes: we go through the dark by holding each other's blanket."[19]

Fourth, the exercise of subjectivity and power by blacks acts against those who dominate them: A struggle for justice is an inevitable expression of black redemption, as is suffering in the cause of justice. Fifth, the redemption of the land is part of the realization of black humanity: As creation itself was material, so the new creation is material. Finally, the land vitally binds a community with the bodily remains of the departed—the living dead, the ancestors. The unity in community with the ancestors, the "founding fathers of black existence," provokes the redemptive role of memory, a "reconnection of the black umbilical cord of history."[20] It establishes a synchronically and diachronically real community as a mark of true humanity.

Do his categories illuminate the actual beliefs of ordinary, relatively untrained, believers such as those at Amawoti? If not, what are the differences?

1. The Question of Particular Identity under Oppression

The particularity of Jesus's birth is very significant for the Amawoti BEC. Repeated statements exemplify or expand on the birth narrative and the BEC's own experiences:

> Mandla: I think it was strange that angels came to people who were not high class; they didn't come to the high priest. It is a symbol showing us that when Jesus comes on earth, he won't treat himself as high class.
>
> Nondyebo: This gave the shepherds hope, that if a child was born in a place like this, they would have a chance to see him. If he had been born in Addington hospital [the major hospital in the city of Durban], they would need permission to see him or there may be guards there. This says to we who are low class, who people say are useless, to Jesus we are most important.[21]

This exchange took place before the dramatic changes in South Africa, and it reflects the powerful sense of exclusion from mainstream society of communities such as Amawoti. They recognize in the birth narrative something pointing to their own worth or subjectivity. This leads them to identify with Zionist AICs because these "churches of the spirit" (*amosonto amoya*) are seen as much closer to the people than the other churches, the "churches of the law" (*amosonto omthetho*).[22]

There are surely multiple explanations for this perception, but among those specifically noted during the course of the BEC's life are the closer proximity of Zionist church leaders to the daily life of the people, their consequent identification with the needs and struggles of the local community, their organic grasp of the language and discourse patterns of the local community, and their ability to fill the shape of the Christian gospel with African traditional religious and cultural content.[23]

Thus the members of the BEC view Jesus' redemptive, salvific activity as historically efficacious in the life of their community and in the broader body politic. Yet they do not forget their African roots, even as their understanding of their African tradition is reconstructed. Hermeneutically, this is what one should expect. It is perhaps best exemplified in a conversation about the traditional process of mediation with God.

Three biblical texts (Rom. 5:12-14, 1 Cor. 15:21-22, Gen. 2:16-17) convince the BEC that Jesus Christ provides direct communication with God. This is important, because it abolishes discrimination between priests and people by undermining the priestly claim of mediator between God and the people. It also overcomes the gap between the people and God in traditional African notions that communication with God goes via the ancestors. The BEC noted that the latter problem was particularly acute for women, who by tradition were required first to approach an uncle or grandfather who would then intercede with the ancestors. The ancestors would in turn communicate with God (*Umvelingqangi*). By removing this triple bypass, Jesus undercuts sexual discrimination.

African tradition is explicitly questioned in this specific instance. Yet it would be simplistic to consider the issue resolved so easily. The BEC carefully states: "Jesus did not come to destroy all African traditions. There are those traditions that God detests. . . . But there are also those traditional customs that God likes."[24] This nuance is important.

What conclusions may one draw from this discussion? First, a reappropriation of African tradition and culture is important to the question of identity in a reconstructed communal life. Second, this is likely to include a hermeneutics that reconstructs African tradition and culture in accordance with contemporary norms of emancipation. Thus, besides emancipatory impulses contained within African tradition (such as the ideal of *ubuntu*, a complex concept meaning roughly "full humanness, in communion with others"[25]), there is an unavoidable encounter with the influences of the Enlightenment and with norms of other cultures, including emancipatory tendencies within Western culture. The BEC does not spurn this encounter. Third, such hermeneutical activity arises in the practical reflections of the BEC, and it does not depend upon significant inputs from externally located, "mainstream" denominations. This has important implications for ecumenical policies and for state agencies concerned with the role of religion in reconstruction and development.

2. The Use of Creative Power

Political theologies, liberation theologies, feminist theologies, and Black theologians such as Mofokeng have attacked others for their de-emphasis of power. All share a consensus: Theologies that de-emphasize power undergird the position of the dominant group, whose power is already ensured.[26]

For the BEC, power is a common theme. The group readily names those who exercise negative power over them: the oppressor, Satan, the rich, vigilantes, and preachers and pastors. Preachers and pastors are belittled frequently in their Bible studies. At no stage, however, can one discern overt bitterness, hatred, or vitriol. Their focus instead is on their capacity to tap and generate power themselves, power to stand against those who dominate, dehumanize, or destroy them. It is important for the BEC that such people or forces be concretely identified. As the group poignantly noted during a time of immense repression, "Satan must be identifiable. Identification comes in seeing what is happening in the struggle for power between Satan and Jesus, for example, a government spy who works for the kingdom of Satan."[27] Revenge is not encouraged, however, nor does one find any sense of fatefulness, anomie, or resignation, despite many material reasons for just such symptoms of powerlessness.

What is the BEC's positive view of power? Interpreting the notion of *reign of God,* they claim that positive power happens where the community is organized, where they "use good ways to meet needs," where changes for the better are made, where one finds "people who build people" and "leaders who are servants of the community."[28] They read Scripture to reinforce a belief in creative power as power *for* (not power *over*) the other. This is power given to them for positive ends, not power residing in an external agency somewhere else. Religious experience here clearly contributes to a highly positive and progressive view of the task of reconstructing society.

Later the BEC links the question of power directly to need, through the aphorism "give us this day our daily bread."[29] In a fascinating hermeneutical shift in interpreting this line from the Lord's Prayer, they equate daily bread with power. *Daily bread* certainly means basic material needs, which must be met if one is to "go to church and praise Him" ("then our stomach will be full and we can concentrate"). But, the group asks, "Is power a basic need? Can we live without it?" Yes, in some sense, but not in another, because cooperative, constructive power is needed to secure some basic human needs. Thus the BEC extols the idea of power as power to work, the fundamental economic activity. One cannot meet basic human needs if one does not have the power to get a job, for example. The implications of this statement are great for soteriology (in relation to unemployment and its effects on a human being), as well as for questions of the reconstruction of society.

There is no naive view of power here, nor a simplistic view of power as that which enables one to get what one wants. Power, the group thought, is the "power to challenge things not good for oneself or for others" and the "power to recognize things good for self and others." One is reminded of Paul Tillich's theological definition of power as the power of being, infused by the power to discern being against non-being.[30] Nelson Mandela is mentioned as a good example of the power of being over non-being in his suffering "all those years in jail" for others whose support he thereby earns, in itself another form of power, this time in solidarity with others.

3. Solidarity with Others

Reading Luke's version of the Lord's Prayer, the BEC noted that though they might not have much in the way of money or food, they were able to survive because they "had God." In a bourgeois setting, to have God might mean something like a spiritual or personal sense of comfort. For the BEC it meant that "maybe God has already talked to a neighbor who will have a plate ready for me when I come." As another group member put it: "Daily bread can mean being strong in God. When one gets bread, one must take half and give half to someone who needs it."[31]

This sense that one's daily bread is also for others who might need it, and that God's strength enables one to enter into this kind of sharing, is contrasted frequently with the behavior and attitude the group expects from the rich. BEC members take it for granted that God's redemptive activity must affect the material conditions of those who do not have enough. For the BEC, difficult choices in the context of scarce resources are possible because of genuine religious commitment.

Economics deals with multiple demands in the face of a scarce supply of resources. Implicit in these views, therefore, is a conviction that the realm of economics is the realm of God's redemptive activity. It is also the realm of sin when one betrays God's redemptive intention in the way one uses and manages economic goods. Solidarity with others must then be both spiritual (expressed in an ethic, an attitude to life, a particular consciousness) and material (with tangible effects).

Justice is thereby invoked—specifically, the need to take a stand for others and to exhibit the courage this might require. This view is captured most clearly in a BEC discussion about a group of women from the larger community who had developed a communal subsistence farming project to supplement their meager income. A distinct possibility existed that a man named Ngomezulu might want to claim title to the land farmed by the women, though it was government owned. Ngomezulu was feared and hated. He had taken brutal revenge on those who thwarted his designs, relying upon apartheid structures to back him. The BEC was concerned that the women would be too scared to prevent him taking over their small plot. "But Jesus says that even if you are scared, you need to tell that person, you need to speak out and say you don't like that thing. We need to fear Satan, not Jesus; the ladies of the gardening group are God's tool, because they are working together."[32]

Thus practices that bind people together in solidarity in service of the cause of justice are redemptive in themselves, not simply because they meet an immediate need but because they exhibit the desired character. In this particular sense, the BEC demonstrates an innate, incipient theological wisdom whose most articulate form may be found in the link Jürgen Moltmann makes between hope (what is anticipated) and planning (living out that anticipation in the world).[33] The self-awareness of this hope is evident in a laconic comment on the devil and the church: "But the devil is already beaten. The church forgets that. It's like watching a video of Pirates and Chiefs [two football teams] when you already know what the score will be." Again, this is no cheap idealism. To respond in practice to this hope, says the BEC, is like walking through the forest toward the light: one knows "it is not easy because there are snakes and lions."[34]

4. A Struggle for Justice

That one might encounter snakes and lions on the road to the anticipated reign of God signals the group's awareness of the difficulties and dangers of living out their redemptive vision. A struggle is involved. Albert Nolan has described the symbolic richness of the term *struggle* in South Africa.[35] Engagement in action for liberation is called *the struggle,* carried out against *the system,* the code word for white supremacy and an economic order that favors a rich minority.

Nolan identifies a variety of activities as theologically significant in the struggle, whose most visible and most characteristic manifestation was not violence but singing and dancing ("the hope that is celebrated"). This singing and dancing, however, were more than a celebration of hope; solidarity and unity in the struggle was also celebrated. This participatory experience "rescues people from alienation, isolation and individualism. It restores *ubuntu* (humanness) and the experience of being a living member of a living body."[36]

The link of Nolan's interpretation to my theme lies in what BEC members understand about themselves. For them, Jesus struggled in the cause of justice for all who suffer. Christians are required to take the same route, though it will not be easy. They refer here to the Zulu or Xhosa word for struggle, *umzabalazo*, which means "it is not easy; we need to be deep, involving our mind and our body, comprehensively."[37] Not surprisingly, the notion of *discipleship* emerges as a religious term for engagement in the struggle for justice.

This religious cast alters what might otherwise be a purely utilitarian or deontological ethic into one that reflects an acceptance of ambiguity and an eschatological vision. This is best captured in yet another interpretation of the Lord's Prayer: A necessary struggle produces God's justice where "soldiers do not favor any side, children are well looked after, [and there is] stability, all-embracing peace, happiness, love, equality, religious unity, not so many denominations, sympathy and empathy, no apartheid, no different racial groups in church, no violence, and kindness." In this reconstructed world, "people will come together, animals will be free, people will share, there will be no sickness and suffering, God will be down here with the people, weapons will be on fire, and there will be no babies without an equal life."[38]

An all-encompassing vision of well-being thus defines the soteriological vision of the BEC as well as the actual conditions from which redemption is required. It might be worth noting here that Abraham Maslow's classic definition of a hierarchy of needs does not fit well with what we discover from this BEC, remembering that this is a seriously impoverished community. Perhaps this is because Maslow did not see that spirituality reflects the transcendent dimension of immanent needs and is not a separate need at the top of a hierarchical list.[39]

The struggle for justice is costly. In Dietrich Bonhoeffer's language, there is no cheap grace, no easy reconciliation. For the BEC this seems obvious: "Once you are a Christian, you won't get rest; even if you are a young person, you won't get rest until you die." Thus Bible study must involve more than talk: "Without doing the right thing, without changing what is wrong, it is useless."[40] The suffering that one endures in the process is sanctified by serendipitous acts of redemption. Redemptive suffering is the practical meaning of grace. For the BEC it is both universal ("Jesus is not only in the Church but in the community; God is where the people are, and loves not only Christians and believers") and transcendent ("Like Jesus we must be persistent, even if we are being defeated time and again").[41]

At this point, the incipient theology of the BEC draws together two themes: the birth of Jesus Christ in a humble place among poor people, and the cross. The incarnation, a creative insertion of divine history in the midst of human history, prefigures the cross because the incarnated one appears among "the least," whose history is a history of suffering. The soteriological significance of these linked themes is summed up for the BEC in two juxtaposed statements, both from Bible studies that followed an Easter march through the gravel streets of their local community.

The first statement notes that Jesus was born in "a country of suffering and darkness." But his birth changes this context: "Jesus' birth is educating and free-ing the poor. . . . When the yoke [of oppression] is broken, the cow is very happy, but the farmer is very angry." Jesus' death, on the other hand, is also necessary "so that people can be freed from the things that oppress them here on earth." Both the birth and the death of Jesus contain within them the symbols of the new—the birth because it brings hope on earth, life in the midst of death; the death because it "reminds people that in all that happens to them, sufferings, death, violence, in all this Christ suffered for them too, and that it will all be overcome, really overcome."[42]

5. Remembering

Jesus' suffering and victory were remembered in another way, one with consid-erable symbolic and practical import for the BEC and, indeed, the wider com-munity. This was the organization of an Easter march through Amawoti. The words "do this in remembrance of me" became for the group the occasion to remember the struggles, sufferings, and small victories they had experienced within their community over the years.

The march set off from the primary health office where many of the BEC worked. It stopped at various points of significance for that community: here a young person was assassinated for his political convictions; there people had been shot by the police; here a temporary roadside camp for homeless people, now several years old, contradicted by new, expensive police barracks directly across the road. These and other memories became the loci of the community's own *via dolorosa*, their own stations of the cross. At each station the group stopped, prayed, preached, and sang. More and more local people joined in until there were hundreds.[43]

This event encapsulates all the key themes of our discussion: The formation of an identity, in solidarity, for the sake of justice, in the knowledge that general suffering is wrong but that suffering for the sake of justice is right. The process unleashed creative power to bond the living with those who had died and were now remembered. We are very close to what Mofokeng reaches for in his Black Christology, but also, I think, to an equally consequential and fundamental understanding of redemption found in feminist theology. For feminist theologian Mary Grey, redemption goes beyond political liberation, although it includes it, to human integrity and wholeness, a creative reclaiming of that which has been broken in life, a search for the sources of creative impulse, a move from creation to new creation:

> Redemption suggests the goal, the process and the method of reaching that desired wholeness. It not only comprehends the personal journeys of men and women to maturity and integrity, the structures of society, damaged and corrupted by vested interests and impoverished vision, but also speaks to the wounds of our damaged planet. It grasps every aspect of the cosmos, every dimension of experience, every aspect of living, past, present and future. It is a word which does not pretend that living is pain-free.[44]

Little is said by the BEC about ancestors as such, a key element of African religion. One brief comment compares the last supper of Jesus and his disciples, in its Eucharistic setting, to the slaughtering of cows in memory of the ancestors.[45] The belief in the importance of relating to one's ancestors, particularly those who have gained an aura of special authority, remains vital to the majority of black South Africans.

Why are they largely absent in the BEC discourses? A general taboo within the dominant forms of Christian theology and catechism on the often misunderstood question of ancestors contributes to the relative silence on the matter. Perhaps a profitable exercise for South African Christians as a whole would be to rethink positively the notion of ancestors, along the lines of the Eastern Orthodox understanding of icons as symbols of remembrance of the exemplary Christian lives of those who have gone before.

Ancestors may function as oppressive authority figures, but that is by no means all they are. From one point of view, they may by understood through

Mead's notion of significant others who help construct a social identity. One may add to this Walter Benjamin's insights into the social construction of memory,[46] which he thinks is deepened by an appreciation of the rich experience of those who have gone before us and upon whom we depend, and diminished by their neglect. This is *Erfahrungen* (thick experience), which integrates a sense of the past and expectations of the future, mediated through cultural awareness. It is opposed to *Erlebnisse* (thin experience), unconnected episodic experiences of the moment, without duration, not enriched by the depth of time or cultural awareness.[47]

Benjamin sees contemporary life under the impact of global market economic forces as an expression of the tyranny of thin experience, in "the replacement of coherent narration by dissociated information as the dominant mode of communication." To rediscover thick experience is "a matter of tradition, in collective existence as well as in private life."[48] Benjamin goes on to apply these insights to death. Under modernist conditions, we tend to curtail death, to package it and bury it quickly. We cut short an enduring, experienced memory of the dead. This removal of the dead from memory, Benjamin suggests, deadens our capacity to create new futures. All we have left is the repetition of countless deaths which make no difference to the future. They merely represent "the miserable endlessness of a scroll. Tradition is eliminated from it. It is the quintessence of a passing moment [*Erlebnis*]."[49]

Thus Benjamin believed that revolutionaries who sought to build a new future without respecting the sacrifices previous generations had made were doomed to re-create the evils of the past. The suffering of past generations must be understood, remembered (made part of our corporate body), and in this way given their due respect. This is the route to genuine transformation.

Remembering ancestors may thus be understood as a recovery and a reaffirmation of thick experience in the face of oppression, exploitation, and systemic violence in the lives of a subjugated people. It is both a retention of tradition in the face on an onslaught against it, and a form of resistance at the level of discourse and imagination against the colonization of time itself by a market economy and the modernist project.

The Amawoti BEC does not produce this kind of thinking through reference to ancestors, although it might if the masks of interpretation could be lowered further. But it does do so in the Easter march and the remembering of those in their own community who have suffered and died.

The sixth of Mofokeng's categories, on the recovery of land, finds no reference in Amawoti. Yet jobs and work in general are discussed frequently. This suggests both a redirection of interests to an urbanized, industrialized setting, and a recasting of the issue of ownership in other terms. More than that one cannot really say.

Conclusion

One cannot draw too many conclusions from a limited set of Bible studies. Yet the practical value of this investigation lies in the likelihood that the BEC probably reflects many of the perspectives and experiences of an increasing, and already large, body of South Africans who live in similar conditions. The heuristic value of the Bible studies lies in the reflection on the meaning of the localized religious experience of the BEC members. Their interpretive activity offers an acute insight into the potential of religious life and thought for the needs of reconstruction and development.

The point of dealing with the Bible studies in a systematic fashion—trying to understand the broad framework of the perspective on God, Christ, and redemption—is to provoke the judgment that their theological framework is both coherent and instructive for the theological enterprise as a whole. In this respect, at this stage I offer several judgments about the hermeneutical implications of reading the BEC texts.

1. There is a "priority of praxis over theory" in the christological formulations of the community in Amawoti.[50]

2. Christological formulations are generated by reflections produced in and for a community, rather than in relation to an individual existence.

3. The tradition itself is weighed in the balance of communal considerations, and interpreted accordingly.

4. The location of the community is important for an understanding of truth, so that what is read out of the tradition begins with a commitment of a communal God to the people who are poor, marginalized, and oppressed.

5. This commitment is not exclusive of the rich or powerful, but it does mean that the message of the gospel is not read with the interpretive interests of the rich and the powerful in the foreground.

The interpretive activity of the Amawoti BEC shows us how much the message of the gospel is polysemic.[51] But the polysemy of the text itself is not entirely arbitrary. It is restricted by its semantic structure, its surrounding text, and its location in a canon. In Paul Ricoeur's language, the text has an intentionality of its own: It projects possible worlds.

This is what makes it possible for the text to be interpreted by the poor of Amawoti in a way that also produces valid meaning for the rich. The polysemy of the text implies, in this respect, that the gospel message will be coherent for both the context of the rich and of the poor, but it will address them differently. This dynamic is most evident in the way in which the group understood the trickiness of Jesus, and it clearly opposes any simplistic literalist interpretation of the text.

In one way or another, these are the clues we will follow in a series of theoretical reflections on the problems of incipient theologies. The BEC texts have provided the initial starting point and impetus to raise the hermeneutical questions dealt with in a more general form. Amawoti gives rise to thought.[52]

3. Tradition and Domination

"Sheep are stupid beasts," the Mayor exclaimed with venom. "I have never understood why the founder of your faith should have compared them with ourselves. 'Feed my sheep.' Oh yes, perhaps after all like other good men he was a cynic. 'Feed them well, make them fat, so that they can be eaten in their turn.' 'The Lord is my shepherd.' But if we are sheep why in heaven's name should we trust our shepherd? He's going to guard us from wolves all right, oh yes, but only so that he can sell us later to the butcher."
—Graham Greene, Monsignor Quixote

In all that has been said so far about the contextual and thus contemporary nature of the BEC's reflection on faith, the ghost of tradition lurks. Is tradition good or bad?

Graham Greene's mayor makes statements that, even when not taken in the same cynical vein, hint at the ways in which religion has functioned, at worst as oppression or somewhat less strongly as a constraint on human freedom. Some of the Amawoti texts express a similar view about tradition, particularly in the way in which clergy use it to wield authority. Yet the matter is clearly more complex and nuanced than that.

The notion of tradition emphasizes an enduring deposit of thought and experience to guide present and future generations. The German term *Über-lieferung,* that which is "delivered over" to us, conveys this precisely. Tradition ties a person and a community to a particular past. Tradition in this sense affects the Amawoti BEC from several directions—an African heritage, an imported faith, and a modern constellation of social and economic forces which have shaped their lives long enough to produce new traditions. The complex hermeneutical problems and strategies underlying this reality is our focus.

Tradition–A Provisional Sketch

In the founding narratives that describe the gathering of disciples around Jesus of Nazareth, in the inception of the Christian community proper, and in the literature that precedes and arises from it, the Christian faith appears dialogical in its intent and structure. Its character lies in the forms of communicative interaction that gave it birth rather than in any strict personality cult, enshrined rule book, or cherished collective tradition.

Thus we find parables and narratives as the form of the Gospels, teachings as spoken word contrasted with the Pharasaic dependence on written law, letters as the means of engaging with new communities in the work of Paul. All exemplify a communicative impulse aimed at determining truth through a communicative rationality. This communicative dynamic enabled the expansion of the faith as an extension of the *Word* (of God), which was already a term for communication.[1]

The communicative practice of Christians is extended similarly throughout the history of the faith, with ongoing interpretation of its claims and origins a clear characteristic of the tradition. Its most important results are captured in literature, confessions, creeds, liturgical rituals, symbolic acts, and dogmatic proclamations. That these products of interpretation are sometimes treated as a fixed deposit does not make the trajectory of the Christian faith any less a history of communicative practice. Recorded in one way or another, this communicative practice is the simplest way of describing what counts as Christian tradition.

We should distinguish between two kinds of communication at this point. The recorded tradition of Christians past, like the tradition we are in the process of confirming, altering, or supplementing today, arose from long, complex processes of communication. Some of these processes occurred between contemporaries, others drew on what had gone before. Thus synchronic (explicitly with others in our time) and diachronic (implicitly with others of previous times) communications remain central to a proper appreciation of the actual meaning of the tradition as an inheritance and as a significant choice in the present.

Of course, harmony, peace, and agreement are not always or necessarily present in the process. Indeed, this has often not been the case. Where the process has become particularly heated, a regular occurrence throughout the history of Christianity, disagreement has shaded into disharmony and hostility, sometimes to the point of violent conflict. Thus *tradition* should really be written as *traditions,* for at least since the schism between the Western and Eastern churches, including the splits occasioned by the Reformation in the Western church, one could argue that Christianity has developed distinct variations of the tradition held by the Old Catholic church, itself already a variation on a theme. One can find similar distinctions within the scriptural record itself.

It is clear that the Christian tradition must be understood as dynamic, as an unending development of various trajectories in faith. Some of these trajectories are compatible, some are not; some become dead ends, some are recovered and brought to life again. But none stand still while they live. They live only because they enable human beings who claim the Christian faith as significant, to represent, orient, transform, and communicate their lives in ways they find realistic, meaningful, and hopeful.[2]

In this sense, the tradition is about the discovery of truth. I will argue further that the truth discovered through this communicative practice, that which is recorded in tradition, is neither the whole truth nor the only truth. As something is revealed, much is concealed. Ambiguity and uncertainty remain, no matter how dogmatic claims to truth may be. Uncertainty and insecurity, however, cannot always be tolerated in the face of human needs for assurance, comfort, and stability. Necessarily, therefore, a tradition will concretize itself in enduring claims for the kind of truth it represents. One example, the result of a long and still not wholly complete battle, is the formation of the Biblical canon. If one is not to trivialize the issue, such central accretions of tradition must be taken into account in any contemporary hermeneutics of tradition.

Now we arrive at another complication: The tradition handed down to us as a public record is not the full record. As a public record it both reveals and conceals the truth. This is not merely a matter of epistemology, a question of paradigms, of the limits of language, of hiddenness of being, or of the provisional character of all acting. Particular histories are revealed or concealed in tradition by virtue of the exercise of power and authority over the interpretive act, the products of interpretation, and their recording.

All traditions are particular, and any particular tradition is constructed—by human beings, of course—rather than essential, that is, given in an external source of revelation. One may legitimately ask, therefore, who does the constructing? To what extent is a particular record the reflection of the perspectives and practices of a dominant group, class, or elite? To what extent may it be read as the public record of the marginalized, silenced, and poor sectors of its host societies throughout its history?

As an example, Itumeleng Mosala clearly believes—taking his book on biblical hermeneutics[3] as his credo—that the biblical text leaves out the voices of the oppressed almost entirely. The subaltern does not speak in the scriptural record. If this is so for Scripture, how much more so for the rest of the recorded tradition of the church?

Another example: In African religious history it has been argued with some force that the Donatist movement during the period in which Augustine was most influential in North Africa was crushed in the interests of a centralized power that was about to collapse. The Donatist movement was an attempt by Africans to construct an indigenous Christianity without dependence on the European centers of church authority ultimately defended by Augustine.

This history is seldom read from an African perspective, however. Donatism is usually discussed only in relation to doctrinal disputes with the dominant church (particularly as represented by Augustine) over questions of the purity of faith.[4] Yet as W. H. C. Frend notes, its program of social reform was unmistakable, representing an "equation of social revolutionary zeal coupled with eschatological hopes and the rejection of the established forms of organization of religion."[5] This Augustine did not see or appreciate. He saw himself as bound up with the Roman church authorities in the first place,[6] and it has been said that his "personality and work were the last brilliant product of the Roman way of life in Africa."[7]

Augustine won the battle, though Donatism as a counterhegemonic (heretical) movement only finally disappeared under the impact of the Muslim conquest of North Africa in the eighth century. Thus the tradition here reflects primarily the perspective in the writings of Augustine. The public record strongly mirrors the perspective of the victor and weakly, if at all, reflects the subjugated knowledge of the vanquished.

The subjugation of the Donatist movement had a theological impact as well. With Augustine's victory came the decisive turn in Western Christianity to a dualist view of reality ("the tendency to regard salvation as a private matter and to ignore the world"[8]) and to an introversion, a psychologization of faith.[9] Just as significantly, the Donatist (African) emphasis on wholeness and the integrity of the community was lost.

This example suggests that the products of the communicative practice of faith generally reflect the interests or perspectives of the dominant rather than the interests or perspectives of the dominated. At the same time, the voices of dominated groups are never entirely absent, as Mosala suggests, an important claim for my general argument about the incipient theology of the Amawoti BEC. What presence do they have then? Ironically, perhaps only that which lies in the traces of their absence or in encoded form.[10]

Discerning such presence is a complex task, as historians of popular life well know,[11] especially when one takes into account the question of representation: Whose voices, in the end, do we hear? The voices of the oppressed themselves, or their voices as represented by others? Whatever the answer, the work of James C. Scott and Jean and John Comaroff[12] sufficiently undermines too strong or too one-sided a theory of the hegemony of dominant knowledge to allow the bald-faced claim that all we have in the public record of the Christian tradition is the voice of the dominant elites.[13]

In seeing tradition as communicative practice, we acknowledge a history of contested communication. This contestation is bound up with the limits and actualities of language and being, with the role that power plays in the construction of knowledge, with the human need to conserve certain experiences and claims against a paralyzing abyss of uncertainty or ambiguity, with the possibilities of language and being, and with the role resistance and innovation offer in gaining new knowledge.

In the end, the Christian tradition is simply (though not simplistically) testimony through the centuries by myriad communities of faith and their spokespersons, in crisis and in celebration, in conflict and in conciliation, of what this faith means.

Confronted by Traditions

I have used the term *tradition* largely in the singular, meaning the Christian tradition in general (noting that the Christian tradition is also plural in important respects). Yet more is at stake. We are confronted in practice by different senses of the notion of tradition, and by differing general traditions, in any encounter with a community such as the Amawoti BEC.

Here tradition lives as the heritage by which Christians name themselves. If Christians call themselves thus, they necessarily relate to that particular heritage as the source and touchstone of identity, however critically they may judge parts of its legacy. Otherwise they are left with a superfluous faith or a superficial faith. Here, too, tradition persists through an African cultural endowment (even if transformed and changing) with a similar impact. Tradition, in each case, is not the same thing, in content or historical development.

Thus we have a growing debate in South Africa and elsewhere about the link between liberation and inculturation,[14] a debate that also makes clear that tradition (Christian, African, or any other) may function to oppress or restrain the development of people. It is commonplace in South Africa that Christian tradition, introduced or imposed from Europe and North America, bears in part the double historical burden of being tied to the regional interests of an imperial power and being bound to the explicitly Christian social theory of apartheid.[15]

In reading the Bible together, the Amawoti BEC became aware of the tension between the two trajectories of liberation and inculturation. Teachings or actions of Jesus that were considered culturally different or that posed a challenge to their sense of African identity introduced problems for the group which were not resolved.

The teaching in Matt. 5:27-30 against adultery and lust produced this reaction: "We are a different nation. We need to follow our culture. Having sex freely is right according to our culture, but not according to the Bible."[16] The question is raised whether study of the Bible does not make the group forget their valued African traditions, forcing on them the beliefs of other cultures or nations. Nuances arise. Late in the group's life together, a member notes, "Jesus did not come to destroy all African traditions. There are those traditions that God detests (*amenyanyisayo*). . . . But there are also those traditional customs that God likes."[17] The group could not decide, however, how to sort out the distinction.

The hermeneutics of tradition also appear in the worries of those who fear the dilution, the depreciation, or the corruption of the tradition they take to be holy. Is one not in danger of eclecticism or syncretism if one takes too seriously the kind of theological thinking that emerges from a less than orthodox group such as the Amawoti BEC? How does one deal with AICs whose orthodoxy is even less recognizable to those schooled in Western traditions? Are we not inexorably led to heresy or, worse, the destruction of the very foundations of faith? Is a contextual theology not the thin edge of the wedge?

One of the most sophisticated versions of this kind of questioning comes from George Lindbeck. His rule-theory model for Christian doctrine argues that the received religious tradition provides us with a "grammar of faith" within which we must operate. This grammar places strong limits on what new may be said or not said about revelation. While Lindbeck makes an important point, he seems to miss (1) the unstated and usually unrecognized prejudices and interpretive interests behind any grammar, and (2) the limits to, and ambiguities inherent in, any theological claims anyone makes.[18]

The debates about the nature of (Christian) tradition are both long-standing and numerous. To make them fruitful for my purposes here, we will pursue only a select, related set of questions about tradition, each of which has obvious roots in my dialogue with the Amawoti BEC:

1. In what sense may we describe Christian tradition as essentially a dynamic activity of interpretation (rather than a fixed deposit of truth)?

2. In what sense is the tradition contested and what does this do to its claims for truth?

3. Is popular religion a reliable source for the construction of Christian tradition, and can context be normative for Christian theology?

The central concern is how we are to understand the nature and function of Christian tradition in the faithful reflections the Amawoti BEC carry out. The territory we will cover may be described as treacherous, bordered by the shadowy marsh of popular religion, the bramble thicket of hermeneutics, and the precarious slope of context. The reader may emerge from the other side wet and muddy, scratched and torn, bruised and possibly bloody. Perhaps there is no other way—outside of the sterile, paved road of dogmatic certainties—to deal with tradition in our time without losing either its significance for a grasp of reality or our own integrity as reasoning, feeling human beings.

The Dynamic Interpretation of Tradition

What needs to be said about the dynamic nature of the Christian tradition can be done by considering again the mediated thoughts[19] of the Amawoti BEC on the question of redemption. Our look at the BEC's approach to redemption clearly pointed to an immanent soteriology rather than a transcendent one. Yet a transcendent ethic, pointing to something not yet present in their lives, is also evident in the eschatological language used by the BEC.

Such an ethic enabled them to perceive the limitations of their own actions, the anticipatory nature of their successes, and the historical conditioning of their context. It enabled them to contemplate that which is not, to envision other ways of relating, organizing, and embodying their hopes than those that present conditions one might suggest are possible.

The soteriology we saw emerging revealed a strong link to a communal understanding of life and to solidarity with others, including those who have died. Behavior and belief, practice and proclamation, practical sense and con- templative wisdom—all are difficult to separate in the ensuing religious world- view. As the needs, demands, and crises change in the daily life of the BEC, so too does their interpretive focus, producing a changing, developing view on the meaning of God's redemptive activity.

This, naturally, affects their view on God as such. The term most used for God, we noted, is *Nkosinathi,* meaning "God with us," embodied in their daily lives, Immanuel. The universal and the particular, the infinite and the finite, the actual and the possible—all meet in God's ongoing presence with the community.

The truth of God's revelation depends, therefore, upon whatever the truth of the situation demands. It is not that the situation dictates what counts as truth, but that truth reveals something about the situation which allows for redemptive existence to become real in the life of the community.

Because truth is situationally bound in this way, it conceals at this one point what it might reveal at another point. Truth is dynamic, remains dynamic, and cannot be claimed as known at any point without a substantial, inescapable residue of uncertainty and ambiguity. If this is so, then no moment of revelation is complete, nor are we able to treat any statements we or others make about revelation in that moment as certain, stable, or infallible. The idea that one can claim or proclaim "the whole truth and nothing but the truth" is an idolatry, a usurpation of God's point of view and thus of God.

The same applies to Christian tradition. Each and every element of it must be understood as situationally bound, revealing and concealing simultaneously. No complete truth may be found here, at least not by human beings. Even the most cherished confessions and creeds are bound in this way. They may be understood as expressions of a moment of hard-won truth in a particular time, and they endure for that reason as an inheritance we must digest, consider, and judge. They draw us into a community with a long history of struggle and debate, of error and achievement, and they thereby contribute to our own search for a fully human life in a whole world. But they cannot dictate for all time and for all places what we should say, do, and believe about Christ, God, and the world. Where tradition—including Scripture—is nevertheless used as a dictatorial device, subtle or crude, there violence is done to all three: Christ, God, and the world.

Contested Traditions

One might ask if there is not perhaps some more complete truth to be found precisely in the totality of the development of the tradition. Do not all the moments of truth in the tradition form part of a larger historical whole, a summation of truth first captured in the Bible, to be subsequently expanded by later theological traditions? If so, all Christians would be bound by this totality.

Then this totality could be mastered only by the few, for the tradition is complex, its history is often confused, its lacunae frequently not well understood, and its claims and counterclaims often obscure. We would require domination by an ecclesial elite, certainly not unusual in Christian history. It is precisely out of a critique of such ecclesial contexts of domination that what we today call sociology and critical theory began.[20] More importantly, we then radically diminish ordinary Christians' actual experiences of and reflections on faith. Such a loss is what this book questions and challenges.

The point is contemporary. Juan Luis Segundo, whose reflections arise out of a context not that dissimilar from that of the Amawoti BEC, has suggested that tradition be understood as of a developing totality of truth. Extending his early methodological discussions about theology as "deutero-learning,"[21] he proposes we read the tradition as an educational process, a process of "learning to learn" (deutero-learning).[22] Each element of the tradition, situationally understood, is a further step toward the truth, from the time of the Jewish patriarchs through the New Testament and beyond. For Segundo, this process is infallible, although he adds that the scriptures themselves or "any formula proper to a moment within that process, can contain things that in themselves are 'incomplete and temporary.'"[23]

Segundo attempts to escape the straitjackets of dogma and teaching authority in this way, emphasizing that the tradition testifies not to a fixed set of truths but a process of learning more truth. Yet I am not convinced that he resolves the dilemma sufficiently. Postmodernism, understood as a critique of the paradigms of modernity, helps us grasp the problems with Segundo's approach. For our purposes, the Comaroffs' description of postmodernism is most suggestive. They see postmodernism as assisting in: (1) the need to address the indeterminacies of meaning and action, events, and processes in history; (2) the admonition to regard culture not as an overdetermining, closed system of signs but as a set of polyvalent practices, texts, and images that may, at any time, be contested; (3) the invitation to see power as a many-sided, often elusive and diffuse force that is always implicated in culture, consciousness, and representation; and (4) the importance of treating the writing of histories as a generic mode of making both the past and the present.[24]

The first point emphasizes indeterminacy in all aspects of history. Segundo's proposal for a view on the Christian tradition, including Scripture, retains the notion of infallibility applied to a total learning process. It is this infallible process, inspired and instituted by God, into which we are initiated by scripture and tradition. Why does Segundo take this route? It seems he wishes to avoid wholly discarding the notion of infallibility, perhaps for strategic reasons, while making space for a critique of the content of Roman Catholic ex cathedra pronouncements that claim dogmatic certainty.

However, I can see no a priori grounds in a theory about deutero-learning for accepting the notion that the tradition is fallible in its content but not in its pedagogical intentions. To locate the absolute in a process is still to locate it firmly, securely, without ambiguity or contradiction. A postmodernist critique, as in the first point made by the Comaroffs, correctly disallows a revised essentialist metaphysic.

On to the second point: If we substitute the term *Christian tradition* for the term *culture,* then its texts, liturgies, rituals, creeds, and all other knowledge it contains and transmits must be seen not as a closed system of signs but as polyvalent and contested. Segundo grants the fact of polyvalence in the tradition, noting that theologians, even if not always laypeople, generally take for granted the reality of multiple interpretations and valuations of any doctrine (only thus could one explain how the recorded Christian tradition came into being in its present forms).

Yet the notion of tradition as contested is not clear in Segundo's approach. Contestation implies substantial difference in claims made by Christians, to the point of direct contradiction. Segundo, however, believes the tradition must at every point be understood in relation to the situation and time out of which it arose. Each situation and time contains its own truth, which may not exist and is often not appropriate for another situation or time. It thus appears as if we are dealing with contradictions ("errors"). But in his view these are not errors or contradictions. They are limited, partial truths, valid for their time and place and, insofar as we understand and learn from what those of other times discovered, valid for our time and place too. What is crucial here is the almost obsessional need to find a locus of certainty, of absoluteness, of control, by which to define the world. Against this speaks the second point made by the Comaroffs, not only that truth is partial but also that it is fundamentally a realm of contestation.

The third point they make ("power as a many-sided, often elusive and dif-fuse force . . . always implicated in culture, consciousness, and representation") just as powerfully undercuts the model Segundo proposes as the solution to the problem of tradition. If contestation and diffuse forms of power inhabit our world and the worlds of those who have gone before us, then it is impossible to see how the Christian tradition can be read as a relatively harmonious process of learning to learn in which each moment, understood for itself, adds to truth. The effects of contestation and power suggest that the tradition may be flawed more profoundly than allowed by Segundo, demanding of us a rather more sub-stantial critique of each of its moments.

I would regard as more persuasive Itumeleng Mosala's hermeneutics,[25] which sees in the scriptures texts that conceal, in the interests of power, as much as (if not more than) they reveal. Mosala probably relies too much on an overly structuralist model of domination and hegemony,[26] but the Amawoti BEC Bible studies support his intuition about the contested, power-laden nature of inter-pretation more strongly than they do Segundo's notion that each interpretation has its valid truth.

Segundo's most helpful point concerns the openness of tradition against all attempts to close it down, to narrow it to one meaning either to secure power over another or to protect oneself against potential threats posed by the thoughts, practices, or beliefs of the other. But his solution to the question of inspiration and inerrancy I find unconvincing, binding Christians to a still too limited view of the tradition.[27]

Redemption Revisited: The Impact of Context
Most of the early major battles of the Christian tradition (Gnosticism, Mar-cionism, Montanism, Docetism, the great christological controversies) were bound up with the question of what does and does not count as redemption, and on what grounds. To probe the distance between the classical doctrines in inherited tradition, and what makes sense in local contexts defined by experiences of subjugation, deprivation, and relative powerlessness, it will be useful to return to the question of redemption, in a context not unlike that of the Amawoti BEC, drawing on an insightful study by Ronald Nicol-son. [28]

Nicolson conducts an imaginary dialogue with a young black person (Sipho) in a local South African township.[29] What could Sipho accept as genuinely redemptive in the South African context? Showing that most traditional atone-ment theories are inadequate, Nicolson concludes that Sipho would find a satis-factory theory of salvation only where he finds in Jesus Christ the motivation for doing something about his own condition. Jesus Christ is "a catalyst in a process of autosoteriology, of self-salvation."[30]

Salvation implies that one is saved from something, usually termed *sin* (however defined). Salvation is what God does to redeem sin; it is how God intervenes to make good what has been corrupted, disrupted, or damaged. Sipho's history tells him that God does not intervene directly. Nor can he accept that the humiliation he has suffered because he is black is the result of personal sin. In his case, the sin of others against him is more pertinent.

This much should be obvious from the direction of thought pursued by Nicolson's dialogue with Sipho: If we take Sipho and his like seriously, we must question the received tradition at many points, altering, reconstructing, even rejecting it where necessary. This does not preclude, of course, the task of clarifying the possible value of the tradition, both as a challenge and an insight into our reality.

The Amawoti Bible studies support Nicolson's thesis. There is considerable harmony between many of the elements he sees as necessary in our context and those teased out earlier from the BEC using the categories of Takatso Mofokeng. Moreover, Nicolson grounds the method used with the Amawoti BEC: "Talk about whether and what God is may or may not need to have an empirical base. Talk about what God does surely cannot possibly make sense without such a base."[31]

The transcripts of the BEC dialogues on biblical texts provide us with a first link to that empirical base. I have added the claim that listening to or dialoguing with communities or persons normally regarded as insignificant in their contribution to Christian truth is an essential methodological foundation for testing that truth. Otherwise, supposedly general Christian truths remain those of the powerful, the elite, the trained, and the dominant groups in society and history.

Past tradition was neither uncontested in content nor processes it transmitted as tradition, although this contestation is related to the construction of knowledge on the back of uneven power relations. A paradigmatic case study of the point has been made by Rubem Alves, on Protestantism and repression in Brazil. He analyzes what he calls Right-Doctrine Protestantism (RDP), a blend of Calvinist fundamentalism and pietism brought to Brazil by nineteenth-century missionaries and sustained by others ever since. RDP concentrates theologically on the anxieties of people in personal or social crisis by offering freedom through conversion to a faith that guarantees absolute truth and excludes the possibility of doubt.[32] A "new security system" is constructed with a religious authority as its guardian.

In Brazil this form of Christianity has wreaked havoc with the hopes of the poor and marginalized, and seen the withdrawal of progressive Christian people, their enforced marginalization, or their exclusion from religious institutions. Alves does not blame earnest RDP adherents for this state of affairs. He regards the outcome as "the natural if not inevitable expression of the inherent logic of Right-Doctrine Protestantism."[33]

This logic is grounded in the juridical practices of an institution that disciplines individuals, demanding that they be faithful servants of institutionally defined categories of understanding and practice, which in turn are sacralized through creeds and confessions. The underlying logic Alves defines as "a single, total, closed rationality which provides no way of *naming* contradictions; and what cannot be said, cannot be thought."[34] The ethic attached to this rationality is an ethic of the civil servant. The functional needs of the institution determine the logic of behavior.

Alves concludes that the "suggestion of the serpent" in the biblical myth of the fall, the temptation of absolute knowledge, once heeded unfolds its logic "with syllogistic precision." For him there is only one way out: "We must consciously and deliberately reject truth and certainty before they take hold of us."[35] A redemptive process, accordingly, is one in which an experience of life, growth, and fulfillment in the creative embrace of doubt and change becomes so compelling "that women and men no longer need the security provided by sacred authority and absolute truth."[36] This, at least, is Richard Shaull's summary of Alves's hope in his foreword to the book.

But Shaull asks, does such a redemptive process have any chance of success? The Brazilian case is not encouraging in this respect. Sadly, the spirit Alves champions did not survive in any institutional form. Shaull believes there are two reasons for this. First, those who were part of the movement had no strategy worked out for the survival of their communities. Second, and perhaps more important, he believes that the leadership of this movement (including Shaull himself) and their small communities "were sustained by their newly found social concerns and political activities more than by a compelling new experience of the power of the gospel." They had not articulated a new religious language capable of speaking to people in general.

This is the challenge of grasping the phenomenon of incipient theology, by definition a source of knowledge and wisdom already articulated by ordinary people in religious language. Ordinary people live out of tradition and traditions. To grasp what this means requires a hermeneutical reconstruction. But if paying respect to the importance of tradition is one side of the coin, the other is a hermeneutical suspicion about both the past and the present, if our dependence on tradition is not to foster new forms of oppressive dogma and authority.

The Coherence of Context and Tradition

Where a received tradition fruitfully interacts with the present context as living truth, it is experienced as a healthily constitutive of individuals and communities. Hans-Georg Gadamer reminds us that tradition in this sense must be reinstated alongside critique and deconstruction as a fundamental category of what it means to be human.

Let us pursue the point by way of a contrast. Salvation in the industrialized and individuated ethos of modern developed societies is probably understood more as an internal matter, often with the soul as its focus, than a social one. Moltmann calls this the *cultus privatus*.[37] The cult of privatization is also present in developing societies such as South Africa, to the extent that the Amawoti BEC are sufficiently aware of it in their own context to offer critical comment.

What challenges it? Perhaps the biblical metaphor of the body as the locus of spiritual reality? This at least is suggested by some of the BEC readings. Body firmly locates one in the world. It cannot be extracted from the world of which it is part. The body thereby unites the personal and the communal, the internal and the external. Christian anthropology embraces the body, both in the image of resurrection (the transformation of the body) and in the profound reaction of the early Church to the gnostic and docetic heresies (de-emphasizing body and world). Paul also extensively draws on the metaphor of the body in pointing to the variety of roles and functions members of the community fill, in a holistic vision of reality. The body is also an embodiment of creation itself, linking creative human being to the created earth.[38]

Salvation or redemption cannot be understood as anything less than body: It is concrete, historically located, and materially significant, or it is not salvation. By the same token, we may speak of the condition from which one is redeemed as brokenness: it is the broken body that is redeemed and made whole. This broken body is not atomic, individual, or independent, but corporate, that is, related to other bodies and to the body of the earth itself.[39] The Eucharistic liturgy in which we speak of the body of Jesus "broken for us" (and the blood shed) takes on this meaning and locates it in history, leading necessarily to a corporeal and communal understanding of salvation.

The Amawoti Bible studies point to a strong coherence between this reading of the Christian tradition and the experientially shaped beliefs, values, and significant religious symbols of the BEC. It expresses itself in the close link between the discursive activity of the BEC and their intentional embodied actions in the wider community.[40] This makes the perspectives and practices of the BEC more than just interesting. They offer a good starting point for rereading the Christian tradition.

A local rereading may, of course, emphasize a disembodied, pietistic faith. In this case it is unlikely to display a critical engagement with context. Critical engagement is likely to arise only where the local community enters into a relatively unconstrained discourse of contradictions of practical life (as in Amawoti), or by an encounter with other communities whose reading is different, or by the tools of historical and social analysis. A local theology that closes itself off to such possibilities remains far less instructive for rereading the tradition.

I have proposed that communities such as the Amawoti BEC or the majority of AICs are touchstones (not necessarily the arbitrators!) of an adequate Christian theology. Their knowledge, wisdom, traditions, and practices offer important correctives to the top-down method we normally use in reconstructing society or the church. The social impact of a methodology that pays attention to incipient theologies may be limited. But implicit in it is an ecclesiology and an approach to the construction of knowledge, starting from the base of ordinary believers, which offers possibilities and potentialities for building a democratic citizenry able to participate more fully in decisions about their own lives, and thus in the making of a nation. This would be a credible expression of Christian faith as embodied. It is also a very good reason to explore and build upon the incipient theologies of our people.

An Understanding of Context

The notion of a contextual or situated theology has repeatedly been at the back of previous discussions. Clearly, context is normative for theology. But can context be considered a reliable and defensible norm for theology? What is meant by *context*? Is the term not confused and inherently misleading, one to be avoided?

The term is not precise, yet it has strategic value. In South Africa, at least, during the 1980s the term *contextual* became a widely used code word for resistance theology.[41] Its vagueness requires those who read, hear, or use it to clarify, at least for themselves, what it means. And, the notion of context as normative drives one away from the philosophical universalism that bedevils so much of modern theology. There exist, then, historical, pedagogical, and philosophical reasons for the term. Still, its vagueness demands some clarification of its use in this text.

Context might be taken simply as synonymous with *Sitz im Leben*. Then all one would mean by saying theology is contextual is that it arises in and out of a particular place and time, that it is situated (a descriptive and superficial meaning). If this is all that is meant by *context*, all theology is contextual. If this is all the term conveys, it is trivial because it is self-evident and it is unnecessary because it adds nothing to our understanding.

Context should be read as a critical term, defined by an analytical approach to life worlds. This implies that the meaning of the term goes beyond a descriptive or comparative approach. To analyze a situation requires that one asks questions, among other things, about the material and social conditions that define and ideologically shape knowledge (theology). The answers to such questions contextualize the *Sitz im Leben*.

Such use of the term is not self-evident. It is contested, at least implicitly, by those who take it to mean nothing more than the particularity in time and space of a specific group of people. In this latter perspective, all good theology addresses or arises out of a real situation and is taken to be acceptable in its own right, because it arises and addresses a real human need or fear. Each context produces its own validity claims. No context can be judged by claims arising from a different context.

I oppose such an interpretation. It merely coopts, for false purposes, a notion of context that from the outset was radically critical of theologies bound to specific contexts of domination or oppression. Although I am not wedded to the term, I am bound to this original insight that the term expressed. What context implies in theological discourse, at least as I use it, is similar in one respect to the insights that drive historical-critical approaches to Scripture. A depth investigation of the formative material and social conditions of the situation (text), using the tools of critical and historical analysis, replaces a surface reading. The use of sociological tools adds the theoretical insight that knowledge is ideologically determined, and the practical insight that ideologically determined knowledge may be either oppressive or emancipatory.

One should go further. The precision of the term *context* as I wish to use it lies in an understanding of persons constituted by a "concrete totality," a phrase from Anselm Min[42] who argues on philosophical grounds that the "person as a concrete totality" captures the necessary holistic relationship between mind and matter, body and soul, the spiritual and the material, the private and the public, or the individual and the social that defines any particular human being. To understand a person or people in context requires that we pay attention to this totality, and refuse any reduction of holistic complexity.

A contextual theological analysis must then grasp the situation of particular human beings as a totality, that is, as they construct reality in a specific time and place through language, work, and other practices, and as they are constructed by past histories and present discourses, structures, and actions. Revelation, analogously, is concrete, incarnate, historical—and thus also contextually shaped. It is not an essence given once and for all that merely requires new applications. There is no separation of ethics from doctrine, with only the application of the principles or axioms flowing from the latter.

To be sure, no theologian of substance would question the idea that theological doctrines must be understood, if they are to be understood at all, within a context out of which they arose. They are situated. But, to repeat myself, situatedness is not what I mean by *contextual*.

Contextual theology begins with an emancipatory interest grounded in the real material conditions of oppressed local communities or groups of persons. Theologies that do not begin here, or those that do so at a distance from the real conditions of such groups, are not contextual as I define the term. Their categories, terms, frameworks, and problem solutions would all derive outside the specific local context. Such theologies are not innocent of the link between knowledge and power either, although they may appear or claim to be innocent. They easily exist, therefore, as the practice of an elite group of trained individuals.

My view on the meaning of *context* as privileging the perspective of the poor, the marginalized, the victim draws on two general claims. The first takes note of three characteristic elements in the Christian tradition: (1) Jesus' highly unusual (in his context) privileging of such people in his ministry; (2) the early Christian emphasis on the inseparability of body-mind and world-spirit in the divine redemptive activity—an emphasis given force in the later view on the inseparable humanity and divinity of Christ; and (3) the central significance of the cross, that is, the suffering shared and borne by Jesus for the sake of the world. All three elements are distinctive, and they define the meaning of the Great Commandment, Love God and your neighbor as yourself.

The second general claim depends upon the first. It simply states that redemption is precisely an overcoming of the conditions that enslave, dehumanize, marginalize, and alienate us from our neighbor, our self, and God. Redemption concerns body-mind and world-spirit by sharing and bearing suffering. Our responsibility to this divine task begins at least in an understanding of who suffers, why they suffer, and what those who suffer experience. It does so by confronting the agents and forces of suffering in the name of the comprehensive well-being of all.

Contextual Commitment: A Reduction, or a Norm of Faith?

Joining the terms context and commitment might well prompt the suspicion that Christian faith here functions merely to legitimate a particular set of ideologically determined convictions in the name of a supposed universal truth. This is one argument, for example, against the theological claim of God's preferential option for the poor. Those who defend such a commitment, on the other hand, argue that it is nonexclusive and generally defensible: it expresses the point of the gospel for all, rich and poor.[43]

Whatever the merits of this argument, the related but slightly different point we will pursue concerns the claim that context is normative for Christian theology. We have already noted that context shapes all theology. Asking whether it is normative presses the point considerably further.

To build a response to this question, we begin with the long and honored doctrine of the *sensus fidei,* the sense of the faith present in the people of God generally. The doctrine implies that the magisterium (clergy, theologians, hierarchy) has the role only of defining the actually held common faith of the church. It serves rather than directs the faith of the church at large, seeking to grasp and formulate from below the working of the spirit in the community of faith rather than defining from above what counts as truth. Although this tradition has remained weak in the way dogma often arises, it does support the notion that popular faith and experience, inevitably shaped by the specificity of local and historical contexts, contributes normatively to the construction of dogma.

The notion of the *sensus fidei* is particularly difficult for Protestants who operate with a narrowed notion of the *sola scriptura* as *norma normans* (the "norm of all norms"), or for fundamentalists of any kind who wish to secure a fixed, external, objective locus of revelation upon which they base all truth claims. Still, it offers a clue about how one may value incipient theologies in the contemporary construction of church teaching and ecclesial practices. It remains important in addition, however, to demonstrate the permanent indeterminacy of theological constructions. This would equally well undercut theological and ecclesial hegemonies built upon the control over authorized teachings, and thus create space for reassessing the significance of incipient theologies.

We may approach the problem of the permanent indeterminacy of theological constructions by clarifying first the problem of a culturally or politically determined Christianity. Karl Barth already acutely addressed the issue at the turn of the century. His concern was to establish, against an acculturated liberal theology, an objective ground for the revelation of God which could neither be reduced to a cultural or political moment nor fall prey to Ludwig Feuerbach's penetrating critique of all ideals of God as mere representations of human desire. Barth's passionate battle remains a clear and strong warning against crude partisanship in contextual theologies.

Though his attempts to answer this problem may no longer be adequate, he still provides significant insights. One of them is his conviction that liberal theology had abandoned the essential meaning of the resurrection—that it concerns the body, the physical material reality of human being—for a truncated subjectivism, that is, an emphasis on the moral life and the internal locus of faith. Thus Barth in his 1926 essay introducing Feuerbach's *The Essence of Christianity* notes:

> Feuerbach has had and still has, secretly, a head start over modern theology . . . in the fact that all his solutions or reinterpretations of Christian theology . . . derive from one point where he has the old, and even the oldest, tradition on his side. I speak of his resolute antispiritualism . . . or, positively, of his anthropological realism. . . . He is concerned with the whole reality (heart and stomach) of man. It is only when one is thus concerned that one can in truth speak of God.[44]

The heart might be subjective, but the stomach is concretely material. The one signals possibility (desire) and the other signals actuality (need). Joining the two means that speech in truth of God—doctrine, if you like—is contextual speech. Anthropological realism demands that speech of God—theology—be about the whole of reality. Christian commitment, accordingly, must enter into cultural and political life both as expression (language) and as action (practice). The positive action in history of the God we recognize in Jesus Christ requires of us an analogously responsible action in the world. This action has cultural, political, and philosophical weight (even if only penultimately or provisionally, a point stressed by Dietrich Bonhoeffer).[45]

Barth's critique of liberal theology in its apparent homage to liberal culture therefore has two sides to it. His purpose is not to abstract Christian faith from the world, but to void any claims that the culturally shaped languages and practices stemming from this faith guarantee the truth about God. Theological indeterminacy is intrinsic to theology itself, else it is false theology.

What Barth attacked was not just the content but the method of the liberal theologians. The issue is still with us. All attempts to ground our understanding of the revelation of the gospel via particular cultural or political practices or theories about human beings are prey to the kind of critique Barth leveled at classical liberal theology. This point becomes pertinent in my consideration of the religious life and worldview of the base Christian community of Amawoti.

Is it possible to give full weight to their understanding of the meaning and the content of the Christian faith without falling prey to a culturally and politically determined, specifically local view on revelation? Would this not lead to a relativist quagmire where all claims are equal and none therefore stronger or weaker? Is there some force to religious claims beyond their limited, human context? In other words, can the base Amawoti Christian community's experiences of God be taken as a source of insight on reality itself, something that goes beyond the limits of a particular context to address all contexts?

To be sure, the Amawoti BEC read biblical texts in ways that are not innocent. Whatever truthful insights they may offer from their readings, there would also be error and distortion. Yet this does not gainsay the point. There is no interpretation of biblical text free of interpretive interests, but by the same token, there is no biblical text that is not already an expression of particular interpretive interests. All texts, for this reason, are contextual, in the specific sense that they remain tied to history, to ambiguity, to uncertainty. Once this is granted, it at least becomes possible to think about the possibility that context may also function as a source and norm for theology.

To argue the matter further, we shall pursue the limited task of demonstrating that Christology, in respect of its fundamentals, is already a situated, interpreted tradition—that context shapes not only its content but also its form. If this is true for Christology, it would be true for all tradition.

Christology and the Normativity of Context

Let us restate the thrust of the whole argument to this point: The question is whether the contextually determined theological reflections of people in local base communities can, or should, have an impact on foundational doctrines.

We will tackle this question by tracing the historical dynamic behind all doctrine, via the example of Christology. That there is such a historical dynamic is not new. Jürgen Moltmann, for example, notes in the foreword to his *The Way of Jesus Christ* that the title implies Christology is itself a way, a process, historically conditioned and limited. This dynamic is best grasped, I think, by understanding doctrine as the interpretive activity of human beings.

Interpretation is possible only on the basis of the limits, constraints, and possibilities of a specific cultural milieu and history. It is a human activity. No doctrine, whether communicated in a sacred text or by other elements of a religious tradition, escapes this dynamic. There is no divinely inspired doctrine, if by that one means a direct and unmediated teaching from God. Inspired interpretations are possible, but they remain interpretations and what constitutes their inspiration remains to be determined not once, but again and again.

It is no surprise to the trained theologian, therefore, that the question of who Jesus Christ is receives such a wide range of answers. There is no single interpretation, no easy harmony between interpretations, and no easy route to deciding the validity of each interpretation. The history of the struggles over classical christological controversies alone makes the point clear, as does the range of contemporary critiques of this classical tradition.[46]

The enduring character of what is discovered in one time and place must be established anew in another time and place, and then it may change its character. There is an irrevocable dialectic here between that which bridges contexts and that which is particular to a context. The formulations of Christology cannot be understood as a fixed set of teachings. They are instead the result of a dynamic interplay between a general tradition and particular knowledge. This interplay is where the interpretive task arises, and here is where it finds its focal point.

Consider this dilemma: Christology is the definitive feature of the Christian tradition. Without Christ there is no Christian tradition. Yet Christ is an enigma, in human experience, if not in theory. Let me give examples. James Cone's claim that only the black Christ is the true Christ was an answer to the question about the nature and work of Jesus Christ; so was the sometimes hysterical counterreaction to the idea of a black Christ. Theologies that claim Christ for the poor are countered by those that claim Christ for prosperity.

One may reasonably ask (remembering that these competing claims are not merely intellectual disputes but shape a whole range of practical outcomes), Do

Christians speak of the same Jesus Christ? Modern theology has battled with these and similar questions as much as did Christians of the early church.

Søren Kierkegaard's suggestion that Christ is present in the world incognito indicates an enduring view that we cannot pin Christ down to specifics except indirectly. Bonhoeffer's claim that "Christ takes form in a band of people" adds a communal-relational understanding of Christology to the complexity of christo-logical claims about the identity of Christ and his work. Fyodor Dostoyevsky's description of the true Christ in his famous piece on "The Grand Inquisitor" (in *The Brothers Karamazov*), in which Jesus returns to our world only to be rejected by the church as too demanding, too unrealistic, too radical, reflects a skeptical Christology many of today's Christians would share.

Feminist theology has deconstructed dominant views of the Christ, either by seeing in Jesus a champion against prevailing Jewish patriarchal practices and structures (Elisabeth Schüssler Fiorenza, Rosemary Ruether, Phyllis Trible), or by casting elsewhere for a formal substitute redeemer figure who is intrinsically female (Mary Daly, Carol Christ).

Some have sought a solution in separating Jesus of Nazareth from the Christ of the *kerygma*, as in Albert Nolan's *Jesus before Christianity,* which argues that a radical call of obedience is evidenced in the life of Jesus to resist the dominant, oppressive powers of the world on the side of the poor. Jonathan Draper goes further, drawing on anthropological and sociological insights into the origins of Christianity to argue that the person of Jesus cannot be discovered apart from the community, the "Jesus movement," who recognized in him the charisma of God.[47] Draper's claim is that Christology must be defined by the "central sig-nificance of community in the person and work of Jesus" and by a "priority of praxis over theory" in terms of his works in community.[48]

Others, despairing of knowing the historical Jesus, have placed all emphasis on the Christ of the *kerygma*, the one encountered in faith. Rudolf Bultmann, of course, stands as the preeminent father figure for this position, going so far as to acknowledge that even if we could establish absolutely nothing about the histor-ical Jesus, this would in no way affect the reality and significance of the early church's proclamation of faith in Christ.[49]

More recently, we are faced with the rethinking of the doctrine of the exclu-sivity of Christ as a result of the dialogue with other religious traditions that marks the latter half of this century (prefigured already in Friedrich Schleierma-cher's *Speeches on Religion* some two hundred years ago). In another direction, the kenotic Christologies of Thomas Altizer and others endure among many who would find it acceptable to be described as Christian atheists if this means a rejection of modern theism.[50]

One could add numerous other examples in modern theology, let alone the longer tradition, of theological disputes over the nature and work of Christ.

What this brief account demonstrates is that our understanding of Christ is clearly not a matter of received tradition alone. Not only is the tradition diverse, it is contested at every point.

It is the church as a believing community that declares the person Jesus of Nazareth to be the Christ, and this declaration is in the first instance not a matter of proof but a matter of faith. What we have in *Jesus Christ,* as Bultmann clearly saw, is already an interpreted event. The history of christological disputes and ecumenical formulations is likewise a history of interpretation.

Any particular interpretation, moreover, is not and never was historically neutral. It need no longer be argued that interpretation is interested, that is, shaped by historical conditions and human struggles. In this sense, all Christology is originally centered in life and human being in the world. Past interpretations may no longer work, or they may reappear in wholly new ways. Authorized interpretations may be the stuff of formal christological claims (as in denominational confessions or creeds), but they may not be the same as what is believed locally. The tension between institutionally ratified belief and experienced faith is often great, as every attentive pastor knows.

Churches have ways of institutionalizing the "correct" understanding of Christ, and there can be little doubt that this input into the shaping of the believer's view at the local level plays a role. But so do other factors beyond the control of pastor, priest, creed, or catechism. These other factors are usually deemed of no consequence for theology as such—for example, christological truths—whereas they may occasion increased attempts to correct the error of the other. This error, of course, is seen to lie in any belief not supported by the received orthodoxy or institutionalized dogma. Perhaps, viewed sociologically, this kind of control over belief is necessary to protect and maintain the identity and continuity of the institution.

If, however, received orthodoxies or institutionalized beliefs are diverse and contested interpretations, one may ask why they should not be more open to christological understandings that arise from the local level. Why should contextually derived understandings of Christ not weigh as heavily in our judgments of the truth of our claims for Jesus Christ as does the received tradition?

If local understandings were to carry significant weight, many churches would find it much easier to appreciate and integrate African thought, experience, and tradition into their foundational theological statements. Equally, it would become possible to give due weight to the local base Christian communities' knowledge or wisdom, born of faith and enhanced by human reason as experienced in specific contexts.

The christological tradition present in the readings of the biblical texts by the BEC is consistent. Jesus below (with the people) proves more inspiring and significant than the heavenly Christ figure above. The human Jesus, whose divinity is nevertheless largely unquestioned, fills the foreground.

One hears echoes here of issues at stake in the original christological controversies. We have seen too that the interpretations of Jesus Christ found in Amawoti cannot be divorced from the context out of which these interpretations arise. We might therefore see in their readings something of a critical correlation between contemporary interpretations and classical interpretations of the text.[51] A kind of "conversation" between the past and the present occurs.[52]

This is normal in theology. What is not normal is to allow the voices of this type of marginalized community into the diachronic and synchronic conversation of the Christian community represented by theology, at least in terms of shaping the nature of the conversation. I argue that this is wrong. Proper attention to the faith experience of members of base Christian communities will empower ordinary Christians in ways not only human but also soteriologically significant.

This claim follows Michel Foucault's understanding of the connection between knowledge and power, by suggesting that the knowledge of the church (its theology) offers power to those who are allowed to shape it, and that sharing this power is one form of the empowerment of local communities.[53]

The corollary of this claim is found in the requirement that theological expertise, lying primarily in the hands of clergy, trained laity, and theological intellectuals, must in the first instance be placed in service of ordinary Christians, in solidarity with "the least among us." The momentous implications of such a requirement for the decision-making, theology-shaping courts and commissions of the church cannot be spelled out here, but it should at least be clear that they are momentous.

The community of Christians whose combined wisdom over time makes up the deposit of theology is a broken community.[54] Thus, theological hermeneutics must include rhetorical practices that expose this brokenness in collaboration with those who are broken—personally, politically, and economically. This task includes uncovering the effects of power relations within the Christian community itself. Its aim is intrinsically theological, because it aims at a vision of well-being to be shared by all.

For this to happen, an appropriately sensitive hermeneutics will take perspectives from a local community such as the Amawoti BEC with as much seriousness as the received tradition. One necessarily becomes aware of a plurality of (perhaps contesting or contradictory) voices within the church. This should drive one to give proper weight not only to voices of the past, or to those whose knowledge in the present represents power over others, but also to those voices who are at this point still marginalized or suppressed. Theology becomes real to those who actually suffer poverty, oppression, and marginalization only if it also connects with the specific material and historical conditions that shape their local contexts of life.

Finally, theology is not absent from this base insofar as ordinary Christians reflect upon their faith in the light of their daily experiences, their suffering, their struggle for existence, and their hopes for healing and comprehensive well-being. Their reflection may be, and usually is, that of the theologically untrained mind. It may be naive and precritical; it may be unsystematic and scattered; it may draw incongruently on a range of symbols, rituals, narratives, and ideas that express the encounter with the sacred.

In these senses, the theology present in communities of ordinary Christians may be seen as incipient rather than overtly articulated. But it remains theology. It is this incipient theology that I claim to be the necessary starting point for an authentic contextual theology.

Truth in Tradition and Life

Running through any consideration of tradition is the question of truth and its counterpart deceit. Christians claim that their tradition has some hold on truth, as they have done since the beginning. In what sense does tradition convey or mediate truth? What kind of truth are we talking about?

I have implied that truth is connected to particularities, for example, those expressed through the experience and thoughts of the Amawoti BEC. Is there a truth beyond particularities, something more universal that may be said to endure in the tradition? I have also implied in my definition of context that truth is discovered in an analytical, deep reading of the material and social conditions of existence from the perspective of the poor, the oppressed, the marginalized—a materialist approach to truth. I have also argued for the nonmaterial importance of the religious worldviews of the AICs and communities such as the BEC—an idealist notion of truth.

In my use of Jürgen Habermas's concept of communicative action, truth becomes that which is reached in open, unconstrained communicative consensus, something located in the language and language-like interactions between persons who seek understanding and agreement. Truth is here pragmatic, visible in communicative activity and arrived at through language.

The seemingly random, eclectic mix of notions of truth must now be defended, if it can be. The key to doing so is to show how a materialist and idealist approach may be combined, and how particularities and universals may be understood in relation to each other.

Spirited Existence, Embodied World

> The truth of human experience is that it consists of a dynamic of the actual
> concealing the possible where the possible is constantly being projected by the
> human spirit into the future in acts of understanding.
> —Douglas McGaughey[55]

Enough has been said to make it clear that all of Christian tradition is already
interpreted or mediated by particular, situated human beings. In this light,
Christian tradition may best be grasped as the history of the attempts of the
Christian community to discover truth and to frame their discoveries in the languages, cultures, and symbolic resources of their time. It is the deposit of wisdom
borne of experience transmitted in claims about reality that endure over time,
but it is not the source of known certainties or absolutes.

If truth does not lie in certainties or absolutes, where does it lie? Are our
truth claims always indeterminate, ambiguous, and uncertain? Yes, I think so,
although I believe there is more than pure relativity here. To explain what this
means, and what it implies for the role of communities such as the Amawoti
BEC or the AICs in shaping Christian truth, I turn to the work of Douglas
McGaughey on the role of *aporiai* in theology and the nature of "faith in a
post-metaphysical context."[56]

McGaughey attacks materialist epistemologies which "mathematize" reality.[57] Here reality is seen as quantifiable, measurable, observable, predictable,
manipulable; rationality is understood as causal, calculating. The materialist
paradigm shift is identified with the domination in Europe since Descartes of
Aristotelian nominalism. Epistemologically, this is most simply stated as the
requirement that there be identifiable "evidence" for the truth, demonstrably
located in a particular place. Place is material, actual. Nominalism therefore
requires that nonmaterial experience be discounted as evidence.

Nominalism thus denies that our names for things are anything more than
pointers to a reality outside the naming process (our consciousness, mind, *nous*).
We have to show (locate) what we point to in our language, that is, verify or falsify (Karl Popper) that external reality our names merely signal. We must show
a correspondence between what is thought and what is externally sense-able. If
we cannot locate this external reality, then our experience or thought must be
assumed to be false.

Modern theology is not immune to such ways. Truth in modern theologies
often means verification of its object in the text of scripture or in the dogmatic
tradition (discernible objects), in appropriate behavior (observable results of
faith, as in pietism or liberal theology). Ironically, the search for verification of a
spiritual experience betrays a materialist epistemology. Spirit—consciousness,

mind, *nous*—is unobservable, insensible, intangible, unverifiable. It offers proof of nothing, at least within this paradigm.

The division between what is internal (consciousness, mind, *nous*, experiencing) and what is external (accessible to the senses or objectively available) parallels the fatal divisions between the seen and the unseen, body and mind, worldly and eternal, human and divine. Such divisions are alien to Africa. The same epistemological fault, McGaughey argues, produces the view that science and theology deal with different spheres of truth.[58]

Nominalist notions of truth thus find their reference in actualities: texts, observable behavior or action, language, the deposit of history, and the like. All are object-like manifestations of the real. McGaughey argues with some force, however, that the real includes not only actualities but also possibilities. This clue offers the key to what I want to say about tradition and truth.

Let us begin by noting that we cannot simply go back behind nominalism— as though it had not unleashed material powers of science, industry, and technology we very much want—to a revamped notion that material reality is the product of ideas. Instead we have to rethink the idealist and the materialist paradigms together.

McGaughey proposes to do so by recovering a notion of truth found in Plato's simile of the line.[59] The technical details of McGaughey's argument are unnecessary here. But his point about the simile of the line is crucial because of its implications for his radical interpretation of truth (and analysis of the disease of modern theology).

Plato draws a line between mind and body, spirit and world, ideas and material. The first terms (mind, spirit, ideas—or in the Greek, *nous*) are placed above the line, the second terms (body, world, material) below. Usually, Plato is read to treat the former as true, the latter as mere appearance. McGaughey shows, however, that spirit (consciousness, mind, *nous*) is neither restricted to ideas nor reducible to calculating or contemplative reason.

Plato does not mean to speak of a self-contained mind or abstract reason separated from a world of engagement. Spirituality or *nous* must not—as many interpret Plato[60]—be seen as separate from or superior to body, world, or materiality in any formal or ontological sense. On the contrary, spirituality (consciousness, mind, *nous*) is the capacity to apprehend experience (ordering of the sense phenomena of the material world). It is the condition of knowing body, world, materiality. It is thus also capable of transcending all actualization of body, world, materiality, and is therefore also the source of new possibilities.

Reality, and by implication truth, for Plato consists in what lies both above (consciousness, spirit, mind, *nous*) and below the line (sensible world, materiality). Truth only arises in grasping both the material and the spiritual simultaneously. Reality is a *Gestalt* of mind and body, of spirit and world, not just that which can be empirically or materially ascertained, or just that which can be experienced internally or subjectively at the level of consciousness alone.

The modern spiritual vacuum can be understood as a consequence of the Cartesian split of mind and body, spirit and world—and the triumph of an epistemology that overvalues the second term (body, world). Going back to McGaughey's identification of nominalism as the problem, its epistemological framework would see the spiritual as unreliable, as unverifiable, as mere emotion or illusory experience incapable of guiding us to truth. The modernist paradigm thus reduces truth by excluding, bracketing, or marginalizing subjective factors in favor of an objective correspondence between external occurrence or object and what is named.

The flaw here, of course, is that any truth about material reality already depends upon, and is irredeemably mediated by, a prior imaginative framework both limited and partial. Neither consciousness nor knowledge of the world provides guarantees of truth, for both are filled with ambiguity and unknowability. Consciousness operates with ultimately indefinable universals (Socrates),[61] whereas knowledge of the world is inescapably framed within limited interpretive paradigms, an insight Thomas Kuhn made clear for the natural sciences, which tended to claim unmediated access to reality through experimentation and controlled observation.

What does it mean to speak of indefinable universals? This is the next major step in my argument and requires a revised concept of universals. McGaughey shows that Plato meant by universals not something eternally true or absolutely fixed but hypotheses of tentative approximations, still and always to be confirmed. These are historical hypotheses, not speculative ideas, so the meaning of an idea, or universal, is not grasped "without having grasped it as a possibility for understanding something particular."[62] Universals are then deposited in human history in the form of language that precedes us, and in the form of traditions that identify us. Because both language and tradition define the self in relation to others, universals are inherently social, the work of communicative action.

Clearly, universals do not come down to us from on high. Spirit (*nous*) produces universals and paradigms. It projects possibilities (what is not) in the world, opening up actualities (what is) to enable us to transcend them. This is not transcendence *from* world or body, society or person, but transcendence *within* world or body, society or person. It is an elevation of what is (actualities) into that which is not yet (possibilities). It is the motor of what is new and the source of creativity in the human being. Spirituality understood as *nous*, therefore, can never be merely private, individual, isolated from body and world.

At the same time, actualities of the world or body constrain us and are part of our reality and its truth. The point of Plato's simile of the line is that we cannot escape actuality, or what is.[63] Actualities include traditions—past generations' deposit of experience that endures as true wisdom. Universals in a tradition are then historically generated and defined, making up the prior imaginative frameworks or paradigms we inherit as part of our actuality. But if universals in this sense are enduring but tentative approximations of reality, they are also open to new historical transformations, ranging from minor alterations to outright rejection.

Christian Tradition and the Fragility of Truth

We are now in a position to understand the nature of truth in the Christian tradition. McGaughey defines our prior imaginative framework or paradigm as the "sedimented syntheses" of the past. Quoting Paul Ricoeur, he agrees that "the labor of imagination is not born from nothing. It is bound in one way or another to the tradition's paradigms . . . deployed between the two poles of servile application [so we require a hermeneutics of suspicion] and calculated deviation [a hermeneutics of creative restoration], passing through every degree of 'rule-governed deformation.'"[64]

Everything in this book is a challenge to the servile application of the paradigms of the Christian tradition, and a plea for a calculated deviation from those paradigms. Thus we have employed a hermeneutics of suspicion to analyze factors of power and knowledge, relations of power, representation of the other, and uncritical conversation arising from an encounter with a BEC. The calculated deviation from traditional paradigms goes by way of a restoration of the knowledge of this local community as contribution to the formation of tradition.

The latter goal is enhanced when one recognizes that the Greek word for truth, *aletheia*, means disclosure of that which eludes notice or is unnoticed.[65] Those who are usually not noticed give us access to a broader truth because they often have a better grasp of actuality through the suffering it causes them, and a clearer vision of the kinds of real possibilities that need to be actualized in overcoming this suffering.

The argument up until now has gradually pursued an understanding of truth that fits the way in which the Amawoti BEC works with Christian tradition. It designates Christian tradition as truth when it joins the spiritual and the material, the possible and the actual, in a commitment to "breaking open the hegemony of the actual."[66] The ensuing disclosure (*aletheia*) of reality is the nature of truth. In revealing what has been concealed, however, new concealments occur, in the sense that other possibilities also existed which have not been realized.[67]

The fragility of truth in the Christian tradition thus lies in an inherent tension or dialectic. On the one side, if we acknowledge it, tradition as the deposit of past commitments actualized in fixed texts and creeds constrains us to a heritage that constitutes us (what is). If this is all, however, then tradition is a truncated reality, a dogmatic trap from which spirit strives to escape. It is tradition as law.

On the other side, by "putting on the mind [*nous*, spirit] of Christ" (Paul), we participate in the making of that tradition in the dialectic between what constitutes us and what we constitute. This is the epistemological foundation for a unification between the actual and the possible. It implies that not all possibilities are congruent, and that the actualization of one possibility conceals or prevents the actualization of other available possibilities. This is why the tradition is not simply a harmonious record of the work of the spirit, but also the record of contestation for one possibility against others.

Universals of the received tradition nevertheless remain as a deposit such communities encounter and must deal with, though no longer with any guarantees. This paradox is the nature of our experiencing: we search for understanding, but we always encounter doubt or that which escapes our understanding. This is because universals constitute the basis of our understanding (we inherit them in language, "the great institution that . . . has preceded each and every one of us"[68]), yet simultaneously we constitute the universals out of the particulars of our experience.

So we cannot ultimately depend upon revealed or natural knowledge. As McGaughey notes, this forces us to live by faith. The truth of past tradition, including the scripture, thus lies in the search of human beings for the wholeness that eludes them. The process is what counts (here Segundo's attempt to speak of "deutero-learning" makes sense). The contents of that search—the words, sentences, ideas, and intentions deposited in the records of the tradition—provide us with no guarantees. They remain tentative, always pointing to our "profound unknowing."[69] We have no access to any higher form of knowing. The route to certainty is blocked. Any attempt to smash down the walls that block us inevitably implies that we smash other human beings or nature itself. This is the insight of faith, of non-knowing.

There are two important implications arising from the way in which we have defined universal truths of the tradition. When we lay claim to being Christian, we insert ourselves into the inherited language of the faith. As we search this heritage to make sense of our Christian identity, so we sink our roots into its universals. Further, we necessarily contribute to the establishment, confirmation, or alienation of these universals by constituting them in relation to our own experience. In this Christians continually participate in the development of tradition. This dynamic is its truth.

Second—and this is important enough to bear repeating—the tentative enduring approximations of reality that define what it means to be Christian are themselves highly differentiated and deeply polysemic.[70] The universals of the tradition themselves are ultimately indefinable, systematically eluding our grasp. No statements of this tradition may therefore be taken to the final, certain, unambiguous truth. They guarantee nothing except our historical identity, which if open to possibility (new creation) cannot remain static. We have earlier hinted at this conclusion in pointing to the long tradition of Christian mystics who see theology primarily as apophatic, as search or quest, not assertion or decree, and in the implications of the doctrine of the *sensus fidei*.[71]

Revelation is thus not an event in the past, but an unfolding of the future in the present informed by the past. This unfolding takes place within the real world, that is, within the constraints of actuality, to expose the limits of reality and to open it up to new possibility. The new possibilities, once actualized, conceal other possibilities that might have been actualized but were not. Theology, like the spirituality it accompanies, is thus an ongoing journey, a search for understanding. It is not a repetition of the past, nor even simply a reinterpretation of the past. It takes the *creatio ex nihilo* quite literally as the bringing into existence (actualizing) of that which does not yet exist (possibility).[72]

Finally, if universals are hypotheses or tentative approximations about reality, then the Christian tradition offers us one set of tentative approximations of reality, as well as a way of entering into reality that promises to open up its fullness. Small comfort here for any fundamentalism, for any religious domination of others, for any exclusive claims to truth. As McGaughey puts it, "The spiritual as well as the material dimensions of experience require us to speak of an odyssey of faith seeking understanding, because we do not have direct and immediate access to the material, and the spiritual, at the very least, is rooted in indefinables. But spirit *is* informed by a higher horizon of pragmatic faith."[73]

This does not mean that a restless pluralism is best, a noncommittal faith exemplary. It means only that we recognize our own limits, in spirit and in knowledge, taking on the humility this requires. What this might mean in the context of any particular society, for communities such as the Amawoti BEC, and for the church as a whole, will be taken up in the next two chapters.

4. Asymmetries of Power

We have been too prone to think, in static terms, that cultural superstructures are passive mirrors, mere reflections of substructural productive modes and relations or of the political processes that enforce the dominance of the productively privileged. If we were as dialectical as we claim to be, we would see that it is more a matter of an existential bending back upon ourselves.
—Victor Turner

And yet, even as they are encompassed by the European capitalist system—consumed, ironically, as they consume its goods and texts—these "natives" of other worlds often seek to seize its symbols, to question their authority and integrity, and to reconstruct them in their own image. Sometimes they do so in open defiance; sometimes through strikingly imaginative acts of cultural subversion and re-presentation; sometimes in silent, sullen resistance.
—Jean and John Comaroff[1]

The question of power—imperceptible and indirect, or willful and visible—lurks in the background of previous discussions. Everything about incipient theologies, about the interaction between theologically trained people and untrained laypeople, about speech with the other, is fraught with questions of control, surveillance, authority, disguise. Everywhere we encounter the effects of power in the context of constrained and unequal relations between people.

The concept of power is central in social science, beginning with Auguste Comte's critique of the unholy power wielded by priests to control the way in which reality is represented. The notion of ideology, as the deliberate mystification of the mind in the interests of power, has its origin here too, to be developed most fully by Karl Marx. Concepts of representation, consciousness, and ideology thus enter into discussions of power as well.

Yet our understanding of power remains confused. Among many Christians, power is thought of as suspect, if not decidedly sinful.[2] The Christian suspicion of power, despite valuable theological insights about the limits and evils of power we normally regard as worldly, is questionable and misleading for those who have little formal power. It hides or perpetuates the interests of those whose power is used to dominate others.[3]

Our major concern will be to address the importance of power in asymmetrically distorted relations within the broad Christian community and the significance of power for those most marginalized within this community. We plunge into the same waters as our discussion of incipient theology, from a different stance and at another angle. Now we must confront ourselves either as purveyors of formal power (intentionally or half-aware), or as those who confront and contest formal power with alternative forms of power often not recognized as such.

My interest is twofold: (1) exploring my embeddedness in relations of power as one example of what others who have power within the institution of the church must come to understand about themselves; and (2) grasping the importance, for my work as a theological educator and shaper of church opinion (and for others in analogous positions), of the innovative, creative sources of power to be found among Christians who live on the margins of society and church.

Expressions of Power at the Base

We begin by considering relations of power and empowerment in the Amawoti BEC as studied by Martin Mandew.[4] Power, Mandew shows, consists not only in actions of the dominant as something exercised *over* others, but also in the actions of subordinate groups as power *with* others. He argues that many theories of power (Max Weber, Bertrand Russell, Talcott Parsons, Gerhard Lenski, C. Wright Mills, Stephen Lukes) tend to define power primarily as an attribute or resource of dominant, ruling, or elite groups. To this he contrasts notions of power from Hannah Ahrendt ("communicative power"), Jürgen Habermas ("communicative competence"), and Michel Foucault (pervasive networks of "micro-power").

Mandew seeks patterns of BEC activity that exhibit characteristics drawn from these latter notions of power, arguing that evidence of power and empowerment includes activities which show communicative competence, and a growth in the BEC's contextual knowledge of itself. The latter depends upon Foucault's genealogical method, which searches for three elements in the history of a people: a memory of conflict, expressions of alternative knowledge (to the dominant episteme), and the insurrection of subjugated knowledge (nonofficial, unrecognized knowledge).

Finally, because the discourse of the BEC is so often cast in religious terms, Mandew looks for the way in which religious imagination inserts an excess of being, power, value, and significance into the demands and habits of everyday existence. This "creates a space of abundance and therefore freedom which, however it may be hedged in and protected by custom, taboo and rite, is thereby also made available to inaugurate, if only for the duration of the sacred dance or story, the kingdom of freedom."[5]

Three major loci for the exercise of power or the experience of empowerment in the history of the Amawoti BEC provide the test: the Ilimo Primary Health Care Project out of which the BEC stems; the Bible study group itself; and two Good Friday Easter marches organized with others.

The Ilimo Primary Health Care Project, initially begun by a group of four Baptist churches in 1987,[6] was set up under a coordinator who subsequently moved into the area with his wife to oversee the project. It offered a developmentally sensitive support structure to the community, intending that the community itself should increasingly control the project (in contrast to a simultaneous private sector initiative that later became the target of considerable community hostility and criticism).

The immediate occasion for these initiatives was a series of severe, damaging floods in the area. They occurred when the South African state had launched an extensive, finely calculated and often brutal policy known as Total Strategy, a form of low-intensity conflict warfare to counteract the rapidly growing resistance struggle inside the country and escalating international pressure from outside. Total Strategy planners instituted a system of regional and local control throughout the country under the supervision of Joint Management Centers (JMCs) with the aim of winning the minds and the hearts of local people where possible, and sidelining or removing—to the point of killing, as we now know—those who continued to be uncooperative. In this context, a community-led project such as Ilimo represented a counterorganization—hearts and minds that would not be won—to the local initiatives of the JMC, even if its focus was health care.

Indeed, the military strategists had a point. Over time Ilimo fed into a wide range of locally based and led initiatives, often playing midwife between community groups or representatives and resource-rich agencies or nongovernmental organizations.[7] Its activities extended to environmental health, personal health, leadership development, income-supplementing programs (sewing, garden farming), and assistance to pensioners and disabled persons.

Mandew's analysis of power and empowerment in this context focuses on one thing above all: the conscious intention of staff and helpers of the Ilimo Project to find ways, however limited in the larger picture of oppression and exploitation, of freeing people from the material constraints characteristic of such areas. Inevitably, in the process one faces the political and economic milieu that so strongly defined the material constraints borne by the community. Thinking of Habermas's[8] notion of an emancipatory interest as constitutive of knowledge about the world, it makes sense to call the activities of Ilimo expressions of power and empowerment.

The Bible study group, the second locus of power and empowerment, can legitimately be described as a base ecclesial community (the Ilimo project not, for its practical activities were not ecclesially motivated or directed).[9] It began out of Ilimo in 1988, partly as the initiative of the Ilimo coordinator, then still employed by four Baptist churches.[10] After about three years, having taken on the function of a clearing house for ideas, feelings, emotions, and imagination, its members finally gave it a name: *Funda IBhayebheli Wenze*, meaning "read the Bible and do/act."[11] This self-designation as the "Read and Do (or Implement) Group,"[12] could not be clearer in respect of its self-understanding, its conscious hermeneutical intention.

Mandew describes the communicative activity of the group, powerfully mediated by the Bible studies, as "expropriating the means of symbolic reproduction" in the creation of a "counter-hegemony" to the readings of "oppressors, wrongdoers, and those who seek fame" (the group's description of those who misuse the Bible).[13] He further argues that the Bible study sessions, openly structured and largely free of any dominant commentator, express a communicative practice that engenders democratic values through the enhancement of communicative competence.

The third locus of power and empowerment, the Good Friday Easter marches held in 1991 and 1992, succeeded in bringing politicized community youth and disparaged AIC leaders into a positive relationship with each other with a vitality not previously realized.[14] Rich in symbolic and ritual meaning, these marches were interrupted at regular intervals to pay attention to what we may call self-defined stations of the Cross. At each stopping point, memories were recalled, events noted, speeches made, prayers offered, and symbolic actions performed.

The BEC itself regarded these marches as extraordinary. In an evaluation of community events following the 1992 march,[15] seven major moments of the BEC's life together were delineated. Ranked first were the Easter marches, followed by violence in 1989, floods in 1987, a drought in

1992, a Christmas celebration in 1990, the first Ilimo conference in 1992, and security police raids in 1990. The prime ranking of the Easter marches signals the importance of constructive events for the BEC—those over which it and the community had some control. The marches allowed for theological meanings to inform life struggles in a fresh and empowering way through the imaginative public patterning of memory, the representation of suffering and small victories, and the symbolic transformation of the given reality (including repression and death). Jesus (and thus God) is not only located in the suffering of the community, but:

> Jesus is relocated into the community not only in his moment of triumph but in his own moment of utter vulnerability. . . . God can no longer count on the protection of the churches. God is no longer safe. Furthermore, this relocation of Jesus also implies that God's love has become less exclusive and more accessible. . . . The marchers succeed in ending the monopoly over God's love. Jesus once again rubs shoulders with the wretched of the earth.[16]

In the words of one of the BEC members, "It showed that God does not only love Christians and believers. God loves everybody."[17]

It is not difficult to understand why Mandew regards the Easter marches as a locus of power and empowerment. With the other two loci, we have a fairly convincing case for the notion of power exercised from below, with others, in the face of often overwhelming experiences of power exercised over the community by ruling or dominant elites. We see too, in the language of Jennings, how religious imagination introduces an excess of being, power, value, and significance that may create a "space of abundance and therefore freedom" however hedged in.

While the above analysis of power or empowerment in the Amawoti BEC adds depth to the notion of power, it fails to grasp what power might mean when it is not a conscious act. Using the anthropological studies of Jean and John Comaroff on African Zionist Christianity,[18] I will argue that one has to include forms of power which carry with them no specifically conscious intention or willfulness. A richer interpretation of the nature of religious imagination in contexts of domination and subjugation then emerges.

Before we turn in this direction, we should complete the picture of the Amawoti BEC by turning to their own hermeneutics of power and empowerment as expressed in their Bible study discourses. The BEC members themselves were clearly concerned with power and power relations. Numerous text readings pick up the theme, in one way or another, from the beginning. Their discussions are not systematic, of course, but the overall picture of power across the various readings over time is complex, nuanced, and filled with productive questions.[19]

Power for others is linked to the actions of Jesus, actions taken to be exemplary:

> If Christ came to do all these things [free the oppressed, give sight to the blind and food to the hungry, and so on], did he finish doing it? No, not completely. But Jesus started and we must continue.

Positive power, captured in the image of the reign of God, is not alienated from human beings, but is to be found where

> people build people . . . [where] the community is organized . . . [where] they use good ways to meet needs . . . [where] they make changes . . .[and where] leaders are servants of the community.[20]

Power, then, is immanent in human existence, an anthropological reality predicated, in this case, on a christological interpretation of simultaneous divine intervention, or motivation, and human action.

The effects of human action of this kind may be felt only on a small scale. They are nevertheless seen as valid and valuable.[21] This applies equally to actions whose immediate aim is nothing more than survival. Survival, more than an end in itself, is also the occasion for small deeds which produce empowering inter-actions with others, the beginning of building solidarity. If group members are correct in their view here, we need to redefine what we mean by *power*. The group-envisaged actions that would count as valid and valuable do not normally figure in notions of power, as is most poignantly expressed in an interchange around the third strophe of the Lord's Prayer:

> Nonthabo: "Give us this day our daily bread?" We may not have a lot of money, food, and so on, but by having God, it helps to survive. Maybe God has already talked to a neighbor who will have a plate ready for me when I come.
>
> Bongi: This doesn't mean you can do nothing. Daily bread can mean being strong in God. When one gets bread, one must take half and give half to some-one who needs it.[22]

The Amawoti BEC clearly believe that they themselves are carriers and mul-tipliers of positive power—a means through which power is articulated, to use Foucault's terminology. Some of their women work in a cooperative garden set up to cater for subsistence needs with the support of an outside nongovernmen-tal organization,[23] but under their control (though there are those who contest the right of the women to use the land, in order to wrest it from their control now that it has been made productive). These women are seen as "God's tool, because they are working together."[24]

The Bible study group itself is also perceived as a source of power, its members being called to "preach unity and working together, to do it by example," to resist a world in which "people are made to feel like dogs," to recognize the need to "start small, from something you know." Thus, one member proclaimed, "this group is a sign of the kingdom; when I went around Amawoti I saw signs of hope, signs of God's kingdom, small lights in the darkness."[25] There is considerable realism about the role of the group, however, and a keen awareness of the need to concretize speech or debate in planned practical activity, a theme explored on more than one occasion around the biblical text about the building of one's house on rock, rather than sand, in order to withstand the inevitable storms.[26]

Throughout, positive power is understood dialectically and relationally: It is the "power to challenge things not good for oneself or for others. Also to recognize things good for the self and others."[27] Though I have no textual evidence that the group discussion went much beyond these dialectical associations (good and not good, self and others), it is not hard to see how power understood in this fashion may be linked more broadly to similarly associated concepts of justice and reconciliation, of judgment and communion, of discernment and solidarity.

These brief insights into notions of power and empowerment, expressed through Mandew's analysis of BEC activities and an internal commentary on the BEC's own readings, serve only to introduce the question of power relations in dealing with incipient theologies. They by no means exhaust the question but beg further questions about the power of such a community to access and significantly shape the dominant discourses of the church, to move off the margins, to avoid becoming victims of a hegemonic knowledge (theologies) and practices of domination—thus to express a counterhegemony, forms of resistance, generative worldviews, a power of their own, which has actual significance for them and potential significance for the church at large.

In order, then, to uncover some of the key dynamics concerning power provoked by this encounter with the discursive world of the Amawoti local community, I propose to turn to three complementary arguments: the first is the claim that power is pervasive and that it is positive as well as negative (Michel Foucault); the second explores issues of hegemony and ideology in relation to popular religion (Jean and John Comaroff); the third draws on distinctions between public transcripts, hidden transcripts, and infrapolitics (James C. Scott).

Networks of Power

Churches in South Africa who engaged in protest against the apartheid system often understood themselves as the voice of the oppressed black majority, or at least as a channel for that voice. Voices are not disembodied sounds in an empty ether. Bodies speak, persons speak, and these body-persons are located socially and economically in multiple matrices of power, each of which constrains and affects their speech.

The connection of speech and location mirrors the link between knowledge and power (Foucault),[28] or knowledge and interests (Habermas).[29] Foucault and Habermas enable one to understand the (potential and actual) significance of local forms of power or local acts of communicative competence respectively, unlike systemic or structural models of power that treat micro forms of power as historically insignificant.

Raymond Williams's insightful analysis of the notion of the masses adds a particular nuance to this picture.[30] His study demonstrates how the idea of the mass arises with industrialization. The term is essentially negative, based on an inherent distinction between theoretical or activist elites (taken de facto to represent the forces of enlightenment, whether in the liberal or the Marxist form), and the rest (the masses who de facto are taken to be in need of enlightenment or emancipation). This negative image of the masses—as an aggregate without form, a faceless, manipulable, or unaccountable crowd—reproduces what Foucault calls the dominant episteme (form of knowledge).

Such ideas would make it difficult to see the point in investigating the local popular religious experience of ordinary people. The task becomes even more doubtful if one follows those theories of macro-systemic power that tend to regard religion as an archaic or reactionary nuisance rather than a significant factor in history. My turn to Foucault is therefore not surprising, if I wish to understand the actual experience of local expressions of power in the form and manner of the communicative action to which the Amawoti base community bears witness.

Foucault argues that . . . "one should not assume a massive and primal condition of knowledge, a binary structure with 'dominators' on one side and 'dominated' on the other, but rather a multiform production of relations of domination. . . ."[31] To understand the dynamics of change, one must grasp the way in which power functions locally on a "minute and everyday level" outside of the state apparatus.[32] Thus, in a concise and vividly expressive statement, Foucault says:

> Power must be analyzed as something which circulates, or rather as something which only functions in the form of a chain. It is never localized here or there, never in anybody's hands, never appropriated as a commodity or piece of wealth. Power is employed and exercised through a net-like organization. And not only do individuals circulate between its threads; they are always in the position of simultaneously undergoing and exercising this power. They are not only its inert or consenting target; they are always also the elements of its articulation.[33]

Power is not a mysterious force, but the expression of social relations that never stand still, are never fully under anyone's control. Power as a dynamic, unsubstantial matrix embraces everyone, and it is in some measure the effect of the agency of everyone. Foucault's view implies that no person is without the capacity to exercise power. If, however, we are to avoid a binary model of consciousness in which power is defined merely as the effect of a conscious intention, a willed act, then we need to go further to understand power as something that functions across the spectrum of consciousness.

Power may originate in a conscious, intentional act that demonstrates "the [relative] capacity to shape the actions and perceptions of others by exercising control over the production, circulation and consumption of signs and objects, over the making of both subjectivities and realities."[34] It may also be present in the everyday, seeming natural and ineffable and thus recognized only through its effects. These effects, the Comaroffs suggest, would be recognized "in their negative guise, as constraints; in their neutral guise, as conventions; and, in their positive guise, as values."

The Comaroffs describe the first mode of conscious, intentional acts as agentive power, the second of seemingly everyday habits as nonagentive power. They further link agentive power to the concept of ideology and nonagentive power to the notion of hegemony: "Hegemony homogenizes; ideology articulates."[35] In the case of hegemony, control and its effects are not visible, they are naturalized. If this is true of hegemony, it must also in some sense be true of counterhegemonic ideas and practices. The means to exercise or resist power is of course not equally available to everyone. Power is uneven, unbalanced, asymmetric. Still—and this is the important point—power is to be found everywhere, both negatively as something acting on us and positively as something we exercise or articulate.

This takes us toward understanding how ideas and practices of the BEC may in fact partake in the exercise of power in the nonagentive mode. It also allows a glimpse of why it is that dominant groups, despite the agentive power they might wield, are never free of the need to reinforce their authority. They are always concerned to "redress contradictions, to limit the eruption of alternative meanings and critical awareness."[36]

What goes on in the BEC and similar communities (including, one may surmise, in AICs) can thus be understood much more positively than might first appear warranted.[37] To demonstrate the point, we will ask about the positive meaning of power for local African religious base communities, not forgetting that there are also significant negative effects of power and that the asymmetries of power generally work against them.

The BEC has not been studied enough with a sufficient range of disciplinary tools to make clear judgments. We will therefore pursue the point obliquely, by looking at the potential meaning of the religious experience of AICs as a test case. AICs are not quite the same kind of congregation as that which makes up the Amawoti Bible study group. Yet if it can be said of AICs that there is a network of power articulated in and running through their expressions of religious life, then it can be said of communities such as Amawoti too. Indeed, we may note that the two Easter marches through Amawoti rapidly became a joint enterprise with AIC churches and their leaders, with the effect of bringing youth and civic organizations, all directly organized around political struggles, into productive contact with the AICs.

Glenda Kruss, studying the socioeconomic contexts of AICs, has suggested that the Zionist movement tends to be most powerful among aspirant petty-bourgeoisie and recently urbanized peasant farmers.[38] Amawoti fits this identification fairly well; the Zionist churches are easily the most representative in the community. In this context, James Kiernan (a cultural anthropologist) offers us some important clues to local expressions of power in AICs through his studies of local Zionist congregations in the area.

Kiernan argues that Zionism grows rapidly because it offers to a poor, recently dislocated and marginalized urban class a dynamic way of integrating their lives, in the realistic knowledge that they will suffer ongoing deprivation and have to fend for themselves as best they can. Zionist churches thus attract because they "provide a healing service which the poor can afford." The small, strong, and lively form of grassroots organization typical of Zionist churches also offers a "sense of a reconstituted order," as well as a "source of inspiration and an appetite for living." Life is ordered within such communities under twin principles of "self-help and mutual aid" which, Kiernan demonstrates, are "applied to a number of different levels: moral, material, corporeal and mystical."[39]

There are ways in which Zionist groups seek to exercise some control over their lives. First, they teach and practice strong discipline over socially and economically disruptive behavior, such as excess alcohol consumption, smoking, and promiscuity.[40] Second, they help increase earning power through control of wasteful expenditure, producing a slight correlative increase in financial surplus. Third, this allows Zionist communities to defray expenses incurred in the life cycle of families and individuals (in particular, births, marriages, and funerals), particularly by a "highly visible marshaling of collective support" in situations of need. In sum, "Zionism enables individuals to associate freely and voluntarily with others in a real community of common interest to secure economic, social and spiritual well-being."[41] All of these aspects of the Zionist religious life and experience are micro expressions of positive power.

In following Kiernan's path into understanding Zionism, we have to reconceive of the notion of power as something that operates, as Foucault said, on a "minute and everyday level." This complicates any notion of power

reductionistically focused on direct and conscious involvement in emancipatory struggles at a macro level, even when its specific acts are local. Zionism
is clearly not an expression of the exercise of political power in this latter
sense. As Goba rightly perceived, Zionists generally are distinctly uncon-
cerned with macro-political problems. "One does not become a Zionist to do
away with apartheid, to stop migration or to get better jobs for everybody,"
Kiernan notes. "One becomes a Zionist in order to gain some control over
one's own life and circumstances; this is what is consciously sought."[42]

Zionist religion does not contribute directly to movements for social transformation. It remains open whether it ever will, if Kiernan is right that the
movement is characterized by conditions of marginalization, for active involvement in a larger political movement is a move away from marginalization and a
point of contact with a different identity. Perhaps, despite its comparative value,
the Zionist analogy can take us no further in trying to understand the nature of
power in the functioning of the Amawoti BEC, a community that developed
much of its interpretive activity around larger political concerns.

Still, if we now look at the question of power operating on the everyday,
micro level in the communicative activity of the Amawoti BEC, we find concerns
similar to the Zionists, even if in different form. For example, BEC members
decided that resources should be provided by my researchers and colleagues in
the School of Theology to assist them in developing a training program under
their control. The first need they identified (by a largely female group) was training in presiding over funerals, a meaningful life-cycle ritual for familial and social
cohesion. In Amawoti, funerals were important for these women because ministers and priests who might otherwise handle situations of sudden death (children
and old people in particular) are frequently not available. They are AIC clerics
who work during the week, often commuting only at weekends or month's end
from distant places of work. Those who die cannot wait until the clerics return.
The women, who are available and who carry the heaviest burden of care, are
ordinarily not allowed to conduct funerals or administer last rites. Training, they
believe, would give them the necessary competence.

Competence, in this context, is power. It involves a capacity of the self, not
derived in dependency upon others, to manage a life situation in a manner that
sustains and strengthens the community in the face of a specific need. The question of gender, and the way in which gender structures power relations and
defines needs, presents itself here. On the one hand, gender concerns as such are
seldom the conscious focus of the Bible study group discussion.[43] On the other
hand, it is striking that the group was made up mainly of women–the group's
executive committee was led by a woman with considerable influence in the
community—and the first need for training is identified as one that touches
upon the lives of women in particular.

Of further interest is what one might call the organic refusal to separate personal and social existence. Discussions in the Bible studies deal with crime, personal greed, health concerns, a lifestyle on the part of many clergy that flies in the face of the community's nature, and the like. Matters concerning political violence, police actions, economic dislocation, and so on are equally the topics of debate. Strikingly, the two categories—personal and social—flow in and out of each other with no artificial distinction. Allowing that Zionism takes no direct interest in civic politics and struggles on a grand scale, the link between personal and social life is not wholly dissimilar.

Other parallels may be drawn between Zionism and the life of the Amawoti BEC, but more important at this point are the insights about local forms of micro power expressed through religious life and language. This does not yet take us far enough, however. Kiernan's work, for example, seems insufficiently cognizant of the full range of relations of power. He helps illumine the ways in which "merely religious" practices encapsulate empowering mechanisms for coping with urban and peri-urban life on the part of marginalized groups. But his tendency to a structuralist/functionalist rather than historical analysis leaves us without sufficient understanding of dimensions of resistance in popular religious practice.

We must turn elsewhere, to the work by Jean and John Comaroff on Zionism among the Tshidi clan of the Botswana, and to the theoretical reflections of James C. Scott on hidden transcripts.

Power and the Reproduction of Meaning

Modernization, urbanization, industrialization—so-called advanced forms of life—are terms often contrasted with their supposed opposites, namely, traditionalism, rural decline, peasant or subsistence economies, by implication backward forms of life. Backwardness also applies, in this context, to cultural, linguistic, and symbolic expressions of meaning. This applies to religious, and thus theological, reflection as much as to anything else. By and large, this was the view of white colonists and settlers, and this heritage still makes it difficult for economically privileged Christians to appreciate the production of meaning among those who stand on the other side of this divide.

The Amawoti community consists of people who stand on this other side, people who are therefore likely to be seen as less advanced, sophisticated, or cultured in their thought and practice than the dominant classes. The argument of this essay has been to show this view to be ultimately shallow. Yet there are important distinctions to be drawn between forms of life or social organization if we are to avoid a romanticized or reductionist interpretation of meaning.

The forms of organization or life with which we are now familiar are the product of decades of interaction, sometimes violent.[44] A major part of this interaction now consists of attempts of all kinds by people within environments such as Amawoti to find a place within the dominant order which will allow them to meet at least their basic needs, more if possible. The articulation between various systemic, structural, and organizational forms of life is complex and they cannot adequately be interpreted by single-narrative theories. In order to understand and apply this insight to the situation of the BEC, we turn to the concept of articulation developed by Jean Comaroff in her study of the Tshidi clan within Tswana society.

Comaroff criticizes what I have called reductionist approaches because:

> Forces and relations of production are disengaged, in such an approach from their embeddedness in wider orders of material, ideological and moral relations; consequently, the dynamic interplay of these relations . . . is reduced to a mechanical determinism. Instead, I use the concept of articulation to imply the multilevel process of engagement which follows the conjuncture of socio-cultural systems . . . whether this be between local formations or between local and global orders.[45]

Her particular concern is to convey, through a study of the Tshidi encounter with the British Empire, the sense in which interacting systems are joined with each other, or mutually affect each other, in ways no party fully controls. One may say, analogous to Foucault's notion of dispersed networks of power, that power works in both directions.[46]

> The encounter between Tswana and Brit is then not characterized simply by the hegemony of one formation over another, but by relations and orders of relations in which equivalent weight is given to "the interplay both of systemic contradictions and of conflicts of experience and value."[47]

To grasp Comaroff's approach to uncovering the relations between the Tshidi and the Brits is to appropriate another way of analyzing the significance of the communicative action of the BEC. Comaroff's work helps in another sense too. What happens in Tshidi society under the impact of conquest and colonization is that their attempts to establish some control over the conditions of the encounter, particularly at the level of experience and value, give rise to expressions of Zionist Christianity. Domination is part of this move, but so is resistance, provided we utilize a much more nuanced notion of resistance than one that implies direct, conscious, politically motivated action.

Comaroff is at pains to say that Zionist Christianity must be understood, at least in part, as embodying forms of resistance either overlooked or methodologically excluded by binary models of domination and subordination. Thus she sees in Tswana Zionism "a particular instance of a universal process of symbolic construction—the repositioning of signs in sequences of practice, 'texts' which both press new associations and reproduce conventional meanings."[48] These are historically efficacious, and that is the key point.

The texts of the Amawoti Bible studies may also be understood as attempts to press new associations that illuminate BEC members' experienced reality and generate new insights about appropriate communicative actions or practical strategies of benefit to the community at large. Their readings of the biblical texts, variously informed by a Christian heritage, may be seen to reproduce conventional meanings, mixing tradition and innovation.[49] The religious life of the BEC, embedded as it is in their local context, reproduces meaning on contested terrain. It is a complex battleground that, however unequal the forces, is saturated by ever shifting, ever changing configurations of power and empowerment.

Specific needs and hopes of the BEC are articulated in and through the Bible study process. It shapes their personal and social aspirations and their strategic thinking. It represents an attempt at reconstruction which will overcome their relative loss of control over their lives and environment. Comaroff again grasps this point precisely in her analysis of the Tshidi:

> The purposive act of reconstruction, on the part of the non-elite, focuses mainly on the attempt to heal dislocations at the level of experience, dislocations which derive from the failure of the prevailing sign system to provide a model for their subjectivity, for their meaningful and material being. . . . efforts are made to restructure activity so as to regain a sense of control. Repositories of value, like the Zionist's money, are resituated within practices that promise to redirect their flow back to the impoverished, thus healing their affliction.[50]

These are forms of power, "mechanisms of power that function outside, below and alongside" state apparatuses and the like.[51] Even among the most marginalized communities there are those practices and discourses that escape the hegemonic attempt to establish power over the local forms or arts of resistance.

Well and good, we might say, these local arts of resistance may partially escape the reach of hegemonically driven ideologies, systems, and structures. But is that not a rather minimal claim? Do they also challenge these ideologies, systems, and structures as a counterpower that offers something to reconstruction at the macro level?

The experience of the BEC in Amawoti suggests that this may indeed happen, but this is difficult to assess. Certainly, many such communities engaged in similar ways must have some effect on society, but perhaps at this point more cannot be said. Their activity remains significant, however, inasmuch as their religious life mounts a protest "in the domain of everyday practice [that] escapes direct control," as Comaroff argues. "Such resistance, . . . while it might not confront the concentrated forces of domination, defies the penetration of the hegemonic system into the structures of the 'natural' world."[52]

We may concur with one final judgment made by Comaroff, this time quoting Bourdieu, which underscores the point of this essay in respect of the communicative competence and action of the Amawoti Bible study group:

> The failure to recognize that there exist mechanisms capable of reproducing the political order independently of direct intervention has condemned us to ignore a whole range of conduct concerned with power.[53]

Essentially, our task is to arrive at the kind of nuanced understandings of popular religion and hegemony that will take us beyond current impasses in trying to grasp the links between liberation and inculturation, conscious resistance and attempts at survival, broad structural struggles at the macro level and multiple minor battles at the micro level.

Popular Religion and the Notion of Hegemony

The notion of popular religion may be used to describe what the Amawoti BEC practice. Yet I have spoken about their incipient theology, which is not the same thing. Another widely used notion in recent years is that of a people's theology. It appears necessary, therefore, to clarify possible confusions in terminology in order to define the significance of incipient theology more strongly.

Incipient theologies do express something of popular religion. Rather, I mean specifically the thinking about their faith of ordinary, theologically untrained Christians—a consciously reflective, though not necessarily systematic or analytic, activity. Popular religion I take to be more general, including the religious experiences and practices—visions, dreams, rituals, moral codes, personal convictions, relational patterns, and organizational operations—that express for ordinary Christians their encounter with the sacred. Local theologies and popular religion will overlap in practice, the former drawing into its reflective processes various elements of popular religion. They may or may not draw upon orthodox theology and faith, and if they do, it will be to varying degrees.[54]

The idea of a people's theology, in South Africa at least, was a reaction to a non-contextualized theological milieu that dominated public understanding and, indeed, ecclesial educational models in South Africa. Among Christians who supported the liberation struggle against the apartheid regime, this idea functioned as a slogan for resistance, to challenge Christians to take their place on the side of the people, meaning the black population in general and its politically active leadership in particular.

One might also designate as people's theology the thought of indigenous African churches. In their earliest form in the Ethiopian movement,[55] their theology was in fact not far from the notion of resistance, rooted in a politically conscious struggle against white-dominated missions and colonial society.

The idea of a people's theology has never been precise. Its activist form does not sit easily with the thought of the AICs, the churches of the people. It has remained a vague slogan, despite occasional attempts to give it a clear conceptual foundation (as in Albert Nolan's *God in South Africa*). One major reason for the ambiguity or indefiniteness of the notion of a people's theology lies in the fact that the actual religious experience of the bulk of the black population was not, and is not, that of a prophetically led struggle of liberation. Black Christianity, found primarily in thousands of AICs and similar local Christian groups, most commonly revolves around needs of belonging, identity, healing, mutual support, communal integration, and, at the limits of daily experience, survival.

The use of concepts such as hegemony and domination, usually located within macro-social theories of the grand narrative type, has frequently led to a jaundiced perspective on popular religion of all forms.[56] The tendency has been to regard popular religion, especially among the oppressed, as not so much wrong as deficient—a mental cage paralleling the imprisoning conditions of the material deprivation oppression defines. The Marxian metaphor "opium of the oppressed" has, therefore, been a common view on popular religion. Its corollary is this: the oppressed need conscientization to free them from this mental cage in order that they may participate fully in the material struggle for liberation.

The idea that popular religion is deficient, at least in terms of social transformation, leads to a serious, consequential separation between practitioners of popular religion and political activists or intellectual avant-garde. It cannot be healthy, either theologically or politically or humanly speaking, especially when activists and the avant-garde want to see themselves as fundamental to the populace in the struggle to overcome domination. If a theory of popular religion prevents a practical symbiosis of the populace and the intellectual or activist, then the theory may need revision. This is the initial impulse for the discussion that follows.

The question concerns the actual and potential significance of popular religion for social transformation. It requires a reconsideration of too strong, or too narrow, a notion of hegemony, particularly in the form of the Marxian dictum that the ideas of the ruling classes are the ruling ideas of the time (to which is linked the notion of false consciousness).[57] Too strong a notion of hegemony implies that the ideas of ordinary people, if not properly channeled and developed by critical intellectuals and activists, will express a naive, false understanding of reality.

Nuancing our Sense of Hegemony

Jean and John Comaroff usefully link the idea of hegemony to consciousness by suggesting that hegemony is constructed over a long period of time through the "assertion of control over various modes of symbolic production." What might at one time have been a conscious, strategic propagation of a particular worldview or ideology gradually takes on such a sense of naturalness that it becomes part of a background understanding of the way things are. It becomes unconscious or invisible. The "repetition of signs and practices" leads to habituation, and they become so deeply inscribed in everyday routine that they may no longer be seen as forms of control—or seen at all.[58] This is hegemony.

But it is only one side of the story. Hegemony is not exhaustive of consciousness, even under the most severe conditions of oppression. Hegemonic ideas and practices are challenged, thwarted, altered, used against themselves, ignored or overcome, in the tiniest corners of social existence. As my experience with the Amawoti BEC would confirm, hegemony is never total. It is always threatened by the vitality that remains in the forms of life it thwarts. "The hegemonic is constantly being made—and, by the same token, unmade; it is realized through the balancing of competing forces, not the crushing calculus of class domination. . . . [It] is always intrinsically unstable, always vulnerable."[59]

The capacity to recognize, uncover, or decode the forms of power on the side of the dominated by which they express the balance of competing forces is critical to the perspective I have adopted throughout this book. It challenges both my own past theoretical foundations and all perspectives that see a community such as the BEC (or the AICs, for that matter) either as unlikely to contribute to social change, or as reactionary and conservative rather than emancipatory and progressive.[60] This judgment presents us with an unresolved tension. This tension, Robin Petersen suggests, occurs because of a dual set of analytical norms.

A sociocultural norm values the languages, ideas, symbols, and practices of Africans who, never fully absorbed into the world of the colonizer and conqueror, have carved out their own cultural niches in a colonized context of conquest. An ethico-political norm values strategic practice—a conscious, intentional political resistance to the dominant elites and their discourses above all. Popular religion as in the AICs may be positively viewed under a sociocultural norm, but not necessarily under an ethico-political norm. Petersen shows this tension to be widely present in liberation theologies.[61]

Takatso Mofokeng also criticizes the classical, negative Marxist view of religion from the point of view of Black Theology. He notes, "Oppressed black people continuously remold religious ideas which are imposed upon them and produce a religion that is capable of functioning as a defensive as well as combative ideological weapon." Yet he simultaneously warns against going too far in this direction, calling for Black Theology to "consider incorporating only those elements which appeal to and sustain the black poor and most powerless in their struggle for survival."[62] In such a view, space has been opened up for the seemingly necessary kind of nuanced interpretation of hegemony and domination. In the words of Jean Comaroff, "If we confine our historical enquiry to the zero-sum heroics of revolution successfully achieved, we discount the vast proportion of human social action which is played out, perforce, on a more humble scale."[63]

The problem with cruder, one-sided understandings of hegemony as ideas and practices imposed through the "crushing calculus of class domination" is that it cannot take account of evidence to the contrary, of which there is an abundance. The root of the problem lies in a binary, Cartesian theory of consciousness that opposes the conscious and the unconscious, which sees something as "all or none, true or false, present or absent."[64] The persuasive solution to the problem, offered by the Comaroffs, is to view consciousness along a continuum, the one extreme of which corresponds to the traditional notion of hegemony (wholly unconscious background), the other to the traditional notion of ideology (wholly conscious strategy).

Most important is what lies between, that which is neither wholly strategic and consciously willed ("conspired") nor wholly unconscious ("natural"). This is what I believe the Amawoti BEC readings to represent, ranging across the spectrum of consciousness. They represent, in the words of the Comaroffs,

> . . . the realm of partial recognition, of inchoate awareness, of ambiguous perception, and, sometimes, of creative tension: that liminal space of human experience in which people discern acts and facts but cannot or do not order them into narrative descriptions or even into articulate conceptions of the world; in which signs and events are observed, but in a hazy, translucent light; in which individuals or groups know that something is happening to them but find it difficult to put their fingers on quite what it is. It is from this realm, we suggest, that silent signifiers and unmarked practices may rise to the level of explicit consciousness, of ideological assertion, and become the subject of overt political and social contestation—or from which they may recede into the hegemonic, to languish there unremarked for the time being. . . . It is also the realm from which emanate the poetics of history, the innovative impulses of the bricoleur and the organic intellectual, the novel imaginary called upon to bear the content of symbolic struggles.[65]

This rich paragraph also describes very well, better than I can, a hermeneutical framework suitable to grasping the religious life, experience, and practice of a community such as the Amawoti BEC. It expresses the intuition behind the concept of incipient theology: that much more than meets the eye is going on among those whose discourses and practices dominant elites usually regard as relatively unimportant, and that we risk losing a great deal if we do not pay attention to it.

Behind the Public Face

What meets the eye may be described as the publicly available discourses and practices of a group of people. What more is going on? James C. Scott's highly suggestive work on the arts of resistance will help us probe this. He too seeks to understand the nature of the power relations, through years of empirical anthropological work in a wide variety of contexts of domination. His insights help deepen the concept of incipient theology.

Let us begin with a particular reading of Luke 18:35-43 given by the Amawoti base ecclesial community. The text tells the story of a blind man sitting on a road outside Jericho. On hearing that Jesus was passing by, the man loudly called on him to have mercy and heal his blindness. The crowd sternly ordered the man to be quiet, but Jesus heard the cry and demanded that the man be brought to him.

A common, almost normative reading of the text for many Christians interprets it as demonstrating the importance of faith in Jesus as portrayed by the blind man, the need to believe in order to be saved. This is not the meaning of the text for the BEC.

> The blind man would not stop shouting, even though the people tried to stop him. Today people are helpless, unemployed, looking for money, fetching water. People ask "who, who" is going to help, and others tell them to keep quiet.[66]

The BEC see in the narrative an account of attempts to shut down communicative action: The crowd demand that the blind man be silent. The BEC members also respond to the blind man's refusal to be silenced by interjecting their own contemporary cries. The narrative emboldens them: Jesus listens to the cry of the blind man over the shouts of the crowd. The BEC interpretation begins with their own experience of the effect of uneven relations of power to produce a reading that one would be hard-pressed to find in biblical commentaries, lectionaries, or devotional literature.

The narrative suggests a second line of thought, about a possible breach in what one may take to be the normal relationship between the blind man and those around him. The blind man shouts while the crowd tries to silence him. Is he breaking custom by his behavior, a custom that sees his affliction as punishment from God and thus legitimate grounds for being marginalized? We do not know. The thought is not present in the BEC's reading of the text, but it leads us to ask about the normal conditions of discursive power. There provocative implication is that we are dealing with at least two levels of discourse, or better, with a continuum of discursive practice whose one end is public, the other hidden.

How are we to understand such a continuum? We may surmise that the crowd's attempt to silence the blind man reflects a customary pattern of public behavior, and that his breaching of convention is what elicits a reaction from the crowd. What is normally hidden is now brought into the open. What is going on here?

Here Scott's anthropological work becomes most helpful. Reflecting on years of fieldwork, he questions the validity of the empirical data anthropologists and other social scientists collect. He wonders if we are hearing and seeing the true story or whether, by virtue of the limits of the standard methods of social science, a story is missing. Scott's own answer is clear: We often do not hear the true story of a community or group of people, for very good reasons. Behind the public face, hidden from view except to those who know how to decode what is happening or who have privileged access to secluded activities, something else is going on.

He argues that too often the empirical data collected by social scientists consists of what has been made public by those who are the subjects of study. His own work produces clear evidence that publicly available data constitutes only half the story. In the contexts of domination and subjugation Scott studies, he points out that neither everyday forms of resistance nor occasional insurrection can be understood without reference to the sequestered social sites at which such resistance can be nurtured and given meaning.[67]

Resistance that is not a conscious strategic activity, which goes by another name, he believes to be widely present in half-aware practices he calls arts of resistance. Like the Comaroffs, Scott moves us into territory requiring deeply nuanced and complex understandings of the nature and effects of power.

Scott proposes the innovative and fruitful metaphor of "hidden transcripts" to describe the kind of discursive or practical activity hidden from dominated groups.[68] Between the hidden and the public transcript is a whole area of coded activities or arts of resistance. Scott calls this infrapolitics, and it includes such categories as disguise and surveillance.

A poignant South African example of the hidden transcript and infrapolitics can be seen in Nelson Mandela's eloquent testimony about his days living underground in South Africa before he was finally captured, sentenced, and sent to prison. He compares underground subversive activity to what was normal for a black South African:

You cannot be yourself; you must fully inhabit whatever role you have assumed. In some ways, this was not much of an adaptation for a black man in South Africa. Under apartheid, a black man lived a shadowy life between legality, between openness and concealment. To be a black man in South Africa meant not to trust anything, which was not unlike living underground for one's entire life.[69]

Scott argues that anthropology and social science usually study the public transcript. The researcher usually enters a particular group or community from the outside as trained experts with a research agenda of their own. It is to be expected that they are seen as a potential threat, a suspicion never overcome even in the most intimate settings. What they hear, see, and record is not wrong, but it is likely to miss the hidden transcript. It is just as likely to misinterpret the public transcript.[70] To get behind the public face to what is hidden, to correctly decode the discourse and practices of infrapolitics, is a mighty task, never possible to achieve fully or with certainty.

In Scott's words, "We may consider the dominant discourse as a plastic idiom or dialect that is capable of carrying an enormous variety of meanings, including those that are subversive of their use as intended by the dominant."[71] The point is relevant to others who engage in interpreting or representing the other in public forums or private circles. It is thus directly relevant to my own interpretive work in relation to the Amawoti BEC.

Have I constructed the subjectivity of the Bible study group in my own image? In representing my interpretation of the Bible study materials from the Amawoti group as an authentic expression of the religious language and perspective of a marginalized group within the Christian tradition, do I not continually misrepresent them, and thus also mislead the reader? Faced with the same question to which Scott responds, I must ask whether and to what extent the data derived from the Bible study transcripts of the Amawoti BEC is anything more than the public transcript. What do I miss in or misread into the encoded forms of expression of the infrapolitical activity of the community?

Clearly, I believe that I have tapped something authentic within the BEC and that I am able to communicate it with some faithfulness. How is one to judge my belief or claims, however? There is no easy answer to this. Even when one introduces scientific or theoretical controls into the process (a material context, a semantic context, and a participatory research process, for example),[72] Scott's question remains. All of the methods adopted to establish these kinds of interpretive controls may be dealing with the public transcript only, and to a greater or lesser extent with encoded infrapolitics.

The whole truth of the matter must include a decoding of infrapolitics and a grasp of the hidden transcript.[73] As long as a hidden transcript exists, or disguise and surveillance mark the communicative interaction of dominant and subordinate groups—as long as relations of power are sufficiently uneven, unbalanced, or asymmetric as to militate against a full and open public declaration of the aspirations, hopes, and perspectives of the subordinate or dominated—so long is one's understanding of the oppressed or marginalized group or person limited, incomplete, and perhaps wrong.

Scott's thesis is supported, in different form, by Jean and John Comaroff. They show in their study of the encounter between the Tshidi and the Brits that resistance occurs in a spectrum of consciousness. It must be understood along an analogous and parallel continuum of actions. "At one end is organized protest, explicit moments and movements of dissent that are easily recognizable as 'political' by Western lights. At the other are gestures of tacit refusal and iconoclasm, gestures that sullenly and silently contest the forms of an existing hegemony."[74] Echoes of Scott's distinction between the public and the hidden transcript may be heard.

As the Comaroffs put it:

> For the most part, . . . the ripostes of the colonized hover in the space between the tacit and the articulate, the direct and the indirect. And far from being a mere reflection—or a reflex expression—of historical consciousness, these acts are a practical means of producing it.[75]

In my study and interpretation of the Amawoti Bible studies one may say I am hoist by my own theoretical petard. Theologians, church leaders, and the like, including local clergy, are very often in the same position vis-à-vis their congregation as I am in my relation to the Amawoti Bible study group. They face the same questions, especially if they find themselves speaking on behalf of those whom they lead or teach.

The questions raised here about power, about responsibility in regard to the perspectives and voices of oppressed or marginalized groups, about interpretation and representation, are as pertinent to the training and functioning of church leadership of whatever kind, lay and clerical, as they are to the research process.

To put the point provocatively, applying Scott's words to my own religious context (the church, and in my case its theological training),

> What we confront, then, in the public transcript, is a strange kind of ideological debate about justice and dignity in which one party has a severe speech impediment induced by power relations. If we wish to hear this side of the dialogue we shall have to learn its dialect and codes. Above all, recovering this discourse requires a grasp of the arts of political disguise.[76]

The speech impediment to which Scott refers, a disturbing metaphor in itself, is established and sustained by demanding of church members an allegiance to a truth allegedly determined from above (thus divinely legitimated) which is deemed to be held securely in the hands of those given the responsibility of maintaining this truth (the guardians of the faith whose knowledge therefore becomes an exercise of power over others), and which must be defended against the vagaries of time and experience (thus denying the practical religious experience and perspectives of ordinary Christians as sources of truth). To quote Scott one more time:

> Unless one can penetrate the official transcript of both subordinates and elites, a reading of the social [read religious] evidence will almost always represent a confirmation of the status quo in hegemonic terms.[77]

It is not difficult to see why phenomena such as the African indigenous churches find no central place, if any, in the life of the settler origin churches, or why they are regarded with such suspicion when they make their presence felt. It is perhaps also possible now to understand why the BEC with whom I dialogue offers an insight into another kind of approach, one less shaped by unacknowledged (and probably mostly unconscious) practices of domination within the churches and one more open to stepping across the boundary domination erects between us.

The possibility of stepping across this kind of boundary is not merely an ideal, a typically utopian proclamation drawn from a Christian eschatology without its feet on the ground, though the point of this chapter has been to highlight the ambiguities, dangers, and pitfalls involved in such a journey. There are many people who have lived lives of integrity in giving testimony to this possibility. This is contested territory, even when those in authority fail, or refuse, to recognize it.

Perhaps those who have bridged this boundary with some success are less accepted for this testimony than many others who, living at the base, see no point in confronting the inertia of suspicious and latently hostile ecclesial authorities, or who, careful of their careers, their status, or a conservative congregation, follow the traditional, established routes into ministry and mission and into church leadership. Yet there are many lives that offer exemplary guidelines, even in their failures, for the kind of practice toward which the discussion in this chapter leans.

They are the significant others who need to be internalized,[78] who need to be understood and modeled. Because I have known such people, and know that they too are part of the church ecumenical, it is appropriate to point to this reality at the end of a discussion on the nature of power and empowerment in the context of a base ecclesial community and the AICs.

5. Voices of the Other

Credence is also trust. . . . This trust will, in turn, be a trust in the power to say, in the power to do, in the power to recognize oneself as a character in a narrative, in the power, finally, to respond to the accusation in the form of the accusative: "It's me here". . .

—Paul Ricoeur[1]

In the encounter of the Amawoti BEC members with each other, with the group facilitator, and with myself and my research students, a claim for selfhood becomes inevitable. As was clear in our negotiations with representatives of the BEC about whether or not they would agree to our research on their Bible study discourses, two fundamental questions were asked by the BEC committee: What does it mean for us? and Who are you (why should we trust you)?

Both questions have to do with our respective status as subjects. What does it mean for us? clearly indicates that the BEC, whose wider community had been the target of several research projects already, were tired of being considered objects of research. They wished to protect their selfhood from reification, from invasion. Could we really recognize them fully, respectfully? The claim for recognition posits both a self, and in relation to the one spoken to, an otherness. What kind of otherness did we represent for the BEC? A threatening, manipulative, and exploitative otherness? Trustworthy mutual conversation partners? In Emmanuel Lévinas's language, the query was about seeing the face of the other.

In this encounter lies a hidden dialectic explored most fully by Paul Ricoeur. Is the other like me (the same, idem-identity) or unlike me (different, ipse-identity)? If sameness dominates the encounter, the other is defined as nothing more than an extension of the self, posing no challenge, no question, no confrontation, no threat. We do not change. When difference is recognized, however, we encounter not just the other but our own selfhood in the making.

If I am constituted in relation to the other, it follows that anything I do to enable or disable the other's power to say (discourse), to do (practice), to recognize the other's self as a full character in a narrative (history), and to respond accordingly (agency) affects both the other and myself. In the case of the engagement with the Amawoti BEC, for example, is there a swamping of some characters and a relative domination by others (for example, by myself and my research students)? To what extent is the power of the BEC undone rather than enabled? Is the result upon which I reflect in this book merely a (my) fiction?[2]

As argued earlier, human beings may be subject to pervasive networks of power, yet they are also the agents of power. As subjects, they intend to do something. Thus, speaking is an act and keeping silent may also be an act (as James C. Scott reminded us). Our focus here is on this part of the encounter with the BEC—their otherness, their face (Lévinas), or to narrow it down, their voice.

There are at least three different levels on which the encounter takes place, each of which introduces its own problems or challenges, and each of which in turn shapes the rest of this argument.[3]

First is the direct, face-to-face meeting of the members of the BEC and my research assistants in the Bible study sessions. The commitment to the other here is quite direct, requiring first-person accountability for participation. Listening is not enough, because participation in the group, if it is to be trusted, also includes giving account of oneself as one speaks to the other from the foreground position of subject.

Subject positions, however, are most often unequal, affected by relations of power that confound speaking to the other. The subject on the foreground depends on levels of trust and distrust, belonging and alienation, domination and subjugation, and the like. Distinctions are necessary in assessing any relationship governed by relative power. We may speak with the other,[4] embracing the struggle for mutuality; we may speak at the other, intending to establish or extend control over the other; we may speak for the other, representing the other but also thereby erasing the other in part. Each of these possibilities has important implications for us, and each will be pursued in turn.

The second level of encounter with the BEC is through my interpretative activity on their Bible study transcripts. The relationship to the other, visible only in the text and not face-to-face, is now indirect and secondary, and quite different. If all we had was the text (as is the case with Scripture, for example), then—accepting Ricoeur's dictum that "the author is dead" and cannot be interrogated—it may not even be possible to recover with conviction the kind of otherness original to it. The written text is polysemous, Ricoeur tells us, containing whatever original meanings it had, a surplus of meaning that allows for interpretations not necessarily seen by the author, and meanings the reader brings to the text.

Therefore, reading the texts of the Amawoti BEC is no straightforward matter. Even if I know something of the group members' contexts, even if I can interrogate their own interpretations to some extent, even if I accept their epistemological privilege in understanding their reality, even if I listen in order to grasp the implications of their perspective, I am still forced to ask: Whose interpretative interests are at stake? How are they connected to material and social interests? Do I actually erase the other in my reading? Erasure is a conscious experience for the BEC, as they make clear in their view on the use of the Bible by those in authority in the church: "It's the way church ministry is carried out—they concentrate on the Bible and not on the community."[5]

Anselm Min notes that a commitment by outsiders, intellectuals, and activists to a practical engagement with local communities against dominating, subjugating discourses and practices may take three forms (leaving aside neutrality or opposition). One he defines as a "specific contribution" mode in which the theologian (intellectual) makes an indirect contribution to the struggles of the poor by engaging as theologian within the realm of theory and theology, according to its own rules and locus, to contest hegemonic discourses. The second mode of engagement, "alternating moments," refers to spending part of one's time working formally as an intellectual, another part in direct political action (for example, a professor and a militant for six months each), thus providing the necessary unity of theory and praxis in an all-embracing project. The "incarnation" mode (the most "complex and most demanding of the three") unites theology and politics through an organic insertion in sharing the life conditions of the poor. It involves a "dislocation of the theologian in terms of class and even space."[6]

All three modes invoke what Min calls "a conversion of perspectives" occasioned by the encounter with the other as other. The nature of this conversion and the particular commitment it draws forth is the second theme we will explore, drawing on Elisabeth Schüssler Fiorenza's distinction between conversation (the metaphor of hermeneutics) and collaboration (the metaphor of rhetoric).

This brings us to the third level at which the issue of the voice of the other must be faced, namely, the general question about what it means for the self to be constructed with and by the other. What is at stake for the self? It is an anthropological question of which the BEC, in its own way, is aware as well. Thus one member suggests, "Wisdom means knowing and thinking about other people." Another speaks of the engagement with the other as a reconstructive commitment: "God sent us into the world to become salt. Those people who have lost their conscience can be changed, like salt in water."[7]

The link of the self with the other also engenders the power to be if one recalls the BEC insight that power that challenges "things not good for oneself or for others" is also power that recognizes "things good for the self and others."[8] This third theme takes the *aporia* of the self and the other as the basis for a revised anthropology capable of grounding necessary engagement with the other by which, in the title of Ricoeur's philosophical ethics, one recognizes oneself as another.

Can We Speak with the Other?

In an influential article, Gayatri Spivak asks whether intellectuals who speak for those they claim to represent are deceiving themselves, as well as those for whom they claim to speak. Can intellectuals speak on behalf of the subaltern, one of inferior quality or status? Suspicious of such representations, she argues that authentic conversation means speaking to the other who in turn speaks to oneself—a communicative interaction between two present subjects.[9]

Normally, in Spivak's view, the master (the expert, researcher, interpreter, authority figure) speaks either for the subaltern, or at the subaltern, who then has no voice of her own. In both cases, the subaltern is not allowed to enter into the dialogue as a full subject in her own right. But, she asks, does the subaltern in any case have the capacity to be strongly present as subject? Her own answer is largely in the negative, but perhaps she goes too far. In developing this point below, I will take her notion of the subaltern as equivalent to "the poor" as this is understood in the widely accepted theological claim in contemporary Christianity of a preferential option for the poor, [10] and her comments on intellectuals as applicable to trained church leadership of one kind or another.

For Spivak, speaking *at* implies no interest in the other except subjugation, and we will not pursue that here. Speaking *for,* or on behalf of, implies some concern for the voice of the subaltern, but it already reifies or objectifies the other. This other is supposedly in need of conscientization and of public representation by those who speak for them and who thereby purport to understand them—activists and intellectuals who believe they know the situation of the subaltern better than the subaltern herself.

Those who speak for the subaltern subject do not acknowledge this, of course, assuming that their speech really is the speech of those they represent. They assume that the subjectivity of the other is publicly available, represented in the first place by their own discourse (*Darstellung*, a performative act), and in the second place, by those who have brought them to consciousness (*Vertretung*, a substitutionary act). The other who is constituted in this way in discourse is viewed as self-knowing, politically canny, that is, able to speak clearly about her situation, while the intellectual only listens and then speaks to others on the subaltern's behalf. The role of the intellectual in actually constructing the subjectivity of the other disappears from view in the process; so does what Spivak calls the "interest" of the intellectual:

> The critique of ideological subject-constitution within the state formations and systems of political economy can now be effaced, as can the active theoretical practice of the "transformation of consciousness." The banality of leftists intellectuals' lists of self-knowing, politically canny subalterns stands revealed: representing them, the intellectuals represent themselves as transparent.[11]

The intellectual, Spivak contends, cannot simply listen to the subaltern—the poor, the oppressed, the marginalized—assuming to be able to communicate or report her reality. Why? First, a report already re-presents what one has heard, linguistically and ideologically constituting the subjectivity of the one listened to through one's own interpretative activity and through the ideological character of this interpretative activity as shaped by social location, political position, and economic realities.

Second, what one hears from the oppressed is also constituted discursively and ideologically, giving no guarantee that their subjectivity has been fully represented (*dargestelt*). The subaltern, Spivak reflects, may not know how to speak of her subjectivity; more profoundly, she may not be able to do so because of thick layers of oppression. Third, claiming that listening and representation offer the genuine voice of the oppressed hides the intellectual's interests in the discourse.

Spivak, following Michel Foucault, calls this kind of intellectual activity "epistemic violence"—the violence of actions taken on the basis of a knowledge of the subaltern presumed to be better than that of the subaltern herself, for the supposed ideal of saving the subaltern from herself.

Spivak, however, concludes that the subaltern cannot speak. Her study of legal and ritual practices in colonial India leads her to believe that the subaltern cannot speak—silence has become virtually ontological in its force. Thus the intellectual must take the risk of representation, but now as a carefully circumscribed task. First must come an act of deconstruction by way of a recognition and admission of one's linguistically and ideologically shaped subjectivity (and interests) in order to clear space for what otherwise cannot be heard. Only then can one deconstruct the speech of the subaltern in relation to her linguistically and ideologically shaped subjectivity (and interests).

Spivak's argument is powerful and persuasive, but she holds perhaps too strong a view of the hegemonic power of the discourse of the dominant. Her notion of the subjugated subject in a context of powerful forces of domination leaves little room for any agency on the part of the subjugated person. Her conception of speaking also seems too limited, appearing to emphasize a

self-conscious capacity of articulation through language. A broader under-standing of discourse or of communicative acts seems necessary.

Are there arguments for my claim that there is something more to the sub-altern subject than Spivak believes to be the case? Can one escape the impasse she describes (that the subaltern finally cannot speak), other than to say that the task of representation remains vital provided it includes the deconstruction of the subjectivity of both the representative and the subaltern?

It does not appear that one can simply claim to have heard the voice of the subaltern in reporting this voice, nor can one claim to be credible on the basis of sincerity alone. Reports and personal credibility are not free of the effects of domination and the problems of representation. Spivak's critique could not be undermined from these directions.

Spivak's critique forces us into a continual hermeneutics of suspicion about any representations of the voice of the other. Having accepted this, however, per-haps her critique can be partially overcome: It can be accepted as a limit upon our claims about the voices of the other without abrogating all validity in such claims. What, then, offers a basis for determining the validity of our claims to have heard the voice of the other? To explore this question further, we turn to the question of interpretative interests and Schüssler Fiorenza's resuscitation of the notion of rhetoric.

Commitment and Collaboration

All interpreters have interests that shape their interpretative activity, overtly or otherwise. Not all interpretative interests are compatible with respect for local wisdom. The question of interpretative interests thus finds its sharpest focus in a consideration of the other by oneself.

In my case, the Amawoti BEC are the other, presented to me in the texts of their Bible studies. I have transformed their otherness, however, by my interpre-tations. I may argue that I represent their views accurately because I wish to respect and, as far as possible, represent their interests. Yet, as we have seen in Spi-vak's analysis of the subaltern subject, this claim is suspect, it must be criticized.

An interpretative commitment is implied, but of what kind? We will con-sider this question by following Schüssler Fiorenza's distinction between con-versation and collaboration.

We should remind ourselves of the interpretative situation in relation to the BEC. Here one is confronted with others who want to know whether their oth-erness will be respected or used for interests no longer under their control: To what ends and for whom is the relationship sought? Whose interests, and which interests, are served by the act of interpretation and its particular strategies?

In fact, the texts of the BEC are already permeated with the interpretative interests of its members, not all similar and not necessarily uncontested. Still, one may say that their internal debates, arguments, and statements demonstrate a fair convergence of generalized interests related to a context of relative poverty and deprivation (concerning crime, violence, powerlessness, voicelessness, subjugation, exploitation, and various forms of oppression). Their marginalization is central to their interpretation. If, as I have argued, perspectives drawn from the margins are vital for the ecumenical church and for society as such, we are committed to privileging particular interpretative interests.

Do we have any solid grounds for privileging the interpretative interests of the marginalized? There are strong arguments in favor of this proposition. Gerald West's analysis of contemporary biblical hermeneutics[12] shows that an overtly acknowledged commitment to the poor, oppressed, marginalized victims of society is vital if we are to enlarge our capacity to read the texts outside of the established categories of the dominant epistemé and thus to engender new, relevant insights. It is a matter of an adequate science of interpretation and not just a question of ideological choices.

West and I[13] see a methodological purpose behind this choice, referring to Gustavo Gutiérrez on the role of experience as the starting point for theological reflection if one is to move from "the current unjust situation to build a different society, freer and more human."[14] Frostin reminds us that the "preferential option for the poor"[15] becomes a way of answering a question always lying behind every theological construction: Who are the interlocutors, the seminal dialogue partners, of theology? Who is the defining other for the theological task?

A liberative theology chooses "nonpersons" (Gutiérrez) as its chief interlocutors: "the poor, the exploited classes, the marginalized races, all the despised cultures."[16] This has profound consequences for a deeper perception of social reality. If transformation, liberation, redemption, salvation, and other related terms are the point of the Christian proclamation (and we avoid the gnostic heresy of regarding the world as irrelevant), then "the experience of those defined as poor is a necessary condition for theological reflection."[17]

It is the necessary "concretely universal" perspective, says Anselm Min. Why? Because all perspectives are "necessarily concretized in a particular group," and within the limits of any one epoch or society some perspectives embody "the essential human crisis of the time in which all groups are involved." The poor or the marginalized are the bearers of this concretely universal perspective on theological grounds (as even the Vatican accepts, Min notes), on ethical grounds (because the "dignity of humans *as* humans . . . is most at stake in the poor"), and on structural grounds (poverty is not a natural but a historical condition predicated upon unjust social arrangements).[18]

Thus a perspective rooted in the objective life of the poor is universal because in *their* suffering is also at stake *our* contemporary human destiny—a preferential commitment to the perspective from poverty, but a nonexclusive one. Conversely, one either prefers another kind of commitment entirely (to a nation, class, the rich, and ethnic group, and so on) or adopts an ahistorical conception of reality supposedly void of all commitments. The first alternative cannot be defended nearly as well nor as universally, if at all; the second cannot be philosophically sustained.

The Amawoti BEC, in their own way, are quite conscious of the significance of particularity and commitment. On one occasion they discussed the question of who God's people are, and in what way God may be partisan. Their conclusion was that there are three categories of God's people: (1) all those who are created by God, whom God loves; (2) followers of God; and (3) special groups for whom God came, like the poor and the blind.

> There is a difference between God's followers and the people that Jesus came for. He wanted to change their situation. For the poor, it was good news, and the blind were able to see. Jesus describes his mission and shows his followers what their mission is.[19]

That God came for special groups is not incidental but central to their soteriological understanding:

> [Facilitator]: If Jesus came into Amawoti how would people recognize him as king or leader?
>
> [Group]: He cares for the poor and outcast; leaders feel threatened. He gives poor people hope and challenges leaders.[20]

Some see such claims as far too particularistic.[21] Sharon Welch defends them on the basis of a circumscribed "ethic of risk."[22] The risk lies not in a particular choice—all positions make a choice of some sort—but in standing in solidarity with marginal communities. By contrast, those who stand with "universal humanity" (an abstract concept as opposed to specific historically and materially situated human beings) tend to stand with the status quo and an "ethic of control."[23] An ethical choice, a "risk" in Welch's view, is all that can ground the privileging of a particular perspective.

Welch's argument draws on well-founded postmodernist critiques of the modern desire for control and certainty. But one may add other kinds of arguments, too. In particular, Schüssler Fiorenza's challenge to shift from a hermeneutics of conversation to a rhetorics of collaboration is helpful in expanding on the specific theme of the voice or speech of the self and other. It is a move from particularity in general to the particularity of marginal communities.

Conversation, Schüssler Fiorenza contends, is the basic metaphor underlying interpretative interests.[24] Conversation, however, implies no commitment to anything other than dialogue. We have already explored how dialogue is itself complicated or distorted by power and interests. Thus Schüssler Fiorenza argues that a hermeneutical model of conversation, though necessary to respect the plurality of experiences and thus the experience of the marginalized other as well, is insufficient. We may be partially constituted in a dialogue with the other, but because we do not all enter the conversation on equal terms, critical collaboration is vital.

Thus, says Schüssler Fiorenza, "the inclusion of the previously excluded as theological subjects . . . calls for a paradigm shift from . . . a hermeneutic[al] model of conversation to a practical model of collaboration."[25] Interpretation must be accompanied by what Schüssler Fiorenza calls a "rhetorical genre."[26] Rhetoric here must not be understood in current colloquial language as something false, an argument lacking rationality, or a validity claim protected from interrogation. Rather, it refers to the early Greek understanding of *passionate argument* in senate debates of the city-state.

The socio-historical location of rhetoric understood in this way is the *polis*, the community of citizens, in which political choices must be made, policies developed and implemented. Critical enquiry is assumed, but so is an overt practical commitment. Because something is really at stake for human beings, passion (and compassion) is a virtue, whereas a lack of passion would be seen as a sign of lacking seriousness.

Rhetorical practices link knowledge with action and passion in three ways. First, they display a referential moment about something, for example, a proclamation about who God is. Second, they display a moment of self-implicature by a speaker or actor in which the intent of the proclamation is linked to the interests of the proclaimer. Third, they display a persuasive moment directed at involving the other: they elicit responses, emotions, interests, judgments, and commitments directed toward a common vision.

How, then, does the rhetorical genre avoid a situation in which choices are made simply on the basis of whatever view currently proves most persuasive, even if it may be wrong (we have enough examples of this in our century)? We can never know all the conditions giving rise to any situation of choosing. Neither can we grasp all the constraints governing alternative choices, nor predict with any certainty whether a particular choice will produce the desired outcomes. Are we not then caught up either in a hopeless plurality of choices on the one hand, or an arbitrary choice on the other?

Schüssler Fiorenza's answer is to turn to the notion of praxis. The meaning of rhetoric now becomes critical collaboration, a notion that drives us away from relativism into making choices that can be defended against other choices. One thus deliberately chooses sides, favoring one party against another. But on what grounds can a decision to take sides be theologically defended? Who decides, and why? What happens to the necessary conversation among all sides which not only a hermeneutical intent but also a valid view on theology demands of the Christian community? Is taking sides not a betrayal of freedom and justice?

Schüssler Fiorenza argues her position against two competing views that challenge the notion of taking sides. One view assumes there are definitive bodies of knowledge that are free of value and thus not subject to practical choices, in which truth is timeless and accessible to all who use the right method in uncovering it. This view is found above all in the philosophical idealism of the Enlightenment as expressed in the ideal of pure reason or universal science. The other view assumes that all bodies of knowledge have equal claim to validity within their own chosen frameworks. This is the radical relativism of some postmodernism as expressed in notions of irreducible difference or irreversible plurality.

Schüssler Fiorenza unpacks "four correctives" to the Enlightenment ideal of pure reason, and, in doing so, a critique of radical postmodernism emerges. Three correctives to the ideal of pure reason, she notes, are widely accepted: the aesthetic-romantic corrective ("intuitive imagination over selective abstraction"), the religious-cultural corrective (tradition as "wisdom and heritage"), and the political-practical corrective (the connection of knowledge to power).[27]

To this she adds a fourth corrective she believes has emerged from the challenges of dominated groups and peoples: the corrective of "minority discourses" (meaning, one may assume, marginalized or suppressed discourses). Its essence is to assert the importance of the situated, particular self against the Enlightenment notion of the universal, transcendent subject "whose disembodied voice is reason." This disembodied voice effectively overrides the particular voices of dominated groups and peoples because they are assumed not to have universal significance. Enlightenment universalism, in the end, thus really represents only the voice of the bourgeoisie writ large.

Schüssler Fiorenza seeks an embodied voice, specifically that which represents the colonized other who must engage in a political and theoretical process of becoming the subject of knowledge and history. For this reason Schüssler Fiorenza distances herself from postmodernist perspectives which she believes tend "to abandon the notion of the subject and the possibility of defining the world."[28]

It is important to note that Schüssler Fiorenza is not an enemy of the gains of the Enlightenment (indeed, her own work depends upon these gains). She makes it clear that her model does not invoke an argument with empirical research, analytical scholarship, or critical abstraction itself. Rather, she attacks an uncritical conception of reason, knowledge, and scholarship which hides the rhetorical character of science even as it marginalizes the four correctives to science as ideological and therefore inadmissible. Wherever reason or science does this, she suggests, it defeats the Enlightenment's own intellectual ideal (critical understanding) and its practical ideal (a just and democratic society).

Critical Collaboration and the Theological Task

Critical collaboration, applied to theology, implies that religious authority claims and identity formations must be investigated to determine to what extent they exhibit "destructive religious discourses."[29] Theological paradigms and texts, even the great christological creeds, are not taken to be innocent from the outset. They cannot simply be discarded if one claims Christian faith, but they contain more than "cultural-linguistic rules" (George Lindbeck). They also reflect contradictory discourses embedded in competing sets of power relations.

Theological discourse, therefore, is no more than guiding reflection upon the symbolic constructs (narratives, rituals, images, and so on) by which faith communicates itself through the ages. Received teachings are thus heuristically significant rather than dogmatically determinant. As David Tracy points out in criticizing Lindbeck's postliberal "rule-theory" of doctrine, this does not imply "a capitulation of traditional religious beliefs to contemporary secular beliefs. Rather, . . . any correlation should be, in principle, one of *mutually critical* corre-lations of an interpretation of the meaning and truth of the tradition and the interpretation of the meaning and truth of the contemporary situation."[30]

This methodological assumption undergirds my claim that the perspectives presented by the base ecclesial community of Amawoti must be taken as seriously as the received tradition. The dialectical relationship between these two moments of theological reflection becomes a vital clue to a theological hermeneutics which respects the plurality of voices within the church and, in doing so, gives proper weight not only to voices of the past, or to those whose knowledge in the present represents power over others, but also to those voices who are at this point still marginalized or suppressed.

The realization that the community of Christians, whose combined knowl-edge over time makes up the deposit of theology, is a broken community leads to the second claim, namely, that the theological hermeneutics we require must be accompanied by rhetorical practices that expose this brokenness and its power effects in collaboration with those who are politically and economically broken. This task is aimed in the first place at uncovering the effects of power relations within the Christian community itself. Its aim is therefore intrinsically theologi-cal, because it aims at a vision of well-being that might be shared for all.

The critical, activist aspect of the task is clear for Schüssler Fiorenza: we are not only to understand religious communities, but also to change them. She clearly assumes that the oppressed person can speak in ways that intellectuals can hear directly. She also believes that the intellectual's role is to constitute her dis-cipline "as a heterogeneous, polyphonic public, [thereby being able] to develop critical collaboration and discursive practices in the interest of a democratic public."

Schüssler Fiorenza's confidence about the avant-garde role of the intellectu-al, albeit clearly stated as in collaborative relationship with the oppressed, seems too much in the end to sustain the actual conditions of power and powerlessness in the discourse situation.[31] If Schüssler Fiorenza's arguments are the corrective to Spivak's pessimism about the capacity of the subaltern to speak, then Spivak's deconstruction of the possibility of a sufficiently strongly foregrounded subject who can speak as subaltern is the permanent destabilization of all claims to soli-darity with the subaltern. This paradoxical position is the truth of commitment to the other in the real world, and the dialectic must be maintained.

The Self and the Other

The dynamics of concrete relationality have thus far been our concern. We now take one step back to ask, What is at stake in seeing the self as constituted by and with the other? To do this, we return to the philosophical ethics of Paul Ricoeur.

Ricoeur begins by designating the self as another, that is, as ontologically constituted by the other. Language practice itself contains expressions of this ontology in the way in which pronouns (I, you), reflexive terms (myself, one-self), and other analogous constructs are used. Each depends upon there being both a self and an other to make sense. Language is by definition communicative practice, never an end in itself, and thus also an expression of the nature of the human being as self and other.[32]

We identify persons in two fundamental ways, says Ricoeur: as sameness, or idem-identity, and as otherness, or ipse-identity.[33] Idem-identity implies perma-nence in time, an unchanging self, a core unaffected by time and space and there-fore unaffected by the other: It is the Cartesian ego. Ipse-identity, on the other hand, simultaneously evokes both the self and the other-than-self ("one cannot be thought of without the other"). The self is constituted with the other in this case. As Ricoeur stresses in the title of his book, *Oneself as Another, as* means more than similarity or comparison. It has the meaning of implication: Selfhood implies an other.[34]

Ricoeur's use of *with the other* is significant. It is clear he opposes the idea held by Lévinas that the self is constituted *by* the other. This position, in Ricoeur's view, has two weaknesses. First, it secretly depends upon a notion of two sub-jects whose selves are presupposed to be independent before they face each other. Second, in this role the other can only face us as a judge who calls us to account: ". . . [because] the initiative of the injunction comes from the other, it is in the *accusative* mode alone that the self is enjoined." Separation rather than relation is the ruling metaphor, implying an "utter dissymmetry between the Same and the Other."[35]

Judgment or accusation blocks real dialogue, real discovery, real openness in the encounter of persons. Ricoeur argues, however, that the self has a capacity for reception, for discrimination, for recognition, and for reciprocity that superposes a relation upon the supposedly absolute distance between the I and the other. A philosophy of the subject always fails, in his view, because it cannot take into account the way in which the I is a kind of I-you from the very beginning—never merely a separate subject.

Ricoeur thus contrasts the notion of self as constituted by otherness with the Cartesian ego, the exemplary philosophy of the independent individual which underlies so much of modernity. In Cartesian thought, the I is a free-floating subjectivity. The capacity to doubt, thus to think, does not depend upon any spatiotemporal location. The supreme I, thus stripped of narrative identity, lies in the *cogito* freed from the constraints of space and time. This great freedom comes at a price. The autonomous I now has no story, no history. It is split off from all actual speakers, from human agents, from the character of narration, from subjects of moral imputation. In truth, says Ricoeur, this metaphysical, hyperbolic I is no one.[36]

In the Cartesian ego we are cut off from the other, from history, from any particular place. This move has produced some astounding feats of the mind in technological inventions and the development of the sciences, but it has also truncated the core of human being. The human being is always part of an existing story and part of the making of new stories. In the context of story, the self is no longer an abstract I but an acting and suffering individual joined in the narrative of life with other individuals—in their otherness and thus in their own selfhood. The autonomy of the self—no longer found in the freedom of thought detached from all boundedness and all concrete stories—is now "tightly bound up with *solicitude* for one's neighbor and with *justice* for each individual."[37]

Without solicitude and justice the self/other becomes merely a body to be manipulated, isolated, dissected, and ultimately destroyed. Erasing otherness, by implication, erases the self. In Martin Buber's classical formulation, both the I and the thou disappear to be reified as an it.[38] Body and selfhood are dissociated at the cost of a reduction of being human to mere materiality or thingness on one side, or mere consciousness or spirit on the other. Both tendencies destroy a view on human beings which affirms a holistic understanding of the person as defined by a "concrete totality" (Min).

The key point in all of this, regarding the Amawoti BEC, is that their (explicit and implicit) demand to be heard in their otherness is also simultaneously a challenge for the self to be partially reconstituted by them. Moreover, the encounter is necessarily mutual, its constitutive effects going in both directions: They are partially reconstituted in their encounter with me as well! The effects of this interaction are important, and so are the effects of our respective social, political, economic, and cultural locations upon the encounter. The relationship can be manipulative or destructive. The hermeneutics of suspicion is never absent (neither theoretically nor practically).

But to the extent that the encounter is between selfhood and otherness, something other than manipulation, utility, or harm is at stake. The relation now becomes a call, a voice addressed to the self for the sake of the self. It becomes the occasion for openness, for learning, for a revision in oneself—for conversion, to use a theological word.

Now, however, a choice faces us. The voices addressed to us are always multiple, often conflicting in what it is they demand we hear. Not all testimonies are equivalent, and not all can be trusted. To whom do we listen? Who are we to believe, and on what grounds?

Testimony, Truth, and Commitment

Ricoeur's anthropology refuses the Cartesian view of the human being as being only one indivisible I opposed to another indivisible I. Selfhood, not subjectivity, is the key: The identity of the subaltern is not that of an I but that of a self constituted dialectically in relation to other selves. One can thus discern in a person's claims about themselves grounds for believing them, for two reasons. First, one has some recourse to those others who permeate the selfhood of the speaker. Second, one has some kind of access to the world in which the speaker and her others are located. Both points of reference may be tested, the first by paying attention to the wider world of the self/other, the second by analyzing the way in which the self is embodied in the concrete material and social conditions of a particular time and place.

These two tests place strict limits on what can be claimed in the encounter with the other, of course. One has no guarantees here, no certainties. Nevertheless, an encounter with otherness is rich in potential, which is why I argue for the incipient theologies of groups such as the Amawoti BEC. Moral obligation and ethical constancy meet here in what Ricoeur instructively sees as the deep human necessity to "recognize oneself as being enjoined to *live well with and for others in just institutions and to esteem oneself as the bearer of this wish*."[39]

How does this recognition come? It begins with the determinative question: Who is this other whom I encounter? It cannot be answered abstractly, objectively, or indeed merely subjectively. It is answered in speaking, in attestation, in giving testimony of oneself in concrete contexts. Testimony, if genuinely oriented to an encounter with the other in concrete contexts, claims to be true speech. Truth here is credibility in the act of speaking and the relation of speaking to other general acts and practices.

Herein resides the only ground for a hermeneutics of restoration, that testimony of the self is given to the other. It links speaking and acting, as Ricoeur notes throughout his work, because speaking is an expression of being, as is acting. It is one and the same being who speaks and acts.[40]

In the Amawoti BEC discourses, it becomes clear that neither their texts nor mine contain a fixed, certain truth. What we have is a testimony, contextually located, constitutive of them, myself, and our readers—as long as there is an openness to being constituted in the encounter. The text projects a world of otherness into which the reader is invited. If the resulting encounter is not one of sameness but of otherness, then the self of the reader is thereby also constituted anew, both mentally and practically. The interlocutory relation to the historical person who speaks, where one has really listened, produces two complementary recognitions: One's own self changes, and one is called into a relationship of responsibility or accountability. There is both an anthropological and an ethical imperative here.

This calls for a kind of commitment that goes beyond mere listening to constancy of one's own self. I have already referred to commitment to the other as confronting oneself with a kind of ongoing conversion. It seems theologically reasonable to equate this commitment to constancy in oneself to *discipleship,* whose practical meaning is "esteem for oneself" as the bearer of the wish to "live well with and for others in just institutions."

Both forms of commitment, conversion and constancy, depend upon attestation and trust; both are maintained only by repeatedly returning to the task of restoration in the face of ongoing suspicion. This is the key dialectic: neither restoration nor suspicion is made anthropologically or epistemologically prior to each other. Instead, both are held in dynamic equilibrium in order that what one has heard remains the voice of the other and not simply an extension of one's own subjectivity, and in order that the voice of the other may be heard as a voice for oneself.

It is possible to regard commitment to the other purely as a response to an injunction that comes from outside the self: the face of the other confronting us as judge. For Lévinas this is the only mode of otherness that matters. Because it is wholly external, we can neither erase the face of the other from view nor overcome its radical otherness. There is no epiphany of the other here, only a trace. There is something powerful in this claim: It prevents us forever from assimilating the other to ourselves, forcing a chasm between us and the other which the hermeneutics of suspicion requires, and undermining practices that function only as another instance of imposition upon the other (as in the problems of representation highlighted by Spivak).

For Lévinas's "The model of all otherness is the other person," Ricoeur poses an alternative based on the structure of selfhood as already being enjoined, that is, oneself as another.[41] This ontological rooting of otherness in the self comes to expression as self-attestation: the claim to be true to oneself in the encounter with the other. Ricoeur argues that without self-attestation, the injunction from the other no longer enjoins oneself because the self is given no voice in the encounter. The voice of the other is only of reciprocal significance for the self if the self also has a voice.

This voice Ricoeur calls conscience. If conscience does not exist, and if it does not find expression in the attestation of the self to its own truth, then "the injunction [of the face and voice of the other] risks not being heard and the self not being affected in the mode of being-enjoined." At stake here is not just the injunction from the other, but also care of the self. With this realization the Golden Rule, Do unto others what you have them do unto you, is linked with second and third terms of the Great Commandment, Love your neighbor as yourself.

Power in Three Kinds

The dialectic between selfhood and otherness presupposes mutuality or reciprocity between persons. Ricoeur sees the norm of reciprocity as a general wisdom on the nature of human being, already prefigured in Hillel's Golden Rule,[42] and implied in the Great Commandment.[43] Reciprocity, however, does not necessarily mean mutuality or equality. The relationship between the self and the other, rooted in a spatiotemporal context, may and often does take the form of an asymmetry of power. Reciprocity thus "stands out against the presupposition of an initial dissymmetry between the protagonists of action—a dissymmetry which places one in the position of agent and the other in that of patient."

The absence of symmetry is the root of the dissolution of the other, beginning with a utilitarian view of the other, and ending in murder. This, says Ricoeur, is the power of one will over another, and seldom is this power over not present to some extent.[44] Power over the other may be socially institutionalized, but it does not constitute an ethical norm for persons. It implies something done to the other, no longer in solicitude (friendship) but as a form of domination, descending a slope as far as torture, the extreme form of abuse. *Power over* is equivalent to "the diminishing or destruction of others' power to do," and may be just as easily in discourse as in action. It is precisely against experiences of power over the self and others that the norm of reciprocity has been constructed throughout history and in various societies.

We are now able to see two other meanings of power in Ricoeur's notion of the self and the other. The first is power to do, the power to act, the capacity of a human being to become an author of action (with all the ambiguities that may be attached). The second is power in common, the capacity of a community to exercise its desire to live or act together.

We may also relate these categories to Spivak's question about the capacity of the subaltern to speak. Spivak, we recall, distinguishes between three modes of speaking: speaking to (implying two equally foregrounded subjects), speaking at, and speaking for. The latter two modes are clearly forms of power over the other, even if speaking for the other is a sublimated, less obvious mode of power (it takes discourse out of the hands of the those on whose behalf one speaks, thus diminishing their own power to do).

Modes of speaking thus emerge as inherently linked with kinds of power. The modes of speaking adopted by the Amawoti BEC produce a stronger sense of self and of the other, a stronger power in common which also translates into a power to do. Through a long process of self-constitution that depends upon a history of growing consciousness through communicative action, the BEC has developed a foregrounded subjectivity (Spivak) strong enough to speak to others outside this community (including other groups around the country and, in one case, an international forum).

Nevertheless, we cannot forget that the kind of society in which the dissymmetry of power and relations of power is overcome does not yet exist— "the republic is not a fact" (Ricoeur). The dialectic of the self and the other inherently implies the goal already annunciated earlier, namely, to live well with and for others in just institutions and to esteem oneself as the bearer of this wish. But the fact that this goal remains unreached, an eschatological reality, makes suffering a defining condition of human existence.

The Priority of Those Who Suffer

The perspective of people who suffer the injustices of others and of society as such is vital to the kind of selfhood and otherness the church claims to be Christian and proclaims in Jesus Christ. Ricoeur also emphasizes in his anthropology the nature of the other as acting and suffering. This is an unusual move. Why should we commit ourselves to being constituted by the otherness of the one who suffers? No simple answers can be given, but perhaps a persuasive proposal can be made.

Let us recall Ricoeur's point that the identity of the self is not ahistorical, point-like, but constituted through time and in space with others. The self, therefore, has an inherently narrative identity: it is "entangled in stories."[45] Ricoeur's study on time and narrative makes clear that there is no ethically neutral narrative, just as there is no ethically neutral interpretation, no value-free science.

The narratives of our lives record not just encounters between persons, but also the effects of the three forms of power discussed. The self grows or diminishes according to the kind of power exercised. Ricoeur defines *power to do* as the crux of what it means to be a self, and *power in common* as the effect of reciprocity between the self and the other. This teleological and communal conception of the ethics of selfhood points to the anthropological basis of a fulfilled, whole life, just as much as it directs our attention to the fact that the fulfilled life is an eschatological reality rather than a present one. Dissymmetry, not symmetry, between the self and the other is the rule.

The other person confronts us, to follow Lévinas, by her or his face: "It's me here!" But, so Ricoeur argues, the relational dissymmetry between the self and the other means that the other stands here as judge, enjoining the self to respond. If this response takes the form of power over the other, suffering results. Because the other already exists in dissymmetrical relations, suffering now becomes just as distinctive of the other's personhood as acting.

This may be understood by recognizing what Ricoeur means by suffering: "Suffering is not defined solely by physical pain, nor even by mental pain, but by the reduction, even the destruction, of the capacity for acting, of being-able-to-act, experienced as a violation of self-integrity."[46] Suffering cannot be seen as secondary to what it means to be a person. The self constituted with the other is constituted not only by what passes between each by way of actions but also by what is lost to the other—and thus the self—in suffering.[47] Ricoeur makes the point clear: "With the decrease of the power of *acting*, experienced as a decrease of the effort of *existing*, the reign of suffering, properly speaking, commences."[48]

There are implications here for what it means to speak of just institutions. The encounter of the self with the other, if it is not restricted in its reach, goes beyond the particularities of a face-to-face encounter. If we define an institution as the structure of living together in a historical community,[49] then the ethical aim of living well cannot be reduced to interpersonal relations, even though it is bound up with them.

This is the key point in the particular relationship to the Amawoti BEC I have tried to model so far. Attention to the claims of the other means attention to the establishment of institutions of justice. This is not a belated recognition derived from theory. Living well in just institutions is precisely what the members of the Amawoti BEC seek for themselves, and in their encounter with others.

It is not coincidental that growth in selfhood is accompanied by a willingness to engage others in the construction of just institutions. This extends beyond the local community to the heart of my own project, in that the Amawoti representatives who gave permission for this research did so on the expressed wish that what they had experienced and learned in their context become a voice to the churches themselves.

Even as we note this positive intention, we must recall the ever present dissymmetry in this encounter. The hermeneutics of suspicion surfaces again, recognizable in what Ricoeur calls "tragic wisdom." To this point we must repeatedly return, lest we imagine that encounters of the kind described in this book produce just institutions in and of themselves. This would be to overlook the contradictions that remain and their deep effects. Discussing human action as practical wisdom whose vision or aim is the good life,[50] Ricoeur in his ninth study sought to incorporate what had largely been absent till now in his discussion of the self and the other: the reality of conflict.

He turns to Greek tragedy (*Antigone*) to deal with this issue, primarily because the narrative directness of theater forces us to recognize that actual conflicts cannot be analyzed in the abstract. In the narrative we confront persons who act, in their individuality, testing moral judgment in particular situations that demand practical wisdom. In tragedy, the voice heard produces "the shock capable of awakening our mistrust with respect not only to the illusions of the heart but also to the illusions born of the hubris of practical reason itself."[51]

Reason that believes it has only to uncover the hidden mechanisms of domination carried by structures and material forces in order to free the oppressed person partakes of the hubris of which Ricoeur speaks. Without discounting practical reason, Ricoeur asks us to recognize concrete, historical, particular persons as the test of all practical wisdom. The dialectic of the self and the other is thus made prior to the dialectic of reflection and analysis.

When this is the case, tragic wisdom gains its full significance. It breaks the boundaries of analysis and reflection to confront us with "the agonistic ground of human experience." Conflicts of all kinds become visible in their specificity and capacity for generalization. Through them the self and the other are shaped and taught: self-recognition comes "at the price of a difficult apprenticeship acquired over the course of a long voyage through these persistent conflicts, whose universality is inseparable from their particular localization, which is, in every instance, unsurpassable."[52]

A recognition of the otherness of the Amawoti BEC includes, therefore, an understanding of the difficult apprenticeship they have been through in their time together, and a grasp of the particular conditions of their local experience of conflict. Said thus, we may easily translate our task once more into mere reflection and analysis. Tragic wisdom, as long as it is not separated from practical wisdom, faces us with that in human experience which is intractable, nonnegotiable. It introduces an ethical and practical *aporia,* a gap that cannot be closed by arriving at solutions. Tragedy teaches us that there is no solution to everything.

But the conflicts tragic wisdom places at the center of our gaze call not simply for catharsis (a moment of protest, the sudden irruption of a hidden

transcript), but for conviction. The ethics of the self as another require us to take a stand in the face of tragedy. The full implications of this point are precisely captured by Ricoeur, while his analysis of tragedy also shows us the point of conviction and commitment in the dialectic of the self and the other:

> By refusing to contribute a "solution" to the conflicts made insoluble by fiction, tragedy, after having disoriented the gaze, condemns the person of praxis to reorient action, at his or her own risk, in the sense of a practical wisdom in situation that best responds to tragic wisdom. This response . . . makes conviction the haven beyond catharsis.[53]

In Spivak's terms, the self is also foregrounded in the encounter with the other, though not innocently. In Elizabeth Schüssler Fiorenza's terms, the self and the other are drawn by commitment beyond conversation into collaboration. It is this dynamic of self-constitution in responding to the other that makes significant the recovery of the incipient theologies of persons who act and suffer.

On Availability and Face

We have spoken of commitment and constancy in relation to persons acting and suffering as important moments in the dialectic of the self and the other. Power to do as defining of personhood and power in common as the foundation of the self in community have been contrasted with power over the other, assisting us to understand what it is that we might be committed to and why. We further linked commitment and constancy to the aim of living well with and for the other in just institutions. But what keeps this commitment and constancy open? What is to prevent it being arbitrary, subjective, or a rigid principle divorced from actual encounters with persons?

Ricoeur suggests that to avoid treating the notion of self-constancy as a mere play of feeling and to ground it ethically we need an appreciation of the moral significance of the "dialogic-dyadic" structure of self-constancy. Feelings are not constant and cannot ground an ethical stance.[54]

This double bind is only overcome when we recognize that "all commitment is response." The other whose voice calls me to fidelity and trust is the bulwark against arbitrary feeling and the foundation of self-constancy. But this voice only reaches me if I make myself available to it. As in the Golden Rule, availability calls for a reciprocity in initially dissymmetric situations which "establishes the other in the position of someone to whom an obligation is owed, someone who is counting on me and making self-constancy a response to this expectation."[55] This is the irreducible anthropological core of commitment.

The task of recovering incipient theologies is exactly one of making oneself available, particularly to those who suffer, who experience the loss of the power to do, in the belief that key insights will arise that might break open ways to "live well with and for others in just institutions." While one cannot guarantee one's availability (the *aporia* of self-constancy), the dynamic of making oneself available never ceases to thrust itself upon us. It is not a single act, but an ongoing process.

Given conflict and contradictions, given the dissymmetry of relations of power, and given our flawed personal and social condition as captured most poignantly in tragic wisdom, it seems that self-constancy in response to the voice of the other must also be rooted within institutions—that is, if they are to be just. We must ask, for the establishment of the justice that reciprocity demands in the encounter with the other, not What are you? but Who are you? And, we must ask this in a manner that does not push the other from view when our feelings are distracted or changed. Reciprocity as justice must therefore be structurally and institutionally located if it is to be constant.[56] Only then does an encounter with the other produce an enduring, and therefore trustworthy, basis for commitment and availability.

Beyond Actuality: The Spiritual Foundation of Selfhood

We have spoken of the self and the other, in theological terms of the second and third precepts of the Great Commandment, loving one's neighbor as oneself. But what has happened to the first, Love God? Is there a theological moment here that has so far been obscured in the more indirect language of ontology and anthropology? If self-identity is not solely constituted by otherness (just as otherness cannot be reduced to the sameness of self), what remains if not an independent persona? Is there not a sense in which the self is a spiritual being, rather than simply a being constituted by other bodies or other persons (although never separate from them, either)?

First let us note that the self has a voice, and that this voice, as the attestation of the self to be true to itself, may be called conscience. We may suppose that the conscience of the self arises only by virtue of the other, but this would be a mistake. On the one hand, the identity of conscience surely does arise in relation to the other (the self as ipse-identity comes to the fore here). On the other hand, the self as constituted in time also has an enduring identity, a sameness that enables us to recognize in the child the person who has now become an adult.

Though it is never without the impact of the other, this enduring identity of the self is also consciousness of the self. No longer the Cartesian ego, it is the self considering itself and its own possibilities as an acting and suffering being. Yet this happens in the face of the demands to respond to the injunction of the other or to give testimony of oneself. What in the self is capable both of meeting these demands and incorporating the risks?[57] What enables us to transcend what we are to become what we are not yet (as envisaged in Ricoeur's teleological formulations of living well in just institutions)? What enables us not only to survive the demand to change, to be reconstituted in our encounter with the other, to be converted, to take this open-ended realm of risk as the foundation for our living, as the gratuitous condition of growth and fulfillment? What moves us from the actual to the possible?

It should be no surprise that McGaughey speaks of the self as more than the actual.[58] If the actual were all that defines the self, there would be no way to account for a changing self, a self who transcends itself and becomes what it was not. The term *conversion*, for example, would have no experiential reference and therefore no meaning.

McGaughey goes further, noting that the self, unless eliminated, never wholly succumbs or capitulates to violation (the evidence by survivors of extreme torture shows some capacity of resistance, suggesting that death is the only thing that finally erases the self). Equally, the uniqueness of each person, even where there is a similar genetic structure and personal history (as in the case of identical twins), can only be understood if we accept that each person constructs out of the many possibilities present in any one constellation of actualities a particular identity. Consciousness, always consciousness of something,[59] does this. Thus the self also projects its possibilities by choosing one possibility rather than another (how often do we wonder what might have been if we had not made this choice, or had made that choice?).

Of course, possibility is never without the constraint of actuality (even in severe schizophrenia the denial of actuality comes up against the limits set by others and by the world). Further, the self "is not in complete conscious control of its possibilities, for the dynamic of actuality and possibility is a dynamic of manifestation and concealment."[60]

Still, each individual self manifests a mix of actualities and possibilities unique to itself, and this uniqueness is precisely the key to the individual's claim to dignity and integrity. If we do not grant dignity and integrity to the self, then we cannot grant it to the other. If we grant it to one person, then we must grant it to all. In this sense, the reciprocity between the self and the other to which Ricoeur referred is at its root not ethical but spiritual, that is, constitutive of consciousness.

This insight, McGaughey suggests, is inseparable from the acknowledgment of the priority of possibility over actuality in experience: "So long as individuals, genders, races, social groups, societies, and nations only focus on, or are only defined in terms of, actualities, so long will individuals, groups and societies be tempted to cultivate only mis-understanding, distrust, and fear which are the source of oppression, exploitation and attempts at the eradication of the Other."[61] The self who goes beyond actuality is the self who breaks open the possibility for the new, the transformed, to be actualized. This spiritual dynamic allows for the human being to act, in esteeming the self, with and for others toward just institutions. Spirituality is the self transcending itself for the sake of the self and, by implication, the other.

The possibilities of human spirit, even where its freedom seems seriously compromised, are immense. There is no guarantee of its continuance, no certainty of its victory, of course. But human spirit, in its greatest depth and power, is the capacity to face the unknown and not be overcome, to risk and not be crushed, and in this way, to be true to the self and the other. "Everything," McGaughey says, "hinges, then . . . on how rigorously one fulfills one's responsibility in the light of the necessary role of imaginative variation (projection of possibilities) in the encounter with the other/Other."[62]

In this realization lies the theological foundation for engaging with the marginalized other, as represented by the Amawoti BEC in this case. Ultimately we join in this kind of conversation, commitment, and risk, and in this expectation of confronting what we do not know, for the sake of human spirit. It is a spiritual journey. If undertaken in honesty and faith, its promise holds out the possibility of enrichment for the church and of re-creation for the world. This, at least, is the conviction with which I emerge through the process by which my self is constituted in the encounter with the incipient theology, thus the otherness, of the Amawoti BEC.

6. Widening the Circle
The Personal and the Public

"How local should theology become?"
—Robert J. Schreiter[1]

"Small," said E. F. Schumacher, "is beautiful."[2] One might, if one follows the thrust of this book, say the same for that which is local. Yet it would be romantic illusion to do so. Local realities and local wisdom, as has often been noted, are no less free of mixed interests and systematic distortions than is discourse and practice at any other level.[3] Since Sigmund Freud, Karl Marx, and Friedrich Nietzsche, we know that perceptions of reality or truth are subject to deception, alienation, and willfulness. This would be true of the views of the Amawoti BEC as well.

Why should we take them seriously? Are specific experiences and reflected wisdom that have shaped their interpretive activity in the local context relevant beyond their particularity or are they restricted to that context? Do they necessarily reach beyond the personal, the particular, and the local to the broader community, including the public sphere of discourse and action that shapes nations and societies? This is no idle question. If incipient theologies are contained at the personal or local level, they are no more interesting than a collection of common stamps—each one colorful, identifiable, and of some limited value, but none generally of significance except to a particular collector.

The Amawoti BEC themselves have come to believe that their discourses and reflections are of wider significance. They have found that their engagement in fashioning a new circle of dignity has allowed a stream of energy to radiate beyond their specific circle, producing positive, empowering effects in their wider community. To be sure, over their years together, members have faced contradictions in their life together, heated disputes on occasion, breakdowns in their communicative activity, even distrust and hostility among individuals. Yet this cannot gainsay what was achieved through their attempts to link their discourse and practice to daily experiences via the medium of religious texts, which posed as many questions and problems as resources for renewed insight.

Still, we may ask, how does their particularity become relevant for the general or the universal? In theological parlance, does their wisdom, drawn from reflection on experience, have a missionary significance for evangelical claims about human beings and the world? In what way is the BEC's integration of personal faith and public life exemplary for Christian proclamation and testimony, and how may this be taken into our understanding of the nature of Christian discourse itself?

We know that Christian discourse, in its plurality, diversity, and contradictory trajectories, cannot be reduced to what happens at the local level. Not only would this make nonsense of tradition as a synchronic and diachronic process of the dialogue of believers; it would also undermine the communicative impulse itself by cutting off the discourse of believers from the *sensus fidei*, ultimately depriving theology of its living roots. As Robert Schreiter notes, "local theology is certainly not anything new to Christianity."[4]

While the operation of the *sensus fidei* may be weak, it is the basis of any historically serious ecclesiology. Either local communities of Christians are part of the church universal,[5] or they are not. If not, then ecclesiology itself falls apart, and with it some of the central tenets of the Christian tradition. If they are, the communicative practice represented by a local theology (the reflection of ordinary believers on their faith in context) is of intrinsic value for Christians beyond this local context, at least provisionally. What is new in the Christian tradition is not local theology, "but a direct awareness and pursuit of it" (Schreiter).

There is some indication that the Amawoti BEC itself recognizes the significance of the wider Christian community both as a recipient of their own reflections and insights, and as contributing to theirs:

> Ms. T: Tomorrow at the workshop church members will be present. It is important to discuss [our] ideas with them too. We can tell the people there what we are thinking of.
>
> Mbuso: Yes, we can sell them our ideas at the workshop, then the people can approve and shape them.[6]

That the public sphere may gain from local wisdom is also understood by the BEC, albeit largely in general terms. They frequently link their newly won insights on the biblical witness to their concerns for the transformation of their social and material conditions. On one occasion, for example, Mbuso comments that the song of Mary (the Magnificat) in Luke 1:51-53 shows that "God is doing something different" in scattering the proud, bringing rulers down, lifting the humble and filling the hungry.[7]

We will pursue the general status of local incipient theologies by beginning with the public sphere, thus avoiding at the outset the separation of the religious or theological moment from its location in the world. This will enable us to understand the complexity of the theological task within the church itself by forcing on us the question of the frequent dualism in Christianity between the church and the world.

Theology in Western Christianity has struggled, in the face of Cartesian method and nominalist epistemologies, to unite such 'founding paradoxes' or *aporiai* of theology as church and world, personal and public, body and mind, internal and external reality, usually emphasizing one or the other side of the pole, or stating each side sequentially without a convincing basis for unifying them.[8] Yet it may well be that the natural language of Christian discourse found in incipient theologies such as that of the Amawoti BEC already connects these poles.

Two claims will be argued: that local theologies of the kind exemplified in this study have a specific place in the wider theological arena of church discourse, and that local theologies have significance for the public witness of the church. This produces a view on various levels of reflection on faith which I will call a *Gestalt* of theology.

Public and Personal: Preliminary Comments

Is the primary location of Christian discourse private or public? If both, how do they fit in a context where the privatization of faith, particularly in capitalist economies, finds strong impulses in the philosophy of individualism and the separation of religion out of economics and politics? David Tracy attempts to deal with the issue in his discussion of the three publics of theology: the church, the academy, and society.

Tracy argues that all theology is public discourse, even if the way in which this discourse is conducted differs. The differences are found in the distinctions between the publics of which Tracy speaks. A privatized theology of the personal realm, or interiority only, is for Tracy a contradiction in terms. Theology is always speech of a kind, and it is always addressed to someone: "For every theologian, by the very acts of speaking and writing, makes a claim to attention."[9] Theology is essentially a communal enterprise.

The person who reflects theologically is never an atomic existence independent of varying social locations and social interests. Moreover, the one who is addressed is always changing too, introducing a plurality of roles, strategies, and plausibility structures into theological discourse itself. Furthermore, Tracy suggests, the very claim of any serious theological discourse to be of significance for central issues in life implicitly addresses all three publics. Indeed, Tracy adds, this plurality of publics is not just external but internalized in every person who seeks to do theology.[10]

All theology, therefore, must come to terms ultimately with its public character. Having said that, Tracy's terminology of publics, though helpful, is also potentially misleading in several ways.

First, wrongly read, an emphasis on the public character of theological discourse may sustain the notion that there is also a personal sphere in which theology functions entirely differently, a dichotomy I take to be precisely that which is overcome in the incipient theology of the Amawoti BEC. Second, the description of the three publics as different contexts of plausibility (each with its own kinds of interests and arguments) may perpetuate problematic assumptions about a separation of spheres, reinforcing a split between church and society or church and academy. Third, from the point of view of gendered structures of authority, one has to ask, Who dominates discourse in all three publics? Powerful men, one would have to say. One may say something similar about race and class. The dynamics of power in all three publics tend to marginalize the poor, women, widows, aliens, orphans. A merely functional division of theological discourse into the three publics or reference groups obscures this vital insight (Tracy is aware of the danger, of course).[11]

Tracy does not stress the unity of the publics, but he does note that a theological position is rarely determined entirely by one sphere of discourse alone (and then it is suspect). The normal situation is one "where clear or obscured/elective affinities exist between the distinct publics and distinct plausibility structures of particular theologies."[12] In the Amawoti BEC there are indeed clear links between Tracy's three publics, as well as between the personal and the public, evident in three directions: within the Bible study group, operating with a specifically Christian identity (church); with various civic and political institutions of the local community (society); and with university intellectuals (academy). The process in which the BEC was involved was important precisely because the boundaries between the three reference groups or publics were being breached. It was the unity of the process that seemed crucial, and this included a realization of the need to break the membranes around the different spheres of discourse, to challenge the separation of each into different plausibility structures.[13]

Tracy's claim that theology is always public in some sense, that theology is fundamentally never only personal, private, or interior to the subject, I accept without reservation. However, I use the notion of public somewhat differently in what follows, meaning more the common understanding one finds in governance: Something is public which is of concern to society in reaching agreements about rules, regulations, behaviors, processes, and practices designed to mediate system and life world interests.

In one sense I confine myself, therefore, to one of Tracy's three reference groups, society. I do so to undermine any separation between society, academy, and church. The point is to demonstrate how what happens in Amawoti goes beyond Amawoti itself to address in an integrated fashion Christian existence in all spheres of life. It is this capacity to integrate reality—to overcome the kinds of dichotomies that have so fractured our language and practice—that gives Christian discourse its power, and it is the specific example of the Amawoti BEC that offers insights into how this may happen at local level.

Public Christian discourse necessarily addresses a dual audience: the Christian community itself (edification) and the public at large (apologetics). The two audiences require different forms of address, and imply two different strategies in the development of a public theology.

One strategy, aimed at the public at large, necessarily uses forms of discourse that reach beyond the Christian community, such as interfaith dialogue about the place of religion in a new constitution. Important as it is, this will likely be mainly the discourse of intellectuals, of church leaders, of political and religious activists.[14]

But the ordinary reader, the person in the pew, the marginalized African independent church member in an informal settlement, the semiliterate rural praise singer—in short, the bulk of South Africa's Christians—are unlikely to know of this discourse strategy, let alone participate in it. Public theology in this form, and the policies and structures that may flow from it, will not be owned by them unless it also takes form at the local level of religious experience.

Thus the vital importance of the second strategy of discourse, aimed at the Christian community itself in terms it understands and accepts. Precisely this kind of work was undervalued if not contemptuously thrust aside in the earlier years of an overtly political, outwardly directed, liberation theology. This made it difficult to find an adequate, convincing public role that takes the identity of the church itself seriously. Local realities and forms of struggle, resistance, and survival that are not overtly political are often couched in religious language rather than liberation struggle language. The church does not yet know, especially where its public enemies have become less obvious and more diffuse, how to redefine its role or its focus to incorporate both the macro- and the micro-political context.

To participate in public negotiations and struggles is unquestionably a requirement for public theology. But to do so at the expense of a major effort to bring the issues and debates of such public theology into the center of the life of the local

Christian communities is in the long run a serious error for two reasons: (1) Acts of violence and practices of democratic life are particular, geographically and psycho-socially located among specific people in particular contexts. This is where the necessary forms of discourse to overcome violence and engender democracy are needed. If they are not solidly based at this local level, then regional or national levels of discourse become hollow and thorough social reconstruction itself becomes unlikely. (2) A public theology that does not take the perspective of local communities of the poor, the oppressed, and the marginalized seriously loses its seminal sources of insight and correction.

The church is in need of a prophetic vision that goes beyond protest and is prepared to be constructive, a point also argued in Charles Villa-Vicencio's *A Theology of Reconstruction*.[15] Neither *The Kairos Document* nor its direct successor, *The Road to Damascus*,[16] really goes much beyond protest, yet our present situation calls for a prophetic vision of the future which arises from and is constituted by the historical consciousness of the poor and oppressed. In the same way that poor and oppressed interpreters of the Bible have reconstructed or "refurbished"[17] their Christian faith through the recognition, recovery, and arousal of their suppressed past, so too the suppressed past of the poor and oppressed (including women) must play a significant role in the reconstruction of our society.

A common language, shared images and symbols, and mutually accepted ways of seeing oneself in society, are essential to the well-being of any human community. Yet these things, subject to the dynamics of power, can be subverted as easily as they can be generative. Language may be the bearer of truth and of a search for open communication and constructive human possibilities; or it may carry deceit and a desire for asserting power over and constraining their freedom of the other. When it is the latter, the processes for the formation of a democratic public—a civilian life marked by the capability as well as the possibility of full participation in the ordering of society—will decay. When language is given over to rational-technicist policies of control that objectify people and turn them into factors and figures, the well-being of the community cannot survive. The foundation of human social intercourse, and thus of the political possibility of a healed society, is eroded and ultimately ruptured.

Here, practical critique under conditions of domination emerges not only communicatively but also conflictually, in the form of struggle. The route to a surer foundation for democratic life goes in the opposite direction, by way of resurrecting truth and enabling a critical and self-critical appropriation and transformation or reality.

This, I believe, is what the Amawoti BEC has to teach us about the public significance—yet personal pertinence—of Christian discourse and tradition when it begins at the local level, is bound to everyday life, and is pursued as a practice of communicative action. The BEC demonstrates that this process can be trusted.

A fine claim, but it is yet to be grounded in an adequate epistemology. For this task we turn to Jürgen Habermas's notion of rationality founded in communicative action to help illuminate the dynamics of knowledge construction as intrinsically public even when it seems most personal.

Before we proceed, a caution: Habermas's concern to ground rationality in communicative action embodies an Enlightenment sensibility in the desire to give reason a dominant role in generating an emancipated human existence. Later I will suggest that this restriction must be lifted to make allowance for important ways of incorporating emancipatory discourses that include the irrational, the unsystematic, the ambiguous, and the mystical.

The Social Intelligibility of Local Knowledge

The question of the validity of local knowledge as applied to theology may be put in this form: Does the religious life of a theologically illiterate local community have sufficient intellectual clarity and substance to stand as theological knowledge against, rather than simply under, the knowledge my training represents, a training usually available only to the elites of the church? To answer the question, we draw on insights into the communicative rationality of local discourse, and the link between communicative activity and transformative praxis.

The Rationality of Local Discourse

When we speak of something as common sense, we mean that every human being with reasonable mental capacities has a basic wisdom about life, and we imply that common sense has value. Indeed, for many people common sense has greater practical value for the conduct of everyday life than intellectual cleverness.

Yet common sense may be suspect: It depends upon a background knowledge that is taken for granted. It remains unanalyzed and may conceal as much as, or more than, it reveals. Common sense is normally not aware of the distortion of knowledge, of ideologies or social pathologies, of neurosis or psychopathologies, or of archaic traditions that no longer match the conditions of life. In this light, common sense is not yet rationality, meaning (following Habermas) that it generally does not offer arguments or reasons to support criticizable claims of validity. Common sense, therefore, cannot in and of itself validate the knowledge of local discourse.

The validity of local discourses (such as the Bible studies) as rational appropriations of reality can only be communicatively redeemed—be seen as valid for us as well—after we have critically assessed them. The discourses of the Bible studies represent a self-understanding of the members of the BEC from within, and unless we can be sure that this self-understanding has relevance for us who are without, the decision to listen to this (or any other) particular voice is purely arbitrary. Why should we expect that any systematic learning or consequences should arise for us?

There is an irreducible arbitrariness here. Other communities and contexts are likely to produce different results in respect of the content of the Bible studies and judgments reached through them. Yet something more general may be discerned in the process of the Bible studies. It manifests a communicative activity that confronts and challenges the actions of others, particularly those who see the local community only as an objective, and therefore manipulable, fact in the larger social world, and those who use it to achieve strategic aims of their own irrespective of the actual needs and desires of the local community itself.

The Bible studies of this particular community bring a challenge to all of us. The particularity of this local community, in a social context marked by a long, deep, and painful history of material deprivation and a systematic distortion of consciousness, is the point. The process is the challenge.

The process may be grasped in its depth and its broader implications by considering Habermas's theory of communicative competence. Communicative competence means that one can give good grounds, in argument with others who present their own good grounds, for some judgment or action. Habermas claims, simply, that this is preferable in society to unreflected, instrumental, purposive-rational, manipulative, or deceitful judgments and activity. We will return to this point.

A focus on process does not mean that content is irrelevant. On the contrary, as we have seen in the Bible studies, a coherent religious worldview may be discerned, and the fact of this coherence itself is important. Moreover, it is precisely the contents of this worldview that are of significance for the reconstruction of an indigenous South African theology.

Still, it is in the process that we begin to discern the rationality of this local knowledge (cast in theological categories)—a know-how as opposed to a know-that. Often raised was the "that" of the text (for example: Was Jesus a carpenter, thus not poor? Did Jesus really say what is written?), as might be expected with a group largely theologically illiterate and whose previous knowledge of the Bible was verbal transmitted. Usually, they turned to the group facilitator, a trained person, for help at these points.

But the "that" of the text, often the dominant focus of much biblical exegesis and commentary, was not central. More important to the group was a growing desire to know "how" to understand or read the text in context—not technical skills, but how best to constitute their own understanding, to construct their own knowledge. In short, reading the text became a way of developing a capacity to act in the world, to discover agency.

This struggle to understand was not merely intellectual, that is, a matter of thoughts abstracted from the practical insights of everyday life. It was won in arguments and counterarguments within the group. This kind of rationality is what we must grasp in the working of incipient theologies as I have described them.

Understanding as Rational

The communicative process of argument and counterargument, where the intentions of participants are not instrumental or manipulative (which would subvert the communicative act itself), allows for the use of knowledge (by the speaker or actor), and for the acquisition of knowledge (from another speaker or actor). Thus Habermas argues that ". . . rationality has less to do with the possession of knowledge than with how speaking and acting subjects *acquire and use knowledge.*"[18]

Linguistic utterances (as in the Bible study discourses) and goal-directed actions (such as those that flowed from the regular meetings of the Bible study group) transmit and transfer this knowledge explicitly (in saying something) or implicitly (in doing something). In these two moments of knowledge use and knowledge acquisition, we discern what Habermas, using Melvin Pollner's term, calls "mundane reasoning," that is, everyday, worldly reasoning.

Where those involved in mundane reasoning seek communicatively to achieve consensus to understand what is meant and to coordinate actions around what is claimed, they exhibit the conditions for rationality. They arrive at judgments and take appropriate actions on the basis of arguments about criticizable validity claims. "On this model," says Habermas, "rational expressions have the character of meaningful actions, intelligible in their context, through which the actor relates to something in the objective world."[19] This fits the kind of reasoning we may discern in the Amawoti Bible study discourses.

Rationality here calls forth an understanding of context. To be able to provide grounds for one's judgment or action one must be able not only to enter into argument; one must be able to show what is intelligible about it, that is, what makes it worth acknowledging as a sound argument. This intelligibility resides not just in the semantic structures of language, nor in a merely formal logic, but in the relation of language to the objective world. If there is no connection for the hearer to an intersubjectively shared background knowledge arising out of everyday practice, the intelligibility of a statement or claim is lost.

The *intersubjectively shared background* of speakers and actors defines their "life world," a taken-for-granted substratum without which any communication of action with others would be impossible.[20] This life world includes culture, society, and personality. The maintenance of life world happens through both processes of symbolic reproduction (for example, language, ritual, and so on) and material reproduction (technology, labor, and so on). In respect of the process of the Bible studies, it is the idea of symbolic reproduction that interests me.

The process of the reproduction of the symbolic structures of the life world, which happens in different ways, "connects up new situations with the existing conditions of the life world."[21] With this as our clue, we may suggest that the following points describe the social matrix guiding the production of symbolic structures in the Amawoti Bible study discourses.

First, they arise out of, and are situated in, the life world of the community. For the majority of Africans this life world is in principle strongly communitarian, embracing both the living and the dead, and including the wisdom of ancestors and elders.[22]

Second, the discourses bring to the group's attention selected aspects of the taken-for-granted, shared background knowledge of its life world. These aspects move to the foreground, becoming conscious.

Third, this move to the foreground of previously unreflected elements of the life world introduces the possibility of questioning and probing, that is, criticizing them.

Fourth, the mode of discourse in the Bible studies was carefully facilitated and developed over a long period to promote and ultimately establish a process of communication that allows for open argument and counterargument as the basis for testing claims made.

Fifth, this made possible an encounter between traditions (biblically transmitted tradition, local group tradition, and more generally, aspects of African tradition) in the context of a social environment shaped by severe negative imbalances in material resources and access to power. The encounter also took account of personal dimensions in both tradition and everyday life.

Sixth, the links between the cultural, social, and personal elements of the life world were often pursued by trying to understand what a claim made in one sphere, for example, concerning personal responsibility for theft, might imply for another sphere, for example, the struggle against poverty.

These six observations make it clear that the base ecclesial community, through the Bible study process, was involved in two key overarching activities. First, they engaged in reproducing the symbolic structures of their life world by trying to connect it to new situations,[23] drawing strongly on the semantic openings provided by a rich source of metaphorical and symbolic interpretive categories found in the biblical narratives and parables. Second, they did so through a communicative process that encouraged, and frequently required, arguments with good grounds for making a particular validity claim, met by counterarguments of a similar kind. In both senses—a coherent linking between life world and situation, and a grounded exchange of ideas between speakers—we see communicative rationality at work:

The rationality inherent in this practice is seen in the fact that a communicatively achieved agreement must be based in the end on reasons. And the rationality of those who participate in this communicative practice is determined by whether, if necessary, they could, under suitable circumstances, provide reasons for their expressions.[24]

With this, I argue that the Bible study process of the local community we have been discussing must be understood in its own terms as a source of rational insight into their cultural, social, and personal context.

If we take the concept of life world seriously, their cultural, social, and personal context is not theirs alone, though specific situations (thematically defined aspects of the life world) might be unique to them. Their life world is shared by many others, at least by the broad population of South Africa, inasmuch as the interaction between groups and peoples over decades and centuries has created a general set of conditions we all take for granted as part of our background.

Further, because they raise criticizable validity claims in relation to their life world (to the extent that their discourse demonstrates a communicative rationality), those of us who take them seriously will have to make judgments, also in a communicatively rational process, about their claims, understood in their contextual intelligibility.

Communicative Action and Praxis

The rationality of incipient theology as seen in the Amawoti BEC, and the significance of the communicative competence they have developed, seems clear. What, however, is its link to transformative action, or praxis? How does the discourse and reflection of the group in their Bible studies organically express itself in activity in the public sphere?

The question is particularly relevant if, as many are wont, we assume that Bible studies or the like produce little more than discussion and no practical action, or if we argue that religious discourse is a source of obfuscation and false consciousness, built upon traditions that are archaic (superseded by scientific ways of thinking) and oppressive (imposed by the colonizer or dominating power). It needs to be shown why this is not necessarily so.

The Bible study process of the BEC clearly was the basis of its communicative action: it was acknowledged by members and observers to be the key to their capacity to empower themselves and those around them, and to organize themselves effectively around a number of needs and struggles in the broader community, encompassing educational, civic, political, and developmental (economic) spheres of their life world.

It is possible to theorize what this meant, and thereby make their experience generalizable. We would need to begin by noting that instrumental or strategic rationality is only one form of link between theory and praxis, communicative rationality another.

Communicative rationality allows for a discursively formed public will, that is, a consensus that arises through "appropriately interpreted, *generalizable* interests, by which I mean needs *that can be communicatively shared.*"[25] Here interpretive activity is central to the uncovering and establishing of interests, and to arriving at a consensus on how one regulates these interests. With this, communicative action links practical questions to justifiable norms. Justifiable norms can be distinguished from those norms that "merely stabilize relations of force."[26] This is to suggest that social interaction aimed at finding practical responses to particular goals and aims (teleological action) has its place, among other things, in the coordination of goal-directed actions.[27]

Clearly, then, discursive or communicative activities that support the coordination of goal-directed actions are thereby joined with social action. One may distinguish, however, between different kinds of social action and, correlatively, between different kinds of discursive activity (it is not the same thing to order someone to do something as it is to agree together on something).

> Concepts of social action are distinguished . . . according to how they specify the coordination among the goal-directed actions of different participants: as the interlacing of egocentric calculations of utility . . . ; as a socially integrating agreement about values and norms instilled through cultural tradition and socialization; as a consensual relation between players and their publics; or as reaching understanding in the sense of a cooperative process of interpretation.[28]

A utilitarian approach, essentially calculating, thus does not fit with a communicative action approach. Neither does an approach that depends upon the weight of cultural tradition or patterns of socialization. Cooperative processes of interpretation which produce understanding is clearly the form of goal-directed action coordination Habermas believes to have the greatest value in structuring social relations that are transformative and cognizant of both life worlds and systems. My reading of the BEC process suggests that it is precisely this form of coordination of goal-directed actions that they exhibit wherever their discourse was linked (as it was regularly) to specific practical concerns within their wider community.

We thus see how speech, or the reading of texts, may be linked to praxis. The nature of this praxis most often lies in a defense of life worlds against the media of money and power which steer systems, and in finding mechanisms that would regulate the interface between life world and system interests. Institutions, networks, and communicative processes are the kinds of outcomes one can expect at a practical level, rather than factories, irrigation projects, and so on. These outcomes do affect system imperatives, however, either in a challenge at the political level (including processes of empowerment and democratization), or in an attempt to construct alternatives within the interstices of system-driven structures (such as the women's cooperative vegetable-farming group set up with the Ilimo Project).

Equally important, the practice of communicatively coordinating goal-directed actions allows those involved to recognize disturbances in the life world such as loss of meaning, delegitimization, confusion, anomie, and so on, although recognition does not yet imply that anything changes. On this point, Habermas suggests that communicative practice is also learning practice.[29] In the process in which people debate, argue, persuade, and reach understanding, contested validity claims are gradually clarified, criticized, and vindicated. This allows participants, and the group as a whole, to improve their grasp of a situation and their capacity to respond to it. Practice thus acquires a dynamic of development (what Habermas calls "improvement") in the communicative process.

Finally, to round out the picture, it is useful to consider Habermas's alternative to Max Weber's typology of action. Habermas suggests that one may distinguish between action with a high degree of rationality (being able to give reasons for one's arguments in support of actions) and that with a low degree; and between action coordinated through interest positions and that which comes through normative agreements.[30] This produces a fourfold typology of action. Where the degree of rationality in actions is low, one finds either de facto customary action coordinated through interest positions, or conventional action coordinated through normative agreements. Where the degree of rationality in actions is high, one finds either strategic action coordinated through interest positions, or postconventional action based on agreement.

In relation to the Amawoti BEC, this schema suggests that much of the reading, discourse, planning, and action of the Amawoti BEC can be described as postconventional action. Members exhibit a high degree of communicative rationality in their arguments with each other and in their interpretations of text and context. Their own residual African traditions and whatever Christian traditions they work with are never static and are repeatedly questioned. Seldom do they fall back on customary roles and ways of acting, nor do they rely merely on the authority of tradition or convention in their search for understanding their local context and how to engage with it. This, of course, is what might disturb those who do depend upon customary or conventional actions and agreements, and why aspects of the BEC's interpretation of the Christian tradition will not rest easy with many Christians.

One may add that the BEC did at times operate as if all that mattered was finding the right tools and institutions to achieve a practical goal. Precisely then they began to feel the absence of the discursive, communicative activity represented by the engagement in the Bible studies. They tended, as they put it, to get too involved along instrumental lines in trying to make things happen. This negatively affected their sense of vision, to the point where they would return to the Bible study process in order, once again, to engage in reconstructing communicatively their understanding of what they were about and their capacity to coordinate their actions.

The link between communicative action and praxis in the Amawoti BEC experience seems to me profound and important. Where it happens, individual success (though not set aside) is subordinated to communal action through the harmonization of plans of action "on the basis of [the negotiation of] common situation definitions, . . . an essential element of the interpretive accomplishments required for communicative action."[31]

The process also represents a contribution to the democratization of the populace because it releases the participants from dependency on existing normative contexts and traditionally based institutions—from "the obligation of consensus."[32] Participants, if they do not depend upon normative traditions and conventions to coordinate their actions, must do so by reaching understanding through agreements. In this light, the socially transformative significance of religion lies in the potent symbolic (spiritual) resources it is able to offer as a basis of emancipatory praxis. The transformative potential of religion is realized through the "energies of social solidarity attached to religious symbolism," expressed "in and through communicative action," when these energies are transferred to institutions and persons in the form of moral authority.[33]

I have tried to argue that incipient theologies, in their communicative rationality and contextual intelligibility, are a potential source of such moral authority, especially when they express the voices and presences of those who are usually absent in the development of public policy and the construction of the social institutions that sustain us—including the church. Our insights into the communicative rationality of local knowledge and theologies also raise questions about the nature of the church itself. Our next move is to consider an ecclesiology befitting this analysis.

"Starting in Galilee": Incipient Theology from the Margins

With the advent of mass media and television in particular, we increasingly encounter the world as an overwhelming place with prodigious numbers of people, tragedies, wars, events, and perspectives. Even as we learn more about the circumstances of particular individuals whom we will never encounter and specific communities with whom we will never engage, so our capacity to see persons rather than statistics is diminished. The effect increases whenever carefully designed advertisements are juxtaposed with the random activities and ambiguities of human experiences, until we begin to lose our capacity to distinguish between the two things.[34] Some even doubt whether we have any means to know any longer what is real and what not.[35]

Modern political life does not escape these effects. One reaction in recent years has been an emphasis on small groups, local democracy, and human agency at the micro level. The trend is also visible within the churches, as is perhaps most clearly declared in the documents of the Latin American Catholic Bishops assembly in Puebla in the late seventies. Their assembly affirmed the vital importance for the church of the base Christian communities out of which liberation theology arose, described as "centers of communion and participation."[36]

In the implied understanding that such centers should find a relation to the larger church lies the link between such communities and their larger ecclesial and social context. The definition of BECs as centers of communion and participation was not just a useful slogan; it was clearly placed within the framework of an ecclesiological statement, carrying both dogmatic and practical implications. It represents an emphasis on local activity and reflection as a defining locus for what it means to take the church seriously. My attempt to give to incipient theologies a similar status stands in continuity with this tradition.

To begin at the base, to begin where people are marginalized, to begin where centers of communion and participation offer practical, locally embodied hope of agency and a new life, is to start in Galilee. Local communities are the practical ground within which particularity is grasped as essential for truth (*aletheia*, an uncovering of what is normally concealed). It is the appropriate departure point for a fully developed contextual theology.

This requires a new paradigm in theology, as many have noted in the last couple of decades.[37] The paradigm is not yet established, and the pull to return to the familiar territory of a past paradigm that still dominates is strong: the risks are fewer, the costs less, the unknown reduced to a minimum. It includes taking into account the "contrast experiences"[38] which offer a critique of contemplative or scientific-technological ways of knowing, and secondarily, which assert the nonexclusive priority of perspective of those who suffer. It is to take seriously Elisabeth Schüssler Fiorenza's notion of the "fourth corrective" provided by subjugated discourses.

Desmond Tutu clearly expresses this point through Black Theology's refutation of "the silent claims by the white man to ipso facto give his values and measures universal validity":

> Our scientific strivings must make room for subjectivity, for commitment, for the intuitive comprehension of matters which are hardly comprehensible for the alienated objectivity of the non-committed.[39]

We are used to working with two basic, alternative paradigms of method in theology, both of which are inadequate and do great damage to the theological enterprise in the face of challenges to "begin in Galilee," where commitment to a marginalized people and a challenge to the centers of power and authority are unavoidable. The one paradigm searches for a theology that can be objectively, that is, universally, grounded in its claims for truth. The other searches for a special sphere of life for theology that may rescue its true content from the challenge of relativity in the modern world. Both strategies scrabble for a hold on truth without securing it.

Both paradigms are a response to what Richard Bernstein calls "Cartesian anxiety": the dread of the journey of the soul in the search for "some fixed point, some stable rock upon which we can secure our lives against the vicissitudes that constantly threaten us." Modernity, under the influence of the Cartesian anxiety, says Bernstein, has functioned with a

> grand and seductive Either/Or. Either there is some support for our being, a fixed foundation for our knowledge, or we cannot escape the forces of darkness that envelop us with madness, with intellectual and moral chaos.[40]

This Cartesian anxiety drives us to choose between a clearly established, objective ground for truth, or the chasm of relativity within which all truths are permitted and no truth is established. Theologies that have tried to defend the objectivity of their truth claims against modern relativities by recourse to revelation or authorized doctrine reflect simply a closure of reason in theology, a cutting off of theology from all interlocutors but itself.

Bernstein argues that these alternatives (objectivism and relativism) posit a dichotomy both misleading and distorted. We should exorcise the notion that we must choose between objectivist stability and relativist madness. This, says Bernstein, first and foremost is not a theoretical task but a practical one with moral intention in establishing the appropriate rationality, community, and solidarity. This in turn depends upon a practical base of communal life:

> A community or a polis is not something that can be made or engineered by some form of techne or by the administration of society. . . . The coming into being of a type of public life that can strengthen solidarity, public freedom, a willingness to talk and to listen, mutual debate, and a commitment to rational persuasion presupposes the incipient forms of such communal life.[41]

To move beyond objectivism and relativism, therefore, means to foster and nurture "those forms of communal life in which dialogue, conversation, *phronesis*, practical discourse, and judgment are concretely embodied in everyday practices."[42]

This is the original locus of the democratic impulse on the one hand, and of the rooting of a democratic polity in actual life worlds on the other. It would be an idealist mistake to understand this task as in some way separate from transformation of the material conditions of any actual context. Given our earlier analysis of the asymmetric relations of power, it would also be a mistake to ignore the fragility of the kind of communities envisaged in the face of the powers and structures that seek to coopt, pervert, or destroy them.

Still, to succumb to such powers and structures is the "highway of despair," as Bernstein puts it. There is every necessity to be wholly aware of the fragility of all constructive attempts at practically embodying a *telos* of emancipation or liberation, but there is no intrinsic reason to regard them as totally futile.

Thus the real choice is not between objectivism and relativism but between fatedness (a resignation of human agency in the face of power) and hopefulness (the resuscitation of human agency toward empowerment). The search for an objective ground for the revelatory claims of the church in the face of contemporary relativity is in this reckoning misplaced. The battle against fatedness and the task of representing hope are much more to the point.[43]

Most theologies that take as fundamental to the theological task the choice between fatedness and hopefulness in the concrete contradictions of life and death in the world propagate one or other form of local community or small group in which communicative action is a practical possibility as a key to their ecclesiology. Woman Church, Base Ecclesial Community, Streetfront Church, House Church, Review Groups, Abrahamic Minorities—these and similar images and metaphors are the names given to this impulse. Here is a reaching for the dialogical communities of which Bernstein speaks.

What obstructs the growth and development of such communities is objectivism and relativism. The call to theological objectivism, one side of the alternative, is likely to take the form of the reassertion of traditional authority by ecclesiastical powers. The choice of relativism, on the other hand, is likely to lead to a loss of distinctive values in the marketplace of alternative ideologies and commitments and a resultant paralysis of action.[44]

Let us summarize. If we are to develop a schema for the reconstruction of ecclesiology, it must be done by focusing on specific local communities that embody, or seek to embody, the values proposed in the model of communicative action as they reinterpret and reconstruct their faith understandings according to practical life in their context.

Inevitably, because these dialogical communities are constantly "being distorted, undermined, and systematically blocked from coming into existence,"[45] we must also take into account a confrontation with the powers and forces at work which undermine the potentiality and possibility of such communities. This is what makes theology constructed along these lines a practical as well as a theoretical task.

This may appear wholly idealistic if such communities were not empirically available. But in fact they are, and the Amawoti BEC is but one example. The method required by theology, as proposed here, thus already has a material base in the church within which a practical program and policy may be located and out of which its results may flow. To locate oneself where this material base may be found, in the dialogical communities of Bernstein, is what it means to "start in Galilee."

"Dealing with Herod/Pilate": The Public Task of the Church

We may well begin with local ecclesial communities and their incipient theologies, but, to draw on the biblical image, how is the peasant or woodworker of Galilee, the exemplar of the marginalized person, to connect her or his local understandings and communicative action to what happens in the courts of Herod or at the centers of power in Jerusalem? Is not Galilee of no account?

What follows attempts to discuss this issue along two lines. The first strand, drawing on the work of Paul Ricoeur among others, argues for a hermeneutics of the Word which is simultaneously a predication of action in the world. The second, dependent on Averil Cameron's analysis of the significance of Christianity in the collapse of the Roman Empire, uncovers the rhetorical nature of Christian discourse in the public sphere. The two approaches taken together reinforce much of what has already been said.

A World before Us

We will begin with a consideration of the range of language in its practical usage. By *language* I refer to the range of practices Theodore Jennings calls "linguisticality"[46]—all human activity that may be understood as analogous to language, including *language* as semantic structure, *discourse* as speech, and *word-event* as the givenness of reality (which language conveys imperfectly).

Linguisticality points to the multiple ways of communicating a meaning. Effective communication is the task of finding those ways that will reduce polysemy to a single meaning or set of meanings, in the moment of understanding. It includes the ongoing pursuit of questions or interrogations until it is established just what is meant.

The key point concerns our understanding of the role of such communication in social relations. Jennings notes two important points of consensus in recent debates. First, there is a widespread and persuasive "critique of the notion that language simply 'reflects' either objects or phenomena of consciousness." Second, we face an "insistence that language is . . . irreducibly constitutive of our experience and thought."[47]

At the same time, language is a problematic medium of communication, a fact beautifully captured by T. S. Eliot: "Words strain, Crack and sometimes break, under the burden, Under the tension, slip, slide, perish, Decay with imprecision, will not stay in place, Will not stay still."[48] The predicament is this: in speaking (or doing anything analogous to speaking) we express ourselves or our sociality. That is, we draw out of the givenness of existence a word that objectifies what is given and thus makes it available to others (communicates something). Yet this word itself, in the act of coming to expression, is already alienated from existence and from the subjectivity of experience.[49] Something is revealed and, simultaneously, something is concealed, in the speech act. Speech constructs and deconstructs reality at once.

Jennings talks of the linguisticality of existence as the pervasive need to express ourselves, whether in desire or deceit, consciously or unconsciously. Outside of this linguistic world there is no coming to consciousness. Therefore, Jennings argues,

> Even experiences difficult to "put into words" have a linguistic character and may even be generated by language. One may be "told" both by words and deeds of rejection that one is unworthy. One may "internalize" this as a pervasive sense of guilt. One may find it exceedingly difficult to articulate this pervasive sense. But it is not "outside" language. It is produced within language and may even be exorcized by analytic or therapeutic strategies known, significantly, as "talk-therapy."[50]

The clue to the link between language and praxis here is in the move toward the idea of therapy. It indicates that what is wrong or broken in our existence (expressed in language) may be put right or healed by the same means through which its presence emerges—language. Habermas, influenced by the critical psycho-social theories of his forerunners in the Frankfurt School, pursues the same insights via his social metaphor of communicative competence and its emancipatory, or healing, effect. He thus understands communicative competence as an important counter to practices of domination even if the forces of domination go well beyond the psyche or language. This is language as praxis.

With Ricoeur we may also locate the notion of action within hermeneutics itself, inherent in the interpretive impulse. To the extent that the BEC pursued the tensions within the hermeneutical enterprise, one may say that they were bound to uncover and explore the link between language (what they said) and action (what they did). The communicative process, where it is not truncated or restricted to the repetition of what one already knows, where one allows one's own world to be confronted by another, can be trusted. It does not require outside intervention to force a link between interpretive activity and practical action.

Ricoeur establishes this ambitious claim by using Wilhelm Dilthey's distinction between explanation or *erklären* (the logic and coherence of what is interpreted) and understanding or *verstehen* (the meaning and meaningfulness of what is stated). He makes the fertile suggestion that action can be treated as analogous to texts.[51] Like a text, an action is a meaningful entity that is construed as a whole to inform an interpretation of reality. Like a text, this interpretation may emerge as a conflict of interpretations, and the act one interprets, severed from its original moment (or author), may have a life of its own.

Thus actions become data for interpretation, data requiring explanation (a search for their logic) and understanding (an appropriation of their meaning for us). Both explanation and understanding are bound up in interpretation, which means that an act, as a datum of experience for knowledge, "possesses an internal structure as well as projecting a possible world, a potential mode of human existence which can be unfolded through the process of interpretation."[52]

Thus, in social science as in hermeneutics, "we proceed from naive interpretations to critical interpretations, from surface interpretation to depth interpretations *through* structural analysis." This does not come easily: ". . . meaningful patterns which a depth interpretation want to grasp cannot be understood without a kind of personal commitment"—not the commitment of immediacy, emotion or feeling, but that which links explanation (objective procedures) to the "power of disclosing a world."[53]

This power is most apparent when an act is recorded or remembered in language, in ritual, and so on. Thus, for example, the Easter marches the Amawoti BEC facilitated within the larger community in 1991 and 1992 may be seen to be linguistic events that interpret past actions and point to new ones. Past action thus becomes socialized knowledge, and this knowledge communicatively interprets new actions.

If this applies to contemporary actions, it also applies to sedimented actions (in literature or oral tradition, for example) which precede them and which they encounter in the form of the projection of another world upon their world. This is the nature of tradition. It is what happens in the reading of biblical text.

There is a historical sense to this process, and a contemporary reference in the world. Sense and reference together illumine our situation as discourse, that is, by addressing others in order to generate meaning. When action, rather than a strict text, is the focus of the hermeneutical process, Ricoeur suggests, "a meaningful action is an action the *importance* of which goes 'beyond' its *relevance* to its initial situation."[54] Human actions, whether contemporary or sedimented as knowledge in valued traditions, therefore open up new references and receive fresh relevance from them, thus calling for fresh interpretations that decide their meaning. As Ricoeur suggests, "all significant events and deeds are, in this way, opened to this kind of practical interpretation through present praxis."[55] Time and narrative, as Ricoeur's later work makes clear,[56] structure key aspects of this arena. Interpretation is always and everywhere spatiotemporal; the one who does the interpreting is always and everywhere shaped by narrative or story—history or herstory.

Not all interpretations are equal, of course, for actions, like texts, allow only a limited field of possible constructions of meaning, and "it is always possible to argue for or against an interpretation, to confront interpretations, to arbitrate between them, and to seek an agreement, even if this agreement remains beyond our reach."[57] When an interpretation no longer stands before a tribunal to whom an appeal can be made, then the conflict of interpretations is resolved unilaterally, as a last word. This we call violence.[58]

With this point established, we now need to recall the earlier claim that language also carries within it a therapeutic or emancipatory intent and capacity. Linguisticality—language and language-like communicative actions—not only plays a role in establishing our world for us (it enables us to express, interpret, and thus take hold of what is, or actuality), it plays a role in transforming our world (it enables us to express, plan, and act upon that which is not yet, or possibility).

Constructing the World around Us

How does Christian discourse, necessarily linked to its long tradition, function in the public sphere? In order to theorize this question, at least two conditions need to be met.

We must be able to show that Christian discourse can effectively mediate the complex interaction between life worlds and social systems. We must be able to do so, moreover, from within its own linguistic categories (rather than as a derivation with religious blessing of claims primarily established through other categories in philosophy, physics, sociology, psychology, and so on).

Our starting point is Averil Cameron's analysis of the success of Christianity in replacing classical Graeco-Roman discourse as the dominant discourse of Europe. She contends that materialist interpretations of history that designate discourse as superstructural and thus derivative (determined by material conditions) cannot account for the social power of discourse as seen in the renewal of society after the collapse of Rome. Christianity, she argues, was able under those conditions to provide a "totalizing discourse" for the time, a "systematic moral life plan" and a "transcendent ideological power."[59] Through preaching, teaching, proclamation, liturgy, and ritual communication, it was capable of addressing vital paradoxes of human and social existence and of offering a coherent hermeneutics by which people of the time could imaginatively grasp their life world and the forces that threatened it.

How does Cameron argue this claim? Her approach relies upon a mixed literary-hermeneutical reading of history by which she uncovers the rhetorical strategies of Christian discourse that enabled its practical success. The notion of rhetoric, and of rhetoric as strategic practice, provides the key not only to her own analysis, but also to the importance of her work for my concern to define the public character of Christian theology.

By *rhetorical strategies* she means "characteristic means or ways of expression" that may be oral or written, visual or dramatic, or any other form of communicative activity.[60] She therefore investigates and describes the communicative acts that shaped the life world of the newly emerging Christian realm in relation to which structures and institutions of society (the system) found stability in a judicially regulated economic order of a new kind (feudal Christendom). Cameron tells us how Christian theology functioned publicly and shaped the public realm on the basis of its internal identity, using its own forms of language.

At the time, the prevailing structures of Roman law and culture were rigidifying as Roman authorities fought to hold on to an increasingly threatened empire. This meant that the Roman order became progressively incapable of meeting the demands of the new era, in part because of the breakdown of the slave economy. In this context, Christian discourse, contrary to the declining symbolic world of old Rome, proved to be strongly "elastic."[61]

This elasticity gave Christianity the ability to flexibly express a convincing view of the actualities that dominated the life of citizens and noncitizens alike, and to open up a sufficiently hopeful range of possibilities to gradually enable them to grasp the outlines of a new future. Christian discourse, Cameron argues, was thus singularly fitted, through its vitality, to change and to newness, engendering a literature and a set of practices that expressed the changing life worlds of those it addressed.

What gave it this flexibility and vitality, its elasticity? Cameron locates the necessary dynamic in the inherently "figural character" of Christianity, its ability to communicate through powerful symbols and images, and its strongly "narrative" structure, its ability to tell stories ordinary people could use interpretively.[62] Christian discourse also included another rhetorical strategy of importance for the widespread reception of Christianity, namely, a celebration of the irrational (for example, the cross as victory)—exactly that which classical culture despised. By contrast, classical culture emphasized the intellect, the mind, rationality, or *logos*. But experience is often inaccessible to intellect, the mind, rationality, and *logos*—as postmodernists now argue in a new vein.

Central elements of Christian teaching and narrative discourse engendered a deliberate and creative tension with logical argument, opening up the power of human imagination in the face of crisis. Not only could Christianity be used to demystify reality (explain it in familiar words) and helpfully analyze worlds so that people could make sense of what was happening to them (as in Augustine's massive interpretation of the significance of the rise and fall of Rome in *City of God*). It simultaneously demonstrated a capacity to exploit mystery to open up worlds, which as expressions of new possibilities empowered people through communicative action to construct new worlds.[63]

This dynamic referential quality of the Christian mythos enabled people across a wide social, economic, and intellectual spectrum to relate its claims about the nature and purpose of life to the experiences they were undergoing. *Reference* here was not simply linear, a direct correspondence between language and reality; it was strongly metaphorical, exhibiting a "split reference" (Ricoeur) by which two things logically unrelated to each other are juxtaposed to produce new meaning, breaking open the imagination. Reality was to be seen as paradoxical, one might say. With the failure of the hypostatized values and concepts of the Roman imperial order, this capacity to break through existing categories is seen to be important.

Thus Cameron argues for another important rhetorical strategy characteristic of Christian discourse: the "rhetoric of paradox."[64] Paradox might be seen as a sign of the absence of logic or clear thinking, a mark of ignorance perhaps. But life experience is filled with what are felt to be paradoxes, allowing no resolution of them other than the holding together of their contradictions or the loss of all meaning. Christian theology, McGaughey reminded us, is rooted in a few defining *aporiai*. Its archetypal paradigm lies in the proclamation of an irresolvable riddle as the very location of truth: that God is both divine and human. This essential structure pervades its language and gives it its dialectical character.

The importance of paradox as a strategy for Cameron, when linked to the power of imagination (the figural, metaphorical force of Christian discourse) and the role of mystery, is that it enabled Christian discourse after Constantine to resist "the danger of overassimilation into the public realm."[65] Christian discourse in its fullness could not easily be turned into a predominantly one-sided social or political ideology, because inherent in its discursive categories, its narratives, and its images and symbols was an irreducible dialectical tension between the personal and the public, the seen and the unseen, the actual and the possible, spiritual and material reality.[66]

If Cameron is right about the discursive reasons for the "triumph" of Christianity, we would also have to reconsider the negative view of post-Constantinian Christianity as expressed pejoratively in the concept of Christendom.[67]

A critical disposition against Christendom, often linked to a romanticized view of pre-Constantinian Christianity, enabled many Christians in South Africa to address the struggles of the oppressed, and to challenge the political and military strategies of the apartheid state. But it may be argued with some justification that a dependence on a Constantinian myth about Christianity produced another problem which was never satisfactorily resolved: that of a frequently experienced disjunction between the public and the personal, and a resultant incapacity to address personal aspects of the experiences of struggle.

The gap between activists and ordinary believers often grew as a result, and the personal costs to activists was a constant worry. Burnout, family tensions, political infighting, the interference of personal problems in political activity, the breakdown of important relationships, the effects of detention, the grieving process, the desire for long-term meaning in what one did, and so on—these experiences could only with great difficulty be integrated into public activity or political philosophies and ideologies, if at all. Eventually, liberation theologians began looking for rhetorical strategies that would incorporate spirituality, conversion, and personal relationships—what some called "the human factor"—into their Christian discourse.[68]

The personal factor had been subsumed under the political factor. Moreover, it was extremely difficult to establish a link between the two if it did not already exist, and equally difficult to reestablish it once it had been broken. The resulting frustration was exacerbated by the obvious success, during the same period, of many rapidly growing Pentecostal, charismatic, and conservative evangelical groups to meet personal needs. Their success, in turn, invariably led to a loss among their adherents of the other pole which was so dear to liberation theologians and progressive Christians, namely, the political. In both directions Christian discourse lost its way.

In this context, Cameron's claim concerning the capacity of Christian discourse after the collapse of the Roman Empire to unite the personal and the public aspects of reality becomes tantalizing. It defines something important in the nature of Christian discourse: its potential to be sufficiently flexible for use as a public and political instrument, and simultaneously capable of expressing a wide range of private feelings and emotion.

That the dichotomy between the personal and the public has become pervasive seems quite clear in the Amawoti BEC's own perception of the separation of local churches. BEC members are aware of churches where one is encouraged to distance oneself from politics and they do not understand this. "Politics is in the community, and the church is in the community—it's one and the same thing and it cannot be separated," says Sandile, adding that "if you free a person, you can't free only one aspect of their life and not another." Poverty and unemployment, for example, are not just materially harmful but also spiritually damaging: "a person who is starving won't be strong spiritually, " explains Themba, and "for the person without a job, it's not surprising they're not strong spiritually."[69]

If, however, Christian discourse is to effectively unite the polarities of the personal and the public, perhaps one clue lies in locating this discourse in the matrix of particular persons and their places. As Sandile put it in one part of the Bible study discussion, spirituality has to do with "exact places."

Briefly, three further facets of Christian discourse may be useful to the discussion. All three facets may be discerned in the life and work of the Amawoti BEC.

First, Christian discourse is strongly narratological, constructed through story, as is evident in its scripture and its discourse tradition (from which has come an extensive body of literature and literary devices). During the time Cameron investigates, the most significant works tended to focus the attention of the participant or reader on "Lives" and "Acts," the two kinds of story Cameron identifies as preeminent in the Christian tradition.[70]

The second facet Cameron calls the performative, declaratory aspect of Christian rhetoric. This emphasizes drama, liturgy, ritual, song, choral prayer, symbolic demonstrations, and art, in order to bridge the rational and the irrational, knowledge and mystery, thought and feeling, external and internal experience, the personal and the public, the immanent and the transcendent. In recent South African history, the unity of these elements has been found in fasts, resistance funerals, vigils, symbolic marches, struggle songs, and the like. Where this unity works, there is no comparable discourse available, for example, in philosophical postulates, political theory, social analysis, or secular ideological constructs.

The final feature of Christian discourse Cameron calls its "power over the past."[71] Specifically, she means that Christian discourse succeeded in supplanting the discourse of classical antiquity because it bound memories of past glories and achievements of the classical period to the challenges of the present in ways that opened up the possibility of a new future. Memories were reinterpreted,[72] but not expunged wholesale. Cultural capital was respected and incorporated into the newly emerging rhetorical practices, themselves legitimated by system shifts in moving from the slave economy of Rome to the feudal economy of medieval Europe.

What gave Christianity its cultural power was the capacity of its discourse to bridge the eras, to build upon its cultural capital, and to accommodate what seemed valuable in the declining classical culture. Cultural power was its power over the past for the present, by which it could persuasively express the life worlds of those who moved from the ruins of the old empire into the tasks of reconstructing a new Europe.

We are not yet able to define precisely how this capacity may be taken into a strategy of public Christian discourse (with its accompanying practices) in the shift from apartheid to a reconstructed South Africa. But that the subjugated memories need this capacity seems incontrovertible. In the process of further defining what tasks may be involved, it also seems clear that the cultural capital of black South Africans and of other faiths will have to be taken into account and theologically located.

A *Gestalt* of Theology

We may now outline a theological schema that takes seriously the promise of the incipient theologies of local communities for the ecumenical life of the church, including its public role. Let us call it a *Gestalt* of theology: The term signifies a whole greater than its parts. By extension, it implies that a focus on any one or more of the parts without considering their place in the whole is deficient.

To speak of a *Gestalt* of theology is to describe a holistic approach to the theological task, even as it acknowledges the partiality and tentativeness of that task. My purpose in doing so is to offer a view on the different levels of the production of theological insight that accords as much importance to the reflected faith of untrained believers as it does to the intellectual activity of the trained guardians of the tradition.

One may adopt a Pauline eschatological formula to describe the key claim about theological truth contained in this schema: Something has already been revealed, but much has not yet been revealed. The dialectic of revealing and concealing something about truth or reality is essential to the idea that all theological claims are inspired by some appropriation of faith in context, and all are provisional, ambiguous, and even suspect (at least in principle). The theological task cannot therefore be entrusted to any one dominant, hegemonic source of insight and knowledge, and its primary correctives must come from those who most clearly see what has been concealed in any particular context.[73]

Let me mirror this image in my own role and place in the church. As a trained, skilled interpreter of theological tradition or practice, located in a university, with a history of active engagement in public life, I have acquired influence both in the academy and in aspects of the life of the church in South Africa. This gives me some authority and status by which to influence theological production and practical decisions connected to it in one or another organization or institution.

This text represents whatever skills I have acquired in articulating and systematizing an incipient theology in South Africa. But I am not one of those who produce this incipient theology and, as we have seen, this fact places serious limits on the task. If my judgments and conclusions alone (or those of people analogous to my position) were to be relied upon to shape theological discourse, a theological construct will once more be imposed upon the real conditions and experiences of ordinary believers. This is essentially antitheological.

My contribution only becomes real to those who actually live at the base in any society if it also connects with the quite specific material and historical conditions that shape their lives and work. It is from this base that the living force of any adequate contextual theology of the *sensus fidei* will have to come. It has been my contention that theology is not absent from this base, insofar as ordinary Christians reflect upon their faith in the light of their daily experiences and struggle for existence. Their reflection may be, and usually is, that of the theologically untrained mind: it may be naive and precritical; it may be unsystematic and scattered; it may draw incongruently on a range of symbols, rituals, narratives, and ideas that express the encounter with the sacred. In these senses, the theology present in communities of ordinary Christians is incipient rather than overtly articulated. Nevertheless, it remains theology.

It is this incipient theology I have sought to explore more carefully and fully in this book, as the necessary starting point for an authentic contextual theology that takes seriously the complexity of the interaction between tradition, criticism, and popular religion. In doing so, I have tried to show how the doctrinal traditions of the church are altered, affirmed, contradicted, or added to as the BEC theologically reflects on its context.

Megan Walker has conducted a good local exploration that illustrates the point in another context, on the function of the image of Mary among poor black women in a township called Mphophomeni. Walker's study shows that the image of Mary plays an ambiguous role: "the heart of the matter [is] whether Mary remains simply an object of devotion who can dispense favors to people from her heavenly throne, or whether there is the potential for her to become a companion who inspires and motivates people's earthly faith and struggles."[74] For the women of Mpophomeni there is no simple division between these alternatives. The women have learned traditions about Mary from the orthodoxies of the church, mediated primarily through stories, including the Bible, sermons, and songs. Yet they do not simply repeat the orthodoxies of the church. They invent their own interpretations of Mary in relation to the daily realities and struggles of their lives.

If incipient theologies are a necessary starting point, where do they lead? What is their connection to other symbolic and theological productions of the church and their correlative practices? Some summary statements, drawn from our investigations of the incipient theology of the Amawoti BEC, describe the ground rules of the heuristic schema I am proposing as a guide to a fully contextual yet fully ecumenical theology.

1. A properly developed contextual theology cannot be built as an addendum to, or subsection of, a larger ethical system. Its starting point is at the fundamental level of theological anthropology. It is not an applied theological task (depending on an *a priori* set of theological convictions) but itself establishes and clarifies founding theological convictions.

2. The meaning of a fundamental theological anthropology must be found in relation to our time and place. It cannot be established by reference to supposedly universal or eternal ideas abstracted from appearances. In this sense, it partakes in constructing, or anticipating, the wholly new, the possible—that which may arise from nothing.

3. The work of carrying out a grounded contextual theological reflection must begin with the local experiences, actions, and reflections of those who are closest to the realities of their context.

4. Given the redemptive core of the Christian gospel, and its privileging of the unprivileged (the poor, the outcast, those marginalized from the centers of power), the phrase *closest to the realities* should be taken to refer to those who most struggle for life in the face of forces of death. Not a precise definition, this is rather a rhetorical clue for a methodological determination of the perspectives that should govern the initial framing of questions, as well as first answers, in constructing a contextual theology. It is also a general definition, for it is not tied to any historically restricted class, group, or movement, though such a specification necessarily, but temporarily, takes place in every particular context.

5. Only then does it become meaningful to clarify the significance and contribution of more general (past and present) norms, sources, and traditions of the ecumenical Christian faith. As argued earlier, these more general norms and sources are not self-evident: They are plural, polysemic, constructed historically, and contested. They are also present, however vaguely or unarticulated, in incipient theologies (otherwise there would be no reflection upon Christian claims at all).[75]

6. A consideration of these more general norms, sources, and traditions remains equally decisive for a properly constructed contextual theology. They represent the wisdom or experience—flawed or not, oppressive or emancipatory, unexamined or critically articulated—of the wider Christian community both diachronically and synchronically. A local theology incapable of addressing or being drawn into this wider

sphere of communication remains hopelessly trapped in particularity. The logic of its own emancipatory currents is thereby curtailed, made impotent, cut short of having any impact upon those structures and social forces that also define any particular context.[76]

7. The same point may be argued from three other angles. The first is anthropological: Only by locating oneself in relation to the communicative activity of past and present generations is one's own identity, and thus one's particular humanity, established. The second is social-linguistic: Only by understanding the grammar by which past and present generations sought, or seek, to grasp reality is one able to enter into, learn from, and contribute to a learning process in which wisdom grows in the struggle for wholeness and well-being. The third is pragmatic: Only by integrating the communicative activity of past and present generations are one's own contextual limits uncovered, and thus potentially overcome, as the learning process goes on.

8. In this dialectical interaction, a discourse is possible that will allow for a mature contextual theology to emerge. Where such mature contextual theologies have emerged, the methodology described above can usually be seen at work.

9. On the basis of such a methodology, it becomes possible to rethink, and reshape, the catechetical or theological educational task and the organizational practices of the church. A contextual theology that is itself the establishment and clarification of founding theological convictions (number 1 above) necessarily includes a particular ecclesiology with practical intent.

The way this theological framework expresses itself in the link between local theologies and broader theological discourses (national, international, ecumenical) may now be stated in the form of a fourfold matrix of tasks (local, generic, fundamental, missiological). I note them serially, in an order of priority, though in practice each task will occur simultaneously. This matrix also summarizes the intent behind the public communication of my own study of the Amawoti BEC Bible studies.

We begin (methodologically and not temporally) with local theology, with the scattered reflections by local base communities, the way they think about the meaning and significance of their faith in relation to the struggles and hopes of their daily life, and with the practices these reflections (which include ritual and symbolic practices) communicate.

But this local theology remains cut off from the larger Body of Christ unless it enters into conversation with others. Only in this way could it enrich the church and be open to the correction of the experiences and reflections of the wider Christian community. This is the mark of any enduring theology—that it is communal and has universal intent. Universal intent is that of contributing to the enduring insights of the Christian tradition, tentative and approximate as they may be, by lodging them in a critical reconstruction of that tradition in the particular modalities of a local context. The meaning of being Christian, of identifying that to which one may be committed in the struggle against forces of death and for a life more abundant, is at stake.

Thus a local theology requires what I will call a generic theology, that is, a larger framework of explanation into which it fits, and within which it might become edifying or prophetic for the church. Precisely in this interface lies the role I have defined for myself in relation to the Amawoti BEC, a role I would also attribute to all theologically trained facilitators, pastors, priests, and church leaders.

A generic theology locates local theologies within broader theological paradigms, taking them out of the local context and into the wider community of Christians. A generic theology still retains the sense in which theology is located in time and space in a particular class of interests, just like local theology on a smaller scale (all theology is socially located and socially committed, even if by default or omission[77]). But a generic theology refers to the location of local communities in a wider social matrix, in the first case an ecclesial one.

The isolation of a local community from this broader social context is one way dominating power is retained at the center and the creative power of the margins reduced in its potential impact. For all these reasons—and because a local theology is essentially communal in the first place—the term *generic* is preferable to alternatives such as *social, collective,* or *communal,* though each of these latter terms points to something of import for a generic theology.

Once made generic (no longer confined to the local), insights from incipient theologies become available to the church at large. This must affect its proclamation, and thus its fundamental claims about the gospel. At a theological level, this implies that reflection upon faith at the local level, enriched and challenged by dialogue with the wider Christian community, should be able, from the point of view of those who act and suffer, to enter into our very understanding of who Jesus Christ is for us today, what kind of God is revealed in this Christ, what kind of church is adequate to the mission this revelation will call forth.

This I call a foundational theology, a meta-level of explanation and formulation in which the fundamentals of our faith are questioned and clarified, again and again. Some indications of what this might mean have been offered in analyzing the changing understandings in the Amawoti transcripts of God, Christology, and soteriology. More generally, a profound example of this dynamic at work on a global ecumenical level, lies in the now widely accepted idea of the preferential option for the poor as central to the gospel and the New Testament narratives of Jesus—an insight born of the challenge of local ecclesial communities in Latin America but hardly detectable before then in the theological and biblical work of the first half of this century.

We have noted that the way a great many people experience the impact of theology is through the assertion of fundamentals in the first place. Beginning with this inherited fundamental claim, the theologian proceeds to test whether or not any local theology meets it. If it does, it is confirmed as true. If it does not, it is regarded as false or heretical. This is the direct opposite of the method I am seeking, which strives to give maximum weight to the actual faith experiences and reflections of the ordinary believer in relation to the oppressions and emancipatory or redemptive impulses in their local context.

The fourth level, therefore, I describe as a missiological theology. The adjective *missiological* points to two key features of this theological task: First, it requires the active presentation and representation of the learnings and understandings that have been won from local ecclesial communities in dialogue with the ecumenical church. Second, it reflects an active effort to give expression to these learnings and understandings in the alteration of behaviors and practices.

With all that has now been said about the potential significance of local theologies for ecclesiology and fundamental theology, it should be clear that this mission is in the first place directed toward the church and its self-understanding. It is primarily an internal mission. It is the proclamation of what has been learned about the present significance of the Christian faith through the processes I have described. It is a proclamation that remains methodologically open to continuous correction from the ongoing life and practice of the local ecclesial communities as they struggle with oppression and freedom, facing death in all its forms and seeking life wherever it may be found, and as they come to terms with that which constrains them even as new possibilities are uncovered for themselves and for others.

7. Center and Boundary
The Geography of Faith

"We shall not cease from exploration," says T. S. Eliot in *Little Gidding*, "and the end of all our exploring will be to arrive at where we started and know the place for the first time." The profound connection Eliot draws between exploration, arrival, and knowledge—suggesting that each arrival is a new departure—captures something very important about the journey of this book.

We cannot simply interpret incipient theologies once and feel that the task is accomplished. We are driven back to the local community to recontextualize our interpretations, to face again the fundamental questions with which we began. We arrive at where we started, not to stop, secure in our knowledge, but to journey again. This chapter therefore signals only a temporary ending, a mapping of the territory we have covered and left uncovered, to take stock of our position.

We have arrived at a point where a commitment to perspectives on the margins of society, away from centers of power and wealth, becomes fundamental to the theological enterprise. We may have known this, or we may only now come to see why this should be so. This commitment is expressed in the notion of incipient theology.

Wherever Christian groups meet and discuss their problems on the basis of a text or anything analogous (sermon, ritual, performance, confession, and so on), wherever they do so reflectively—accepting, rejecting, reinterpreting, and retelling its message—and wherever they do so in relation to the concrete conditions of their existence, aware of the human being as other and as suffering, there one may discern an incipient theology worth talking about.

Any good pastor, priest, or layworker who takes the time to listen with care to her or his local community already deals with incipient theologies. I have tried to highlight only the fact that paying attention to incipient theologies in their contexts raises profound hermeneutical questions about the nature of the interpretation of faith, and far-reaching practical questions about who does the interpreting, and with what interests.

We have seen that the very nature of incipient theologies drives us to consider their relationship to the tradition upon which they depend. It has become clear that the wisdom of the past, codified in ancient texts and dusty dogmata, can and often does unlock new moments of insight and recognition—even as experience may uncover the ways in which tradition obstructs new insights and suppresses the vitality of new understandings. Let me attempt to say what is at stake here by bringing into focus the contrasting perspectives of Hans-Georg Gadamer (on tradition) and Jürgen Habermas (on critical social theory).

Gadamer has championed the recovery of notions of prejudice, authority, and tradition as essential to historical consciousness, without which we would have no way of relating to history as such. He speaks of human consciousness as ineluctably exposed to and shaped by the effects of history (*wirkungsgeschichtles Bewußtsein*). Our knowledge, therefore, is not derived from pure reflection but builds upon a prior set of historically given frameworks and categories of interpretation—a forestructure of understanding (*Vorstruktur des Verstehens*).

Gadamer's attempt to rehabilitate the place of tradition has been strongly challenged by Habermas, who defends the Enlightenment view of prejudice, authority, and tradition as irrational and therefore contrary to the emancipatory interest that which drives human beings to overcome existing constraints and oppressions. For Habermas the notion of interests rather than prejudice is the key to unlocking historical dynamics of knowledge. Ideology rather than misunderstanding (Gadamer) is what systematically distorts human communication.

Paul Ricoeur considers this debate helpful for a hermeneutical approach that includes both the moment of suspicion or critique (Habermas) and the moment of trust or reconstruction (Gadamer). Both positions raise legitimate claims, and Ricoeur seeks a rapport between the two. Instead of pitting hermeneutics against the critical sciences, Ricoeur shifts the locus of the debate to argue for a dialectic between the experience of belonging and alienating distanciation.

The details of his argument are unnecessary here. What is important for my purposes is that Ricoeur's interpretation of Habermas locates several moments of internal and external critique within hermeneutics itself: the decontextualizing and recontextualizing of texts, the reconstruction of discourses through depth semantics, the power of a text to open up new realities, and the self-enlargement that happens in exposing oneself to a text through imaginative variations.

He argues that Habermas's separation of the emancipatory interest from the practical interest of the historical-hermeneutical sciences cannot be sustained. Emancipation is not a distinct interest, for it would be quite empty and abstract if it were not situated on the same plane as the historical-hermeneutical sciences, that is, on the plane of communicative action. A critique of systematic distortions in the communicative process cannot, therefore, be separated from grasping the communicative experience itself, and this includes the forestructure of understanding by which actual understanding is in the first place possible.[1] Thus, says Ricoeur:

> The task of the hermeneutics of tradition is to remind the critique of ideology that man [sic] can project his emancipation and anticipate an unlimited and unconstrained communication only on the basis of a creative reinterpretation of cultural heritage. . . .
>
> . . . nothing is more deceptive that the alleged antinomy between an ontology of prior understanding and an eschatology of freedom. . . .
>
> In theological terms, eschatology is nothing without the recitation of acts of deliverance from the past.[2]

The dialectic between tradition and emancipation, predisposition, and interests, and belonging and distanciation, configures much of our earlier discussions. These we may now view from above, mapping the terrain we have passed through in another way.

Mapping the Territory

Theology is reflection on faith in the world in order to make sense of reality. Theology has its own integrity, a wholeness within which the parts not only find a place but are taken up into a vision of completeness. It aims at a *Gestalt* of life. But can this *Gestalt* overcome the dominant dualisms of our time, those which pit the personal against the public, the theoretical against the practical, the local against the denominational, the seen against the unseen?

If one were to take formal theological education as the mirror of theology in our time, the answers are not very clear. Seminaries, universities, and catechetical schools produce theological insights (and errors) as knowledge for the church at large, to be reproduced again by their clientele when they, in turn, take to pulpits and altars. All too often one discerns an almost unshakable confidence that real theology, in the final analysis, is the task of experts, themselves a largely self-selected or hierarchically commissioned elite whose knowledge and status is power over others. Black South Africans know this; women know it; counseling psychologists who see the damage done by repressive theologies know it; others too.

Similarly, formal theological education suffers profoundly from the gap between theory and practice, as much recent writing demonstrates.[3] The

attempts, since the 1950s, of the American Association of Theological Schools to resolve the problem demonstrates clearly that the issue remains unresolved.[4] Modern theological education all too frequently fails to be the liberative, healing *habitus* Farley believes it ought to be.[5]

We find ourselves pushed not only to question the nature and purposes of theological education, but its very rationale—the theological enterprise itself. Perhaps two insights from Karl Barth help us along in seeking adequate responses to the problem, and thus toward an appreciation of the problems inherent in incipient theologies as well as the second-order theological reflections that flow out of them.

Barth described theology as play on the precipice: The seriousness of its intent must not be forgotten, but neither must its practitioners take themselves too seriously. On occasion theology must set aside the serious demands of life for the serendipitous and playful dance of ideas. But we cannot forget in our intellectual wanderings that we do indeed live on a precipice, that life and death is at stake, and that theology should at least have something to do with that.

Barth's second insight addresses the inherent ambiguity in doing theology as an individual, something Barth understood in naming his magnum opus *Church Dogmatics*. Theology, properly conceived, is the Christian community's reflection on their faith. That an individual should construct a theology is thus an inherent contradiction. That we often behave as if only trained individuals have the means or the right to construct a theology is a denigration of the reasonable faith of ordinary Christians. The opposite view is reflected methodologically in what I have tried to say.

It includes a recognition that incipient theologies are not systematic, in the sense of a systematic theology. They are often serendipitous, perhaps with good reason resisting any attempt at systematization. Let me explain.

Long ago a good friend introduced me to classical music through the work of Gustav Mahler—an unusual place to begin for a young person brought up on gospel choruses, counterculture folk music, and sixties rock. But it worked. Perhaps Mahler attracted me because he allowed the unexpected, the contradictory and the unsystematic realities of life to enter into his music without relinquishing a sense of the wholeness of life. The ambiguities with which he lived manifest themselves throughout his symphonies in movements and passages now ending in triumph and beauty, now in tragedy and pain. They form part of the whole. In this he represents for me something required of theology as well.

Mahler was aware of, and critical of, the impulse of moderns to systematize everything into understandable, logically built patterns by which our sense of control over the world is increased and our insecurity in the face of the world temporarily overcome. In a letter to Alma Maria Schindler, then his fiancée and later his wife, written on December 20, 1901, from his Hotel Bellevue room in

Dresden where he was assisting in the preparation of a performance of his *Resurrection* symphony, he bursts out with irritation against the man who is to conduct the performance. The conductor, apparently uncertain about how to direct the symphony, had asked for a program from Mahler.

A program was a formal, written schema that detailed the composer's musical intentions to the conductor, providing a controlled pattern to follow. The brief program Mahler had already provided was extremely sketchy and ambiguous. Apparently it did not offer the desired certainty of interpretation required by the conductor. Mahler, angered and frustrated about the request for clearer interpretative instructions, writes to Alma Maria:

> I'm quite sure that if God were asked to draw up a program of the world he had created he could never do it. At best it would say as little about the nature of God and life as my analysis says about my . . . symphony. In fact, as all religious dogmas do, it leads directly to misunderstanding, to a flattening and coarsening, and in the long run to such distortion that the work, and still more its creator, is utterly unrecognizable.[6]

Mahler's awareness of the severe limitations of his program and of the ultimate futility of every attempt to fix an interpretation of his work could be a paradigm for theology as well. Many well-trained theologians would have little difficulty accepting this. Sadly, however, the same cannot be said for the way in which theology conveys itself to the great majority of Christians.

Dogmas and confessions, we have noted, may well function as discursive forms of knowledge by which to control and limit, with the threat of various sanctions, what may or may not be thought by Christians. In George Lindbeck's language, the "grammar of faith" that provides the rules for acceptable interpretations does more than establish and secure identity. It also derives from relations of power and is implicated in repressive relations of power. Some people do have a particularly privileged access to the records of revelation through their training and their office, and they in turn act as guardians of this deposit. All too often, however, they think of this deposit as *the* truth whose contents act as rules by which the believer is governed.

If, indeed, there is substance to this view, then it is easy to understand why dominant forms of theology are unlikely to make much positive, emancipatory impact on the kind of local community with whom I have been in dialogue. To be sure, one would have to accept to some extent Lindbeck's claim that doctrine functions as a kind of limited language by which the grammar of faith may be discerned as the guide to what does and does not count as being Christian. But we must also accept that the language game is plural, contested, fraught with the effects of systematic distortion and always imbued with unequal relations of power. It may also be beside the point: The impact of formal theology on ordinary Christians, those theologically untrained hundreds of thousands of people whose faith is the life and soul of the church, may well be minimal.

As I have tried to demonstrate throughout this study, the geography of faith may be mapped in terms of a number of dialectics: tradition and innovation, text and context, suspicion and restoration, disclosure and concealment, power and subjugation. These contrasts have helped us to depict the outlines of certain patterns of religious experience and reflection through an encounter with the incipient theology of the Amawoti BEC.

A set of relevant boundaries has also been uncovered: that between trained and untrained believers, between intellectuals and subalterns, between people at the centers of influence and knowledge construction and those on the periphery, between the self and the other. These boundaries are not merely a matter of theory. They cannot be understood adequately except in relation to the human and material boundaries that separate, hurt, and perhaps destroy people. Religion is not innocent.

Ordinary believers in specific contexts offer an important resource for any successful attempt to resolve some of the alienation and pain caused by such boundaries. Bodies are at stake, not just ideas. Christian belief is also at stake, not ultimately, but in its capacity to draw upon and feed back to ordinary people a basis for a hope that transcends all, and a love that extends to all. The human spirit, and with it the reality of the divine spirit, is also at stake. The reflections of this book seek to explore these things, through the eyes especially of marginalized believers.

Does the fact that I have concentrated on one particular community in its specific time and place mean that all we have here is a local theology and nothing more? Does this single case speak to anyone else? Can one extrapolate from such limited particularities to draw more general conclusions of any enduring value?

Mapping the contours of social experience and structures of power, as indeed we have, goes well beyond the particular territory inhabited by the Amawoti BEC. The Archimedean point, I have argued, lies in the potential of their particular experience—of persons acting and suffering, of a community that understands hegemony and domination through the direct experience of their effects—to illuminate the illusions, the distortions, and the contradictions of reality and to offer insight into what is required for spirited existence and for just institutions.

Valid generalizations can and should be made. A postcolonial Christianity cannot allow itself to be marginalized from the general discourse of the church by declining to challenge naturalized hegemonies. By calling it *postcolonial* Christianity, a term strongly present in contemporary literary theory in Africa and elsewhere, I wish to point to the critical impulses arising from those who were colonized against the paradigms of knowledge and power introduced by the colonizer. This is one corrective to the project of modernity. It remaps the territory of our action and reflection and changes our interpretative standpoint. It displaces the imperial claims of the center.

Displacing the Center

Stephen Toulmin tells us the fascinating story of a burial ground in Stockbridge, Massachusetts, where a family grave of unusual symbolic significance lies.[7] Judge Theodore Sedgwick, founding patriarch of the Stockbridge Sedgwicks, is buried under a high-rising obelisk in the center of a great circle. Spreading concentrically outwards are the graves of his descendants, generation upon generation, all laid to rest with their heads facing outward, their feet pointing in toward the obelisk. When they arise and face the judge on Judgment Day, the legend has it that they will have to see no one but Sedgwicks.

As Toulmin laconically notes, this image reflects the modern notion of state organization and the model of Copernican astronomy. The central government, the Solar King, ordains all and wields authority over successive circles of subjects, all of whom know their places and keep their proper orbits. The order of nature and the order of society turn out to be governed by a similar set of laws.

In a strangely comparable way this heliocentric view is a dominant feature in the theological landscape as well, at least in the English-speaking world. It is the conservative form of the privatization of religion under the sway of industrial and financial capitalism. One preeminent popular representation can be found in a widely sung gospel song on which I and thousands of others were brought up:

> Turn your eyes upon Jesus
> Look full in his wonderful face
> And the things of earth will grow strangely dim
> In the light of his glory and grace.[8]

Facing the center, looking at no one but the Christ and those others in the circle who bear his name, the revelatory light throws into shadow the things of this world. The world loses its significance and becomes another object to be ignored or manipulated, in the name of heaven. This inward orientation of faith, often accompanied by a denigration of all that is external (body, world, material reality), reflects itself in many theological constructions.

They are found wherever revelation functions normatively to exclude the world from offering anything more to our theologies than the occasion for the proclamation of what we already know. What is to be known is seen as given by the divine reality alone, one qualitatively different from our reality. The deposit of revelation is then applied to the world. Application requires interpretative transformations, but the orthodox goal of all interpretation is to uncover the essential deposit, not to alter it. Thus the fundamentals of the faith are believed to be secured for transmission down the ages and across the nations.

This dynamic may also be seen in certain formulations of the classical Protestant conviction that grace transforms nature, while nature reveals nothing.[9] Barth took this view to its extreme in his absolute distinction between God and world. He did so for good reasons in his reaction to classical liberal theology, and the lesson he taught remains. But in maintaining this position with great fervor against all tendencies to dilute revelation with nature (his *Nein!* To Emil Brunner's theology of encounter), he cut off all possibilities of recognizing the methodological role of context in shaping fundamental theology.

Ironically, his biography[10] represents one of the most enduring examples of Christian contextual engagements (with trade unions, socialism, and German confessing Christians) irrevocably intertwined with his theological explorations. Yet his *Kirchliche Dogmatik* may be read without grasping its intimate link to the concrete material realities of the world. Hence the ease with which Barth is domesticated—made conservative and reactionary—and the difficulty his radical interpreters have in affecting the wider reception of his theology.[11]

A methodology that excludes from all foundational theological claims anything which is not revelation, understood as an original deposit of faith untouched by the world, makes a contextual theology impossible. Certainly, a theology that addresses contexts is possible; indeed, even a theology which takes the questions of contexts as determinative is possible (Paul Tillich's method of correlation). But a theology that finds answers in a context is ruled out.

This is the superficial picture. But if it can be shown that revelatory insight arising from contexts is quite normal, then we may affirm a theological method that finds answers in a context. To do so, one assumption is essential, namely, that we speak of reality as one, rather than as split between the divine and the worldly. On this basis we may claim that revelation as the given comes to us only in the reality we know. But how do we know it?

If Ricoeur is right in saying that the symbol gives rise to thought,[12] then all human appropriation of grace is conscious—given to our awareness—only insofar as it is imaginatively transformed and reflected upon by human actors in the context of worldly existence.[13] Grace may be the ontological basis of reality, of God's presence in the world—a faith claim. But its validity for human existence in history lies only in our imaginative appropriation of grace and our reflected insight on grace.

Our experience of grace may arise in many ways, but our knowledge of grace comes to us only through symbols and our reflection upon them. Because there is no human being in general and only particular human beings,[14] this in turn is only possible in and out of particular contexts. In this sense, the content of revelation must necessarily be mediated by context, or be contextually shaped.

That our context includes proper attention to the original sources of the Christian faith by which any particular revelatory mediation may be recognized as Christian is a *sine qua non*. But the original sources in theology have never in fact provided more than a fixed point of identification, like the polar star or the Southern Cross, each one relevant only according to the perspective of the viewer.

Identification is the issue, not the content of revelation. Barth saw this clearly in his *Römerbrief*, as he repeatedly seeks content-less metaphors for revelation: the thin red line, the empty river canal, the crater left by impact. There seems no necessary reason, on this basis, to deny the possibility that contextual understanding could change fundamental theology. All that is necessary is that any contextual understanding include the demand to identify itself in relation to the original sources of the faith to be understood as Christian theology at all.[15]

What endures in the original sources are stories, generative symbols, archetypal patterns of existence. They exist not within a fixed solar system, to use a cosmic metaphor, but as swirling clouds of gas with greater or lesser definable fields of gravity which bear differently upon contexts according to the capacity of a particular narrative, symbol, or pattern to disclose reality. The struggle to define relevant fields of gravity is the stuff of church history, of the thought and practice of Christians in particular times and places.

The formation of the canon represents just such a struggle. The Apostles Creed exemplifies one definition of key centers of gravity. Yet every specific concretization of the meaning of one or other element of the creed depends upon something other than the creed itself. Which elements dominate is as much a question of time and place as of tradition, and each element may be hotly contested (a feminist critique of the patriarchal ontology that infuses the creed is one example). Theology thus works in multiple fields of representations whose centers shift from one time or place to another, reflecting the irrevocable relativism of faith.[16]

Jennings has called the field of gravitational forces and defining centers the "Christian mythos."[17] (David Tracy speaks of the "Christian classic," but this tends to limit our view to that which is written.) Multiple potential meanings (or expressions of revelation) present themselves to us in the Christian mythos, but only a certain range of meanings that are possible. Scripture in part constrains the range of meanings, playing a normative role in defining the limits within which theology works. It also provides us with the grammar of our language as Christians, preventing us from claiming for this language something that cannot be found in it. Yet contexts also play a normative role in isolating relevant meanings, of reshaping their gravity and their relationship to other meanings, and of introducing more meaning (Ricoeur).

Only so can one understand the strange fact that studies of the Bible in the first half of this century were by and large blind to what has since become known as the preferential option for the poor in Jesus's ministry and preaching. A mere half-century later, the great denominational gatherings of the church (Evangelical, Ecumenical, Orthodox, and Roman Catholic) have officially accepted that this perspective is indeed scriptural, having the quality of revelational truth.

The paradigm of contextual theology thus simply asserts, in my view, that context shapes not only the questions to be asked, but the alignment of the field of theology, and in this sense, its answers. It does not do so arbitrarily, because its starting point is not reason but faith—not the faith of theologians alone but also the faith of untrained, ordinary Christians. It does not do so dogmatically (according to received tradition alone), because it accords to the untrained, ordinary Christian a genuine measure of reason as she or he reflects on faith, however unsystematically and naively.

Certainly, reflection on one's faith needs the historical dimension (dialogue with the diachronic community) and an ecumenical dimension (dialogue with the synchronic community). But now it is dialogue on different terms. Rather than making the voice of the past wholly determinative (for example, Scripture), it makes a multiplicity of voices essential. The normative role of Scripture is then understood to be found in something other than its revelational character as word of God, for its words both reveal and hide the Word (an insight Luther had already developed clearly). Rather, its normativity lies in the claim that it defines the range of originating narratives and reflections that testify to a series of profound and ultimately definitive encounters with the reality of the sacred. Finally, Scripture also offers symbols, narratives, rituals, and the like, drawn from the contexts of the original recorders of the texts, to enrich our understanding and to shape an identity. Without identity, there is nothing to contribute, nothing that might be called a specifically Christian understanding of life and death.

If we join together the texts of tradition that testify to the enduring wisdom, experience, and sense of reality of a people (our understanding of their universality), and if we read context as meaning particularity, then we may still ask: What is it that holds the universal and the particular together? What counteracts the errors of radical pluralism in which all particularities are granted and difference is stressed to the point where we are left indifferent because it makes all discussion useless?[18] What confronts the mistakes of absolutist universalism in which particularities and difference are overridden with practical consequences, which may include tyranny?

A contexualized anthropology, in this sense, offers us the surest route to answering these questions. Persons are embodied in time and space, occupying particular places.

Claiming Space: Embodied in a Story

To grasp these additional dimensions we turn again to Ricoeur. The contextual interpretation of the bible by the Amawoti BEC may be understood as narrative in four senses: Members of the group bring to it their own story which is already a history with others; the group itself has its own story, part of which has been told here; members' use of biblical text locates their own stories in relation to the group's story; and the biblical story itself is elaborated historically in the stories of Christians across time and space. The link between these dimensions is our concern.

We have already spoken of the Christian tradition as embodying a mythos. Mythos, Ricoeur notes, is not simply a collection of symbols and images, but an emplotment of them.[19] What plots our perceptions and our perspectives at any one time depends upon our location in the grand narratives into which we are born and by which we are brought up, as well as our embodiment in a narrative of the self for which we are in part responsible. Over time, our character may change, but only in relation to our emplotment in a narrative.

As Ricoeur puts it, there is a primacy of emplotment over character. The generalized mythos by which we live is the background to our story of life, while the specific foreground at any particular time and place is constructed on this background (both never being absolute). The universal and the particular are in this way always bound up with each other. One may say, equally, that the personal and the public spheres of life are fundamentally inseparable.

The narrative construction of the self in the world is both discursive and non-discursive, though finally expressed in language or language-like activity. What happens in this process, Ricoeur suggests, is that a fiction is created by which the narrative unity of life is secured.[20] The term *fiction* here does not mean "fake," something artificially constructed outside of real life. On the contrary, real life—at least for human beings[21]—becomes available to our understanding only when it is fashioned on the cloth of the stories available to us, including the possibilities these stories offer for imaginative variations on the narrative journey of the self.

The practical field of our life is thus always shaped by what Ricoeur calls a double-determination in the exchange between the whole and the part.[22] The part is analogous to the particularities of context, where actions and practices shape the story of one's life and contribute to one's understanding of life. The whole may be found in those ideals and projects that endure in one's life and by which particularities are integrated into a larger narrative. The interplay between the two shapes the narrative configuration of life, a unity without which we cannot function. Life projects and fragmentary engagements thus shape the practical field, says Ricoeur,

in accordance with a twofold movement of ascending complexification starting from basic actions and from practices, and of descending specification
starting from the vague and mobile horizon of ideals and projects in light of
which a human life apprehends itself in its oneness.[23]

This twofold movement helps us comprehend the relationship between
local theologies and the grand narratives of the Christian tradition. Our interpretative activity must move in both directions.

One implication: The notion that an adequately grounded theology could
emerge alone from local reflections on practice by an ascending complexification of what is learned is an error on the side of contextualization. In this case,
we can expect nothing from the history of theology, or more broadly, the
Christian tradition itself. But the actual embodiments of universal impulses in
Christianity (keeping in mind the idea of universals as enduring tentative
approximations) are consequential for local theologies. The tension with what
is not local must be consciously maintained.

A second implication: It is insufficient to construct a theology in which
ideals and projects are abstracted from particular realities in order to limit subsequent interpretations, an error on the side of generalization. In this case, we
can expect nothing of theology other than a subjugation of concrete experiences
to new hegemonic interpretations. Once again, the nature of theology as a
reflection of the faith of believers is undermined, and conventions override convictions.

In the twofold movement we have described, potential or inchoate universals
arise out of the processes of history. These are the things of enduring significance
upon which we find agreement. But agreement requires a prior commitment to
arbitration, in discussion, of convictions incorporated in concrete forms of life.[24]
Here Ricoeur comes very close to the ethics of communicative action proposed
by Jürgen Habermas, and indeed he affirms Habermas's discourse ethics as exemplary precisely at this point:[25]

> Only a real discussion, in which convictions are permitted to be elevated
> above conventions, will be able to state, at the end of a long history yet to
> come, which alleged universals will become recognized by "all the persons
> concerned" (Habermas), that is, by the "representative persons" (Rawls) of all
> cultures.

This consideration of the narrative unity of life brings us close to character
and experience of the Amawoti BEC. The validity of local knowledge or wisdom
is now seen to link directly to the larger narratives that make up the Christian
tradition as a whole. The fundamental movement still begins with convictions

rooted in concrete forms of life, but it is completed only in a turn to a few values where the universal and the historical intersect.[26] If the tradition, including the Bible, had no life ideals or projects to offer to particular contexts, it would make no sense to draw upon it. What happens at Amawoti suggests that it does indeed make sense to do so, provided that the discursive framework stays in the foreground and the concrete forms of life remain at the center, that is, provided the embodied story of ordinary people in the material and social conditions of life is given the space it claims.

I am now able to say the following: The integrity of faith, brought into question by suggestions that contexts should be made normative, in fact rests precisely upon a contextual perspective.

Configuring the Boundary

The above argument draws on the integrative power of narrative theory to find an embodied link between the particular and the general. Yet integration or harmony leaves out those boundaries of inequality and injustice that dominant ideologies and oppressive institutions defend. Our mapping would be incomplete without considering these boundaries and their general configuration. To this, we turn to spatial metaphors, using Kathleen Kirby's attempt to think through the boundary, in order to discern the politics of location, subjects, and space.

Spatial tropes, Kirby notes, are increasingly used to construct arguments and political approaches critical of modernist, colonial, and patriarchal oppressions. They are also used in work on cultural marginality. Why this interest in the metaphorical and analytical power of spatial categories? Kirby offers the following potent argument:

> Space brings together the material and the abstract, the body and the mind, the objective interaction of physical subjects and the elusive transience of consciousness (or the unconscious).

It is the way in which we mark and measure interconnection and difference, similarity and distance:

> Space, then, seems to offer a medium for articulating . . . the many facets, or phases, of subjectivity . . . : national origin, geographic and territorial mobility (determined by class, gender, and race), bodily presence and limits, structures of consciousness, and ideological formations of belonging and exclusion.[27]

In fact, one cannot imagine any subject except in some relation to real space, contrary to Cartesian models of the ego located in the interiority of the

mind. Recognizing the space someone occupies and the place by which they are identified is vital to a thoroughly critical attitude, just as it uncovers the pretense of those who claim to be speaking from some absolute space, that is, from no space at all. Kirby's point is particularly pertinent to my sense of contextualized incipient theologies:

> The subject and its form, subjects and their natures, are tied into political commitments and ethical positions by nature of being tied into particular material spaces, like bodies or countries, ghettos or suburbs, kitchens or boardrooms.[28]

Criticism of the occupation of space and the location of power is not merely an intellectual activity of feminist or other trained intellectuals, nor an imposition upon the realities of a community such as the Amawoti BEC. There is evidence in the BEC's reading of gender issues, for example, of precisely the same kind of critical impulse, articulated in less sophisticated language.

It should be noted (if it has not become obvious already) that gender concerns are largely, if not entirely, absent in the Amawoti transcripts. The group itself consisted largely of women, so they were certainly not absent. Their absence in the texts or discourses of the Bible studies marks a particular kind of presence, a silence that speaks volumes. This silence is occasionally broken, though, and when it is it most often signals the depiction of the subjectivity of women through a patriarchal or kyriarchal[29] ordering of power which controls their space and defines their place.

In a discussion on three selected texts, the hidden transcripts of power and the coded language of hegemonic cultural traditions are suddenly broken open as Phumzile bursts out:

> Jesus abolished all discrimination between priests and people—especially women. Direct communication with God is possible through Jesus Christ. Through the African tradition we had a "way" (uhlelo=programme), by means of the ancestors, of communicating with God. This was a gap between the people and God (Umvelingqangi). According to the African tradition a woman had to ask her uncle or grandfather who would pass on her request to the ancestors and in turn the ancestors would pass on the request to Mvelingqangi. Jesus has destroyed that gap. Now everybody has the right to talk with God. Jesus has destroyed sexual discrimination (ukuchwasana ngobulili).[30]

The transcriber of this Bible study session recorded an immediately subsequent intervention by a male member of the group, and the discussion thereafter became confused. The issue did not surface again, at least in this forum. A boundary had been challenged and transgressed. Though temporary and fleeting, the rhetorical force of the expression of this transgression remains, captured in memory and in the text itself. The breaching of the boundary reconfigures the geography of faith at that moment, redefining the established centers of power and authority.

Another dialogue emphasizes the point. This time the group is discussing the question of justice and the demand of the gospel to fight injustice and oppression.[31] They link this struggle to love for the other and the willingness to sacrifice oneself for justice. Abruptly one of the women present asks: "Will you stop exploiting girls?" This startling interruption in what is otherwise a dialogue shaped by general political concerns causes consternation. Three males quickly ask if she is referring to one of them, or perhaps to the whole group, concluding—before she can answer—with a statement that it's a burning issue. But rather than pursuing the issue, the conversation is immediately taken in another direction.

Once again, a silence is broken, an absence is made present, a discourse on sexual violence is inserted into one of political violence. Once again, the moment of disclosure is short and the gap opened is quickly sealed before it becomes a chasm. Order is restored. This is my reading, of course, an interpretation that perhaps penetrates beyond what might have been conscious to any of the participants in that particular dialogue.

This reading, however, helps illuminate my concern for the boundaries that marginalize people. It also allows me to draw a fruitful distinction between space and place derived from Kirby's reading of two key feminist theorists of the subject, Adrienne Rich and Chandra Mohanty.

Place, says Kirby, seems to assume set boundaries that one fills to achieve a solid identity. Place settles space into objects, working to reinscribe the Cartesian monad and the autonomous ego. Later, in reviewing Rich's contribution to the debate, Kirby shows how a physical address of one's home inscribes expanding circles of space subordinate to the centrality of the self.[32] The space designated by Adrienne Rich, a person, is not the same as 14 Edgevale Road, a home. The mapping of these two realities is of a different order. The person and the home are architecturally, subjectively, different; yet both are private. The minute one adds Baltimore or the USA or the Western Hemisphere, the configuration of space changes according to the differing boundaries designated by place. The very use of a personal address, a relatively modern invention, signifies a particular construction of the world. Narratives about gender, class, culture, race, geopolitics, and the like are implied. The self is contextualized by the mapping of space into places.

If this kind of mapping of places is translated into notions of boundaries, it immediately becomes apparent how power/knowledge (Michel Foucault) functions to define centers and peripheries. The configuring of boundaries, of course, is not a one-way process but a result of more or less conscious contestations and temporary agreements or processes of naturalization. Our concern in the search to uncover the significance of incipient theologies, however, has been to discern how the boundaries are configured from the side of those who are marginalized, and what this may mean for those who view these boundaries from centers of power and knowledge. Here is where the metaphor of space shows its disclosive potential.

Returning to Kirby's analysis, we recognize that if place is organic and stable, space is malleable, a fabric of continually shifting sites and boundaries. One implication of using spatial tropes to define subjectivity in relation to concrete locations of power and structures of knowledge is of particular interest for my own project. Kirby points out that the both Rich and Mohanty, the two key figures for her, depend upon geographical metaphors (Mohanty that of two-dimensional cartography, Rich that of three-dimensional architecture).[33] What this does is shift attention away from linguistic metaphors such as writing (or text), thus replacing (imbalanced) binaries with (equalized) pluralities.

The shift to a geography of knowledge construction illuminates my own location, and the fact that it not only transcribes but rescribes the Amawoti experience. The use of spatial tropes in this context materializes and deconstructs the very thing I am about. My own project is revealed as inherently unstable; simultaneously, attention is drawn to, and space thus created for, the project of those who are otherwise ignored.

The configuring of the boundary reconfigures my own work and by implication all similar works (whether in the form of texts, rituals, confessions, proclamations, or any other expressions of power/knowledge). In allowing myself to be constructed by the marginalized voice, I come face-to-face with myself and the demand of the other upon me. But herein lies what Kirby calls the promise of the boundary: "The important element to maintain would be the punctuality of the border; it is not an ontological feature, but an effective, differential one. It holds open space, but the space it materializes is shifting, temporary and replaceable."[34]

From Boundary to Center: Refashioning the Geography of Faith

Many questions remain. Not least among them is the question of the application of the frameworks of understanding and methodologies of interpretation proposed here to contexts defined less by poverty, oppression, and marginalization, and more by affluence, relative freedom, and access to the centers of power. It should not be hard for groups analogous to the Amawoti BEC in other locales to grasp the significance for them of what this study is about, assuming that its substance reaches them in some form or another. But it is hard for those who have little daily experience by which they may recognize themselves in the things of concern to the Amawoti BEC.

Such believers, whatever their local theology, seem to be excluded by the particular epistemological and ontological commitments I have made in my own approach to the issues dealt with here. Their contexts may well offer the litmus test of whatever has been claimed in this study, for if there is nothing here to illuminate those contexts or provide a practical base for working in them, one may well wonder how those who exercise authority, power, and speech in the various church bodies themselves will be challenged by the recovery of incipient theologies among the poor, the oppressed, and the marginalized.

I am both optimistic and pessimistic. Optimism is warranted, I believe, because of the resilience of the human spirit, even in apparently desperate circumstances. The very fact that the Amawoti BEC exists, that someone like myself has been put in a position to learn from its experience and reflections, and that similar learnings among my colleagues have enabled some promising transformation within the confines of a formal theological educational program offers some basis for optimism.

One could go further: The context into which these learnings have been transposed—a school of theology in a university—can hardly be described as defined by poverty, oppression, and marginalization. Yet the impact of the interpretative activity and communal practices of a local base community such as the one at Amawoti remains. What is possible in one such context is in principle possible in every sphere of authority, power, discourse, and knowledge production within the churches.

Nevertheless, pessimism is unavoidable, indeed necessary. The possibility of restoration, of the reconstruction of the ecclesial, goes hand in hand with its actuality, and thus with a hermeneutics of suspicion. Sociological wisdom suggests that institutional imperatives will continue to dominate church practices, including the training of its leadership and the formation of its laity. These imperatives include, inter alia, the need to service (fill) existing congregations, the need to meet the forestructure of traditional expectations of a pastor from a local congregation, the requirement of balancing budgets in the face of widespread lack of financial resources, the need to fit with many—if not most—current models and methods of theological education determined by personnel who either do not have the time, the experience, or the inclination to alter them. One could go on. One might almost say that what I am asking for swims against the tide, a powerful, deeply established drift.

The dialectic between pessimism and optimism—or between a hermeneutics of suspicion and a hermeneutics of reconstruction—is part of our mapping of the terrain of incipient theologies. The offering of this text is primarily an investment in reconstruction, albeit one based on a series of deep suspicions.

The process described throughout this study stands as its litmus test. The communicative activity of the Amawoti BEC is presupposed as exemplary of the kind of process that may be internalized in relation to other communities and contexts.[35] Similarly, my own hermeneutical interaction with the results of this process as captured in the BEC's readings of biblical texts, is presumed to be exemplary of the kind of role all theologically trained church leaders or facilitators at whatever level can carry out.

I have tried to pose, and respond to, the question of how the members of this BEC understand their own being and becoming in relation to their communicatively achieved religious worldview, which is simultaneously an important, perhaps defining, component of their general worldview. My interpretations of their understanding of God, Jesus Christ, and redemption contribute to defining an answer to the question Who are you? That the primary question is *Who?* and not *What?* is an indication of my interest, in the first place, in listening to the other from within rather than defining the other from without in terms of a predetermined analysis (for example, of class, ethnic or gender positions, and structural arrangements).

The question of *What?* finds its place only in a brief analysis of the social location of this community as a secondary, though not unimportant, supplement to the question *Who?* The latter emphasis already suggests that an important focus of the whole study is the agency of those who make up this community, their courage to be (Tillich). They are constituted in the past by the interaction and conflict between traditions that have shaped who they are now, including an encounter with Christianity. Yet the community also adds, in its own activities and behaviors, to the ongoing redefinition of the traditions by which they are constituted. In this way, their own agency also constitutes the present. Their history and its location in a larger history drive us away from any idealistic, noncontextual view of the interpretative task of theology.

This history, we have seen, includes relations of power, dispersed, utilized, and made effective in forms of knowledge. Knowledge as power thus shapes the relationship between a group such as the Amawoti BEC and church institutions. Throughout, I adopt the working hypothesis that the perspectives of the base ecclesial community, as reflections on faith in context, are marginal to the dominant forms of theological discourse. It is this marginalization of what I contend are vital sources of knowledge that I wish to challenge. In doing so, I am concerned to develop an approach that may be generalized beyond the limits of this community and its context.

This is why we are faced with the question of voices of the other and the problem of the representation of the other. By seeking to bridge the boundary between myself and the members of the BEC, I am confronted with the difference between myself and the other. By interpreting that difference, I run the risk of overriding the voice of the other or, worse, creating the impression that my voice is actually theirs. When that happens, the other is effectively erased. Even more, the self is also compromised by the loss of the other. Every pastor, educator, and community agent, it seems to me, needs to come to terms with this issue.

To do so, I have suggested, means distinguishing between conversation (dialogue) and collaboration (solidarity). Collaboration takes the form of a commitment to a partner who may not be equal in respect of access to and use of power. When this happens the dialectic of the self and the other comes to the fore, not as an abstract exercise but in terms of historically located persons who stand in particular, often asymmetric, relations of power to each other.

This, I suggest, is central to the task of recovering incipient theologies and making them part of the reality of a public, ecumenical theological enterprise, no longer marginalized. At the same time, we must expect that incipient theologies will challenge and alter the process by which the church comes to understand and proclaim its truths.

Let me repeat something already suggested at the outset of this investigation. In a way, it signifies something other than repetition. After the journey we have been on, it will hopefully be read with new understanding.

The starting point of the journey is an act of listening, as difficult as this is: To hear the voices of a marginalized black community, in their particularity, and in their context of marginalization and poverty. The result of this listening is necessarily something new.[36]

The theological journey whose parameters have been depicted here, if it is to be made, does not end here. We learn, and in learning we express the creative impulse that marks us as human beings. In error, through doubt, by discovery, and in celebration, we join in the unending pilgrimage that is our lot and our hope—we who, for better or worse, have been made in the image of God.

The reference to the beginning, therefore, is not circular in structure, but spiral. It seeks to return the reader again to the key themes of this study, to enter the process of which it is only one expression, but now without the innocence of the first reading. One may say, then, that it is not the text that counts, but the practice to which it points and which it hopes to engender.

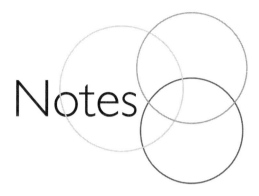

Notes

Introduction

1. This claim is powerfully argued by Mahmood Mamdani in *Citizen and Subject* (Cape Town: David Philip, 1996).

2. Takatso Mofokeng, *The Crucified among the Crossbearers* (Kampen: J. H. Kok, 1983.

3. Base ecclesial community (BEC) is a term derived from the Latin American *comunidades eclesiales de base*. There are some South African variants of what is meant by the term, but none of them have become prominent in theological discourse. I therefore retain the more familiar term, which does have descriptive advantages in emphasizing the three components of a BEC, namely, that it is (a) a local community, (b) which understands itself in some overt way to be part of the Christian family, and (c) which exists at the base of society when society is pictured as a hierarchical pyramid of power and authority. I choose to use the term *ecclesial* rather than *Christian* (as some do), because particular members of this (and similar) communities do not always understand themselves to be Christian, though they are content to be part of a group associated with the church.

4. James R. Cochrane, *Servants of Power* (Johannesburg: Ravan Press, 1987).

5. James C. Scott, *Domination and the Arts of Resistance: Hidden Transcripts* (New Haven, Conn.: Yale University Press, 1990).

1. Salt Stops Ghosts

1. Victor Turner, *The Ritual Process: Structure and Anti-Structure* (New York: Cornell University, 1977), 3.

2. One may call this a postmodernist position, and I certainly do depend upon the insights of many postmodernist theorists. If we may describe postmodernism as a critique internal to the modernist world, then I have been equally influenced by critiques that are external, arising in the conflict between cultures and symbolic worlds and in struggles against domination.

3. This view has been changing, of course, as is perhaps best represented in the dialogues between Fidel Castro and Frei Betto in *Fidel on Religion: Castro Talks on Revolution and Religion with Frei Betto* (New York: Simon & Schuster, 1987).

4. Teresa Okure, "Reflection on Luke 8:40-56," in M. A. Oduyoye and M. A. R. Kanyoro, eds., *The Will to Arise: Women, Tradition and the Church in Africa* (Maryknoll, N.Y.: Orbis, 1992), 226.

5. The acronym AIC is variously designated as African Independent Church, African Indigenous Church, African Instituted Church, and African-initiated Church. Each designation has its proponents and critics, and each its difficulties. I choose the last mentioned simply because it has the virtue of emphasizing a particular agency on the part of the indigenous black population.

6. Jean Comaroff and John Comaroff, *Of Revelation and Revolution: Christianity, Colonialism and Consciousness in South Africa* (Chicago: University of Chicago Press, 1991).

7. James R. Cochrane, *Servants of Power: The Role of English-Speaking Churches in South Africa, 1903–1930* (Johannesburg: Ravan, 1987), 89ff.

8. Studies of these churches have been made with some regularity. (See, for example, Bengt G. M. Sundkler, *Bantu Prophets in South Africa* [London: Oxford University Press, 1961 (2nd Edition)]; C. G. Oosthuizen, *Post-Christianity in Africa: A Theological and Anthropological Study* [London: C. Hurst, 1968]; and Trevor D. Verryn, *A History of the Order of Ethiopia* [Johannesburg: Central Mission Press, 1971].) In the 1960s the Christian Institute of Southern Africa gave support to the establishment of the African Independent Churches Association as a way of bolstering the presence in the public life of the church (cf. Peter Walshe, *Church Versus State in South Africa: The Case of the Christian Institute* [London: Hurst, 1983]). Similarly, during the 1980s the Institute for Contextual Theology supported groups of AICs to help them establish institutes and colleges. But general attitudes of distrust, disinterest or disdain towards AICs from others have not changed a great deal.

9. Representative of the various stages of Black Theology in South Africa are the following works: Mokgethi Motlhabi, ed., *Essays on Black Theology* (Johannesburg: University Christian Movement, 1972); Allan Boesak, *Farewell to Innocence: A Socio-Ethical Study of Black Theology and Power* (Maryknoll, N.Y.: Orbis, 1977); Takatso Mofokeng, *The Crucified among the Crossbearers* (Kampen: J. H. Kok, 1983); Itumeleng Mosala and Buti Tlhagale, eds., *The Unquestionable Right to Be Free* (Maryknoll, N.Y.: Orbis, 1986); Simon Maimela, *Proclaim Freedom to My People* (Johannesburg: Skotaville, 1987); Bonganjalo Goba, *An Agenda for Black Theology: Hermeneutics for Social Change* (Johannesburg: Skotaville, 1988); and Itumeleng Mosala, *Biblical Hermeneutics and Black Theology in South Africa* (Grand Rapids, Mich.: Eerdmans, 1989).

10. Itumeleng Mosala, "The Relevance of African Independent Churches and Their Challenge to Black Theology," in *The Unquestionable Right to Be Free,* Itumeleng Mosala and Buti Tlhagale, eds. (Maryknoll, N.Y.: Orbis, 1986). A word of caution is necessary here: The title of Mosala's work begins, "The Relevance of African Independent Churches," but the text itself speaks of traditional African religions, an altogether different thing. This difference may well be important for any conclusions drawn.

11. I should note that a discussion on Black Theology, pursuing the same line of argument, is also carried out by Robin Petersen in "Time, Resistance and Reconstruction: Rethinking Kairos Theology in South Africa" (Ph.D. diss., University of Chicago, 1995). The

parallels in our interpretations, though developed completely independently, are substantial. Petersen, however, sustains the discussion well beyond the point at which I stop, and includes a much more substantial positive assessment of the contribution of Black Theology than I am able to provide here, given the focus of this book.

12. Bonganjalo Goba, *An Agenda for Black Theology: Hermeneutics for Social Change* (Johannesburg: Skotaville, 1988), 55.

13. Just such a counterrevolutionary example provides the initial focus in Petersen's study of the significance for the "prophetic church" of the AICs: Robin Petersen, "Time, Resistance and Reconstruction: Rethinking Kairos Theology in South Africa" (Ph.D. diss.,University of Chicago, 1995).

14. Various spellings of the name are used locally, including Amaoti and Amouti. Although it is not originally an African name and may be derived from a word given to the area by Indians, an Africanized spelling of the name using current conventions would be Amawoti.

15. Martin Mandew, "Power and Empowerment: Religious Imagination and the Life of a Local Base Ecclesial Community" (Master's thesis, University of Natal, 1993): 65.

16. Ibid., 81ff.

17. The UDF was an umbrella organization for several hundred local groups and movements who were strongly involved in the struggle against the apartheid state during the 1980s. It no longer exists, most of its members having aligned themselves with the African National Congress or with other bodies now allowed to operate legally.

18. Mandew, "Power and Empowerment," 81.

19. The group is more fully described by Graham Philpott, its resident facilitator for six years, in his work *The Kin-dom of God in Amawoti* (Pietermaritzburg, South Africa: Cluster Publications, 1993), 21ff.

20. Mandew, "Power and Empowerment," 83ff.

21. Ibid., 90ff, 99.

22. Ibid., 103ff.

23. Later chapters focus on the questions of "speech" and the "Other."

24. Bible study on Luke 17:20-21, 11 November 1988.

25. Quoted in Jonathan A. Draper, "Social Ambiguity and the Production of Text: Prophets, Teachers, Bishops and Deacons, and the Development of the Jesus Tradition in the Context of the Didache," in *The Didache in Context: Essays on its Text, History and Transmission,* edited by C. N. Jefford. (Leiden: Brill, 1996).

26. Of course, this does not mean that there is no originality in the thought and practice of the community. If that were the case, there would be much less to confront in listening to them than I've argued here.

27. Bible study on Luke 9:57-62, 30 June 1989. Throughout, names used in the dialogues presented are fictitious, though they represent specific persons. The dialogues are verbatim, translated from the original Zulu, and not compositions.

28. Bible study on Matt. 5:13-16, 26 August 1989.

29. Philpott, *Kin-dom of God.*

30. See Gerald O. West, *Biblical Hermeneutics of Liberation: Modes of Reading the Bible,* 2nd ed. (Maryknoll, N.Y.: Orbis, 1995).

31. Emmanuel Martey, *African Theology: Inculturation and Liberation* (Maryknoll, N.Y.: Orbis, 1993).

32. Bible study on Matt. 5:27-30, 1 December 1989.

33. I use this term in the sense of the Eastern Orthodox tradition, accepting the influential and long-standing criticism of Krister Stendahl that Western theology since Augustine has psychologized our understanding of the faith. Orthodox understandings, on the other hand, are often regarded as dependent on a questionable dualism of spirit/matter. If this is so in some cases, it is not always so, and the criticism itself may depend upon a Western prejudice about Greek thought which is now being brought into question. What I mean by *incarnational* may be related to Ion Bria's notion of the "liturgy of life" in which the rhythms of spiritual life are inextricably and ontologically intertwined with the daily rhythms of material, physical existence. The very notion of dualism disappears in this case. Krister Stendahl, "Paul and the Introspective Conscience of the West," in *Paul among Jews and Gentiles* (Philadelphia: Fortress, 1976); Ion Bria, "The Liturgy after the Liturgy," in *Martyria Mission: The Witness of the Orthodox Church Today,* Ion Bria, ed. (Geneva: World Council of Churches, 1980), 66–71.

34. Bible study on Matt. 6:11, 23 February 1990.

35. Bible study on Luke 4:16-22, 28 October 1988.

36. Bible study on Matt: 5:38-42, 19 January 1990.

37. The violence referred to here reflects the struggle for political ascendancy in KwaZulu-Natal, and Amawoti specifically, between Inkatha, a traditionalist movement connected to an apartheid Bantustan, and others linked with the liberation struggle of the United Democratic Front, the Mass Democratic Movement, and the African National Congress.

38. Bible study on Matt. 27:17-28, 11 May 1990.

39. Bible study on Luke 10:25-37, 12 December 1988.

40. Bible study, 28 October 1988.

41. This judgment is not mine but that of various colleagues in Brazil with whom I had occasion to discuss comparative differences between South Africa and Brazil. One of these differences is the effective reach of oppressive political and bureaucratic apparatuses, established under apartheid and earlier legislation. Extensive control over the life of the most rural village was possible and exercised in practice, so that repressive and discriminatory laws had a direct and immediate impact on the lives of all South Africans. Equally, this elicited reaction, rebellion, and an ongoing struggle reaching across the century and into every last village.

Another contributing factor to the relatively high political awareness of black South Africans is the later impact of colonization in South Africa and thus the more recent memory of another order. As recently as 1906, for example, the last war against colonization, the Bambatha Rebellion, took place.

42. I will not duplicate Philpott's work in demonstrating this, but for those who wish to see the way in which select symbols and images interpret reality, and the way in which a language with categories peculiar to the experiences of the Amawoti BEC arises in the process, chapters 4 and 5 of his book are invaluable. Note also that *truth* in this context is roughly equivalent to "adequate to actual experience." Philpott, *Kin-dom of God.*

43. Averil Cameron, *Christianity and the Rhetoric of Empire: The Development of Christian Discourse* (Berkeley: University of California, 1991).

44. José Severino Croatto, *Biblical Hermeneutics: Toward a Theory of Reading as the Production of Meaning* (Maryknoll, N.Y.: Orbis, 1987), 69.

45. Bible study on Matt. 13:44-52, 21 July 1989.

46. Bible study on Matt. 6:11, 23 February 1990.

47. Jürgen Moltmann, *Hope and Planning* (London: SCM, 1971).

48. Bible study on Matt. 7:24-29, 18 September 1989.

49. Bible study on Luke 18:9-14, 5 May 1989.

50. Bible study on Luke 17:20-21, 11 November 1988.

51. Bible study on Luke 11:42-43, 28 July 1989.

52. Bible study on Luke 18:9-14, 5 May 1989.

53. By this stage in the community's life, Inkatha influence was almost nonexistent, most of that movement's key protagonists having been forced out of Amawoti. It is in reflection on the so-called victory of those loyal to the liberation movements mentioned earlier (see note 38) that this comment is made.

54. Bible study on Matt. 7:24-29, 18 September 1989.

55. Bible study meeting, 20 July 1990.

2. Incipient Theologies as Marginal Reflections on Faith

1. Per Frostin takes this term from Edward Schillebeeckx. Per Frostin, *Liberation Theology in Tanzania and South Africa: A First World Interpretation* (Lund, Sweden: Lund University Press, 1988), 94–95.

2. *Knowledge,* in this case, arises out of the expressive, subjective life of persons, in contrast to other kinds of knowledge such as descriptive (scientific) or normative (moral-juridical). I shall later use the work of Jürgen Habermas to distinguish kinds of knowledge more precisely. Jürgen Habermas, *The Theory of Communicative Action: Reason and the Rationalization of Society,* vol. 1 (Boston: Beacon Press, 1984).

3. Such knowledge, following the terminology of Habermas, may be described as goal-directed communicative activity, informed by a particular worldview out of a concrete life world.

4. Theology is reflection on faith. Faith itself is more than orientation (a matter of will or mind) if it is to be soteriologically significant, for it includes being grasped by a new loyalty, a revitalizing reality, a capacity to overcome the constraints of what is (actuality) in order to realize what is not yet (possibility). But that is not my point here.

5. *Faith* defined in this way does not exhaust its meaning in the history of Christian theology. It fulfils a limited but useful role here, restricted to a phenomenological definition of a human commitment or valuation. Faith, for example, is often defined more formally as that which apprehends us from the side of God rather than as our expression of an encounter with the sacred.

6. An initial sketch of some implications for social reconstruction of this privileging of concrete contexts of struggle for basic needs may be found in James R. Cochrane, "Nation-Building: A Sociotheological View," in *Building a New Nation,* edited by W. S. Vorster. (Pretoria: Unisa, 1991).

7. The choice of the image of the "reign of God" as a central organizing focus rested on a belief that the metaphorical richness of the parables in particular would "create space for the group to generate their own meaning of this important symbol in the Christian tradition": Graham Philpott, *Jesus Is Tricky and God Is Undemocratic: The Kin-dom of God in Amawoti* (Pietermaritzburg, South Africa: Cluster Publications, 1993), 26.

8. Texts reflected here are from Genesis, Exodus, Isaiah, Matthew, Mark, Luke, Romans, and 1 Corinthians.

9. The quotations that follow are taken from the Bible study on Matt. 25–34, 25 May 1990.

10. The persistence of the figure of an active, human person of Jesus strengthens the perspective presented here. These examples come from several Bible studies conducted on the following dates: 28 October 1988, Good Friday 1991, 15 November 1991, 22 November 1991, 12 June 1992, 31 July 1992.

11. These latter points arise from a September 1993 interview with the facilitator, Graham Philpott.

12. In South Africa Kairos theology is a good example. Another, in an earlier period, is Black Theology.

13. Takatso Mofokeng, *The Crucified among the Crossbearers* (Kampen: J. H. Kok, 1983), 243. Of course, the role of this story as an indicator of humble beginnings is hardly new. But Mofokeng's point is more profound than this commonplace. It has to do with a particular kind of determining perspective and commitment in theology.

14. Ibid., 11.

15. Ibid., 21–23.

16. Ibid., 43, 223.

17. Ibid., 226.

18. Ibid., 228.

19. Ibid., 234.

20. Ibid., 236.

21. Bible study on Luke 2:8-20, 15 December 1989.

22. These statements were made during a general discussion on the learnings of the BEC from the Bible study process near the end of 1991, that is, after about two years together.

23. The hermeneutical distinction between the *shape* and *content* of the gospel is borrowed indirectly from Eduard Schillebeeckz through Albert Nolan, who sees these terms as more readily understandable equivalents of the classic distinction between *spirit* and *letter* respectively. Albert Nolan, *God in South Africa: The Challenge of the Gospel* (Grand Rapids, Mich.: Eerdmans, 1988), 7–8.

24. Bible study on 1 Cor. 15:21-22, 11 September 1992. I will suggest below that the place of ancestors needs theological redemption too.

25. Bonganjalo Goba, *An Agenda for Black Theology: Hermeneutics for Social Change* (Johannesburg: Skotaville, 1988).

26. Anthony O. Balcomb, *Third Way Theology: Reconciliation, Revolution and Reform in the South African Church* (Pietermaritzburg, South Africa: Cluster Publications, 1993).

27. Bible study on Luke 4:1-13, 21 October 1988. Of course, there is the danger in such images of demonizing the other to the extent that any sense of common humanity is lost, and a crude, merciless justice applied, perhaps even mistakenly.

28. Bible study on Luke 4:16-22, 28 October 1988.

29. Bible study on Matt. 6:11, 23 February 1990.

30. Tillich's view, using the Greek notions of being and non-being, could be read to imply that non-being (which has no power as such), rather than the power of evil, is all that opposes a positive view of power. This would leave in question the reality of negative power as evil and not just the absence of good. However, one may also read the idea of non-being as a metaphor for the effect of the power of evil on human beings, analogous to the notion of dehumanization.

31. Bible study on Luke 11:1-8, 16 December 1988.

32. Bible study on Matt. 10:26-31, 6 October 1989.

33. Jürgen Moltmann, *Hope and Planning* (London: SCM, 1971); Jürgen Moltmann, *The Experiment Hope* (Philadelphia: Fortress, 1975).

34. Bible study on Luke 11:1-13, 9 December 1988.

35. Nolan, *God in South Africa*.

36. Ibid., 158–59.

37. Bible study session (general), Good Friday, 1991.

38. Bible study on Matt. 6:9-10, 16 February 1990.

39. I am indebted to my colleague Klaus Nürnberger for this insight.

40. Bible study on Luke 17:20-21, 11 November 1988.

41. Bible study session (general), Good Friday, 1991.

42. Extracted from general discussions, 15 November 1991, about an Easter march earlier in the year, and the meaning of the life of the group during the course of their time together.

43. A video film of the march, *Amaoti: Place of Suffering and Hope*, was made by John Crossley, Media Resource Center, University of Natal, 1991.

44. Mary Grey, *Redeeming the Dream: Feminism, Redemption and Christian Tradition* (London: SPCK, 1989), 4.

45. Bible study on Luke 22:7-23, 10 March 1989.

46. In Martin Jay, *The Dialectical Imagination: A History of the Frankfurt School and the Institute of Social Research 1923–1950* (London: Heinemann, 1973), 104ff.

47. Both German words when translated into English mean "experience" or "event"; the distinction is only maintained by using the German words.

48. Jay, *Dialectical Imagination*, 208.

49. Ibid., 209.

50. (cf. Draper 1994)

51. Monosemy (one meaning) emerges only in relation to a specific locus of interpretation or context of the interpreter.

52. This way of putting it, a play on Ricoeur's famous aphorism that "the symbol gives rise to thought," was suggested to me by Theodore Jennings. It is a precise and helpful way of describing much of the work of this book.

3. Tradition and Domination

1. The early debate about the ministry of Paul, initially questioned by the Jerusalem leadership, indicates both a tension in this communicative practice (as expressed in the doubts about Paul's missionary enterprise) and finally, a ratification of it.

2. Theodore W. Jennings, *Introduction to Theology: An Invitation to Reflection Upon the Christian Mythos* (London: SPCK and Philadelphia: Fortress, 1976).

3. Itumeleng Mosala, *Biblical Hermeneutics and Black Theology in South Africa* (Grand Rapids, Mich.: Eerdmans, 1989).

4. Jaroslav Pelikan, *The Christian Tradition: A History of the Development of Doctrine, I* (Chicago: Chicago University Press, 1971), 309, for example, notes that there were "many questions of church organization, religious persecution, and even social and tribal rivalry raised by Donatism," but in the several pages he devotes to the controversy, no further mention is made of these questions. A history of ideas wholly replaces the social history of the church here, hiding all matters of the link between power and knowledge in the process.

5. W. H. C. Frend, *Martyrdom and Persecution in the Early Church: A Study of Conflict from the Maccabees to Donatus* (Oxford: Blackwell, 1965), 46.

6. W. H. C. Frend, *The Donatist Church: A Movement of Protest in Roman North Africa* (Oxford: Clarendon, 1985), 242–3.

7. G. Mokhtar, ed., *Ancient Civilizations of Africa. General History of Africa, II* (Berkeley: University of California Press, 1990), 279.

8. David J. Bosch, *Transforming Mission: Paradigm Shifts in Theology of Mission* (Maryknoll, N.Y.: Orbis, 1991), 216.

9. Krister Stendahl, "Paul and the Introspective Conscience of the West," in *Paul among Jews and Gentiles* (Philadelphia: Fortress, 1976).

10. James C. Scott, *Domination and the Arts of Resistance: Hidden Transcripts* (New Haven, Conn.: Yale University Press, 1990).

11. Perhaps the French Annales School is the most extensive modern attempt to overcome the problems associated with recovering popular history. The school has had a primary concern to recover economic and social history, but their methods have focused on collecting extensive detailed data at a micro level on the popular perspectives of the times they investigate, for example, in what is inscribed on gravestones.

12. Scott, *Domination and the Arts of Resistance*; Jean Comaroff and John Comaroff, *Of Revelation and Revolution: Christianity, Colonialism and Consciousness in South Africa* (Chicago: University of Chicago Press, 1991). Also, see chapter 2 in this work.

13. An interesting example of a counterview to Mosala's, in his own field and from another South African, may be found in the ongoing work of Gunther Wittenberg, who argues for a fairly clear trajectory of resistance theology in the records of the First Testament. An exemplary argument may be found in "King Solomon and the Theologians," Inaugural Professorial Lecture presented to the University of Natal, Pietermaritzburg, August 1987, published 1988. A more recent contribution, "The Relevance of Historical Geography for Old Testament Theology with Special Reference to Exodus 34:10-26" (paper presented at Society for Historical Geography, Stellenbosch, South Africa, March 1995), focuses on the "socio-spatial dialectic" of Old Testament theology, and what Wittenberg calls "the struggle

for authoritative resources" (in addition to allocative resources) concentrated in the city and the temple. The "cultic decalogue" of Exodus 3 is thereby reinterpreted as a document of a village-based resistance movement centering on the prophets Elijah and Elisha, and on levitical circles. The "whole document can be understood as reflecting the opposition against the ordering of time-space in the official state cult of Baal." On this reading, the Sabbath commandment reflects a counterhegemonic statement against the state cults control over time and space.

14. Emmanuel Martey, *African Theology: Inculturation and Liberation* (Maryknoll, N.Y.: Orbis, 1993).

15. Every black and white South African who was educated under the authority of the Nationalist Party apartheid government's narrow, racist educational system was told that this was Christian National Education.

16. Bible study on Matt. 5:27-30, 1 December 1989. Whether this claim is true of intact African traditions—and, it probably is not—is not the point here.

17. Bible study on Rom. 5:12-14, 1 Cor. 15:21-22, and Gen. 2:16-17, 11 September 1992.

18. George Lindbeck, *The Nature of Doctrine: Religion and Theology in a Postliberal Age* (Philadelphia: Westminster Press, 1984). Sharon Welch, in different words, suggests that Lindbeck "evades two fundamental problems: (1) the determinative effect in theological work of the theologian's own social and political location within the cultural-linguistic matrix, and (2) the possibility that the 'grammar of faith' is itself oppressive." Sharon D. Welch, *A Feminist Ethic of Risk* (Minneapolis: Fortress Press, 1990), 106.

19. That they are mediated (by me) is inevitable. As Paul Ricoeur has noted, the sense in which the authors of the text have already "died," the interaction between my world and the world projected by the texts, and the consequent creative interpretive activity of mine produce a different understanding from that of the community itself. Paul Ricoeur, *From Text to Action: Essays in Hermeneutics II* (Evanston, Ill.: Northwestern University Press, 1991).

20. In using this language, I do not mean to imply that ecclesial organization, which has to cope with and master as best as possible a wide variety of functions, processes, and procedures, is wrong if not egalitarian. Organizational models may vary considerably in type and structure, and they may include a hierarchy of functions and roles without necessarily producing elitist or oppressive patterns of relations. Countering tendencies to elitism and domination, however, necessarily requires open structures and particular sensitivities to those most disadvantaged by those structures. This is the real challenge, one which is not very often met well.

21. Juan Luis Segundo, *The Liberation of Theology,* John Drury, trans. (Dublin: Gill & Macmillan, 1977).

22. Juan Luis Segundo, *The Liberation of Dogma: Faith, Revelation, and Dogmatic Teaching Authority,* Phillip Berryman, trans. (Maryknoll, N.Y.: Orbis, 1992).

23. Ibid., 76–77.

24. Comaroff, *Of Revelation and Revolution,* 17.

25. Mosala, *Biblical Hermeneutics.*

26. See chapter 5, on power and relations of power, for a critique of macro theories of society and a development of this point.

27. One wonders what feminist hermeneutics would make of Segundo's approach. If, as feminist scholars argue, the scriptures are fundamentally patriarchal—not just in their content, but in the kinds of pedagogies (learning to learn) they exhibit—then surely there can be no talk of an infallible pedagogy in the tradition.

28. Ronald Nicolson, *A Black Future? Jesus and Salvation in South Africa* (London: SCM, 1990).

29. The source of his questions is in fact a real person in the kind of context he describes, but the book he constructs is his own interpretation of the significance of, and possible responses to, these questions. In this sense, the "dialogue" is imaginary.

30. Nicolson, *A Black Future?*, 216.

31. Nicolson, *A Black Future?*, 78.

32. Rubem A. Alves, *Protestantism and Repression: A Brazilian Case Study* (London: SCM, 1985), xiv.

33. Ibid., xv.

34. Ibid., 205.

35. Ibid., 206.

36. Ibid., xvii.

37. Jürgen Moltmann, *A Theology of Hope* (New York: Harper & Row, 1967). Whether this phenomenon is the result of individualism itself, or the squeezing out of public life of destabilizing religious claims by a hegemonic, popular secular culture (for example, liberalism), the point remains.

38. The Markan eschatological image of the earth groaning in anticipation of the new creation makes the link overt. Paul's discussion in Rom. 8:22-24 makes the same point, linking the "groaning of creation in childbirth" with the "redemption of our bodies."

39. Pastoral psychology is slowly incorporating this insight in a shift to family therapy and community psychology, under the impact of the realization that brokenness is never a phenomenon isolated from the larger human and physical environment.

40. Some indication of this linkage has already been made in chapter 2, and it will be strengthened by discussions still to come.

41. The formation in 1980 of the Institute for Contextual Theology, established in Johannesburg but with support from other major centers in South Africa, contributed powerfully to the popularization of the term. What is not well known is that the term *contextual* was adopted at the time, among other reasons, simply because it was more dangerous, at that time of excessive repression, to use terms such as liberation and the like. The very vagueness of the term was its strength.

42. Anselm Min, *Dialectic of Salvation: Issues in Theology of Liberation* (New York: State University of New York Press, 1989).

43. Gustavo Gutiérrez, *The Power of the Poor in History: Selected Writings* (London: SCM, 1983); Jon Sobrino, *The True Church and the Poor* (London: SCM, 1985); Jorgé Pixley and Clodivus Boff, *The Bible, the Church and the Poor: Biblical, Theological and Pastoral Aspects of the Option for the Poor* (Turnbridge Wells, Kent: Burns & Oates, 1989); Min, *Dialectic of Salvation.*

44. Karl Barth, Introduction to *The Essence of Christianity,* by L. Feuerbach (New York: Harper & Row, 1957), xxiv.

45. Dietrich Bonhoeffer, *Ethics* (New York: Macmillan, 1976), 25ff.

46. A good example of such criticism comes from Klaus Nürnberger, who argues for a new interpretation of the Chalcedonian formula on the grounds that the original doctrinal statement, one most definitive of the notion of dogma, is "neither plausible in our patterns of thought, nor functional in the problems we face in our times. It is also not biblical." Nürnberger wants to retain the essential point of Chalcedon, that Jesus Christ is one person in two natures, but the direction he takes uses a language wholly unlike that of Chalcedon and it has radical implications for what the "two natures" doctrine means. Klaus Nürnberger, "The Son Can Do Nothing by Himself: Identification and Authority as Modern Interpretations of the Doctrine of a Divine and Human Nature in the One Person of Christ," *Journal of Theology for Southern Africa* 87 (June 1994): 11.

47. Richard Horsley is a widely influential scholar who adopts this approach. See Richard Horsley, with J. S. Hanson, *Bandits, Prophets and Messiahs: Popular Movements at the Time of Jesus* (San Francisco: Harper, 1988; and Richard Horsley, *Sociology of the Jesus Movement* (New York: Continuum, 1994).

48. Jonathan A. Draper, "Jesus and the Renewal of Local Community in Galilee: Challenge to a Communitarian Christology," *Journal of Theology for Southern Africa* 87 (1994): 29–42.

49. To be fair to Bultmann, one must point out that his extreme view of the centrality of the *kerygma* did not imply complete discontinuity with the historical Jesus. See Rudolph Bultmann, "The Primitive Christian Kerygma and the Historical Jesus," in *The Historical Jesus and the Kerygmatic Christ,* Carl Braaten and R. Harrisville, eds. (Nashville: Abingdon, 1964), 18.

50. On the problem of theism, a technical term for the conceptions of God that arose in post-Reformation metaphysics, see Theodore W. Jennings, *Beyond Theism: A Grammar of God-Language* (New York: Cambridge University Press, 1985); and Janet Soskice, *Metaphor and Religious Language* (Oxford: Clarendon, 1985).

51. The idea of mutually critical correlations between contemporary experience and Christian classics, of course, is that of David Tracy. See David Tracy, *The Analogical Imagination: Christian Theology and the Culture of Pluralism* (London: SCM, 1981).

52. The idea of conversation present in hermeneutics often hides the problem of power relations. Conversation implies an encounter between relative equals, but power relations are usually anything but equal. We will return to this issue later, particularly in chapter 6.

53. Compare Martin Mandew, "Power and Empowerment: Religious Imagination and the Life of a Local Base Ecclesial Community" (master's thesis, University of Natal, 1993).

54. Speaking of a broken community emphasizes that the Christian tradition expresses not a history of harmonious relations, but a complicated history of contestation and struggle within the church itself, and from without it. Moreover, this history cannot be abstracted from the social history of the church, including the effects of political and economic powers on church polity and practice. Going further, I take it that a definition of the community of Christians as broken is not merely a descriptive statement, but an anthropological one that could be discussed under the theological category of sin.

55. Douglas R. McGaughey, *Strangers and Pilgrims: On the Role of Aporiai in Theology* (New York & Berlin: De Gruyter, 1997), 482.

56. Ibid., 443ff, chapter on "Conclusion: Faith in A Post-Metaphysical Context," and 213ff, chapter on "The Aporia of Spirit and Matter" which deals with Plato's simile of the line and notion of universals.

57. Ibid., 447ff.

58. As McGaughey puts it, the epistemological fault finds expression in theology in terms of two sources of knowledge about God: revealed and natural. Nature can teach about the creation of God, but not about the purpose or meaning of life. Hence, revelation complements nature by providing an empirical source of information about salvation, the scriptures. "Truth is learned either from nature or from the scriptures, i.e., there are and must be empirical warrants and backings for all truth claims." McGaughey, *Strangers and Pilgrims*, 445.

59. Ibid., 443, 454. The original simile may be found in Book VI of *The Republic*.

60. McGaughey suggests that the wrong interpretation of Plato, upon which follows a wrong understanding of the much later neo-Platonism and its interaction with Christian theology, arises precisely because the allegory of the cave, which follows in book VII, is not read in the context of the simile of the line. If it were, it could not be interpreted as suggesting that ideas are real and materiality is the mere reflection of ideas or universals.

61. Universals are what our consciousness needs in order to make sense out of the phenomenological flow of events, which otherwise become nonsense in a plethora of independent, arbitrary, and incoherent stimuli without differentiation. Thus universals establish the difference and identity of phenomena by providing us with the coherence we need to make sense of things. It is only in this way that they are universal, however. Universals are not in themselves absolutes, eternal constants, or ontological entities. They remain tentative, ambiguous. Though they establish coherence between things, they cannot themselves be clearly defined. So, for example, we learn to know what a tree is, and can recognize one even if we have never seen its particular type before, but we cannot show in what way all trees are definitively different from all other objects. Botanical categorizations attempt a definitive classification, but their distinctions are themselves chosen selectively within a particular scientific paradigm.

Universals, then, are ultimately indefinable, even though we cannot use them as if they point to definite realities. This becomes the point of Plato's allegory of the cave, which follows directly upon the simile of the line, rather than the usual interpretation of ideas as substantial and materiality as imprecise reflections of ideas.

62. McGaughey, *Strangers and Pilgrims*, 463.

63. Ibid., 458. McGaughey argues that pragmatism fails not because it offers an untenable test of material reality, but because it does not apply the same test to spiritual reality. As he puts it, "try ignoring the paradigmatic universals by which one is able to understand anything and see what happens."

64. Ibid., 450 n. 14.

65. Ibid., 464.

66. Ibid., 460.

67. In the realization that the actualization of one possibility prevents the actualization of other possibilities, one has the epistemological basis for what Habermas calls the "systematic distortion" of communication and action. But, unlike Habermas's project, which seeks to find a model of communicative competence capable of overcoming this limit, this

distortion is also ontological. There is no way around it, for it is the nature of reality. A more limited version of Habermas's systematic distortion may nevertheless be granted as of particular importance, namely, the kinds of distortion that result from the imposition of a manipulative, calculating consciousness which presses its hegemony upon all. This is the point at which a hermeneutics of suspicion becomes vital.

68. Paul Ricoeur, quoted in McGaughey, *Strangers and Pilgrims*, 462.

69. Ibid., 458.

70. There are many Christian traditions, as we have noted earlier, but all mark their claim to be Christian by identifying with some subgroup or other of a broadly definable range of symbols, images, and narratives. Tradition in the singular can thus only be understood along the lines of Ludwig Wittgenstein's well-known notion of family resemblances, and not as a fixed entity.

71. Philippe Denis, for example, points to the view of Vincent of Lerins, a fifth-century writer who argued that "care must be taken that we hold the faith which has been believed everywhere, always and by all." Properly understood, this is not a call to find and hold onto some essential faith by which the people may be corrected, but rather a recognition that what is believed by the people must be taken seriously in the construction of doctrine and, as Denis notes in a development of this argument in later Catholic theory, in its reception. In respect of the latter notion of reception, Denis points out that a doctrine not "received" by local believers—having no impact on them and their understanding of the faith—is a "serious indication that something is wrong . . . with this definition." See Philippe Denis, "Is Democracy Good for the Church? Reflections of an Historian," *Journal of Theology for Southern Africa* 83 (1993): 51, 52.

72. McGaughey thus points out that we need "to speak of God as possibility, i.e., as no-thing, out of which every-thing emerges. This is a *creatio ex nihilo* that is continuous and commences with possibility rather than Aristotelian actuality, i.e., rather than Aristotle's Unmoved Mover which is actual . . . or Process thought's primordial nature . . . of God." He also notes that the key to Descartes's logical arguments for the existence of both the world and of God depend upon the assumption that "something cannot come from nothing." This is the trap of materialist epistemologies from which one cannot escape if one stays with the notion of reality as encompassing only actualities and not possibilities. McGaughey, *Strangers and Pilgrims*, 459 n. 37, 465 n. 45.

73. Ibid., 471, 472 n. 56. In a footnote, McGaughey points out that the Greek distinctions between *nous* (consciousness or reason in Plato's simile of the line), *logos* (the structuring system of universals), and *nomos* (law) help us understand the theologies of Paul and John. In Greek thinking *nous* is higher than either *logos* or *nomos*. I would add that consciousness as understood here is higher than either the paradigms of the tradition (in its texts, creeds, confessions, and so on) or the rules or laws it expounds (in catechisms, canons, disciplinary codes, and the like). This underlines the general point I am making about the role of context, experience, and suppressed knowledge in the shaping of theology.

4. Asymmetries of Power

1. Jean Comaroff and John Comaroff. *Of Revelation and Revolution: Christianity, Colonialism and Consciousness in South Africa* (Chicago: University of Chicago Press, 1991), xii.

2. See Anthony O. Balcomb, *Third Way Theology: Reconciliation, Revolution and Reform in the South African Church* (Pietermaritzburg, South Africa: Cluster Publications, 1993).

3. *Formal power* designates the exercise of power associated with institutional authorities of the state, the economy, and civil society. Formal power is the steering medium, alongside money (see Jürgen Habermas, *The Theory of Communicative Action: Reason and the Rationalization of Society,* vol. 1 [Boston: Beacon Press, 1984]), by which a social system is held in place or defended. A more complex, more nuanced notion of power will emerge during the rest of our discussion.

4. Martin Mandew, "Power and Empowerment: Religious Imagination and the Life of a Local Base Ecclesial Community" (master's thesis, University of Natal, 1993).

5. Theodore W. Jennings, *Introduction to Theology: An Invitation to Reflection Upon the Christian Mythos* (London: SPCK and Philadelphia: Fortress, 1976), 44ff.

6. Mandew, "Power and Empowerment," 83ff.

7. These included sectors of the two campuses of the University of Natal, particularly the Built Environment Support Group in Durban and the Farmers Support Group in Pietermaritzburg.

8. Jürgen Habermas, *Knowledge and Human Interests* (Boston: Beacon, 1971). As those who have read, or read about, Habermas will know, he posited three "knowledge-constitutive interests" in this earlier work: empirical-analytical interests that produce technical and instrumental knowledge; historical-hermeneutical interests that produce practical knowledge (in the Kantian sense); and emancipatory interests that produce critical knowledge. His later two-volume work, *The Theory of Communicative Action* (Habermas, *The Theory of Communicative Action: Reason and the Rationalization of Society,* vol. 1 [Boston: Beacon Press, 1984]); Habermas, *The Theory of Communicative Action: Lifeworld and System: A Critique of Functionalist Reason,* Vol 2 [Boston: Beacon Press, 1987]), altered this framework somewhat, though retaining some of its key impulses.

9. For a longer description of the Ilimo Project and the BEC, refer to chapter 2.

10. All of them withdrew from the project over time, primarily because they did not like losing control to the community, which feared their questionable political activity. These churches, unfortunately, thus lent credibility to the views of the state on such projects, and themselves never understood their own responsibility for society.

11. Mandew, "Power and Empowerment," 90ff.

12. *Iqembu likaFundaWenze* in the original Zulu.

13. Mandew, "Power and Empowerment," 99ff.

14. AIC leaders appear to have been somewhat more positive about the way in which the marches were conducted, including their overtly political content, than were a few ministers of Settler Origin Churches. As the BEC evaluation of the marches notes (Bible study evaluation session, 20 November 1992): "The ministers who were genuinely pleased about the march were those who belong to the churches of the spirit [Zionist]. Those who belong to the churches of the law [the so-called mainline churches] were not happy. . . . The Zionist

ministers are much closer to the people." Also worth noting is that the marchers were joined in 1992 by members of Isaiah Shembe's *AmaNazareta* (Nazarites) Church from its nearby headquarters at Ekuphakemeni.

15. Mandew, "Power and Empowerment," 103ff.

16. Ibid., 108–9.

17. Bible study evaluation session, 20 November 1991.

18. Comaroff and Comaroff, *Of Revelation and Revolution*, 25.

19. The citations from transcripts of biblical studies that follow therefore should not be seen as an analysis of a defined group perspective. Rather, they serve the heuristic role of enabling me to raise questions. In this sense, they provide only nascent clues to possible answers. But, inasmuch as they are clues drawn from the interpretive activity of the BEC, the discussion that follows also represents a second-order level of dialogue with the perspectives of that group.

20. Bible study on Luke 4:1-13, 28 October 1988.

21. "Jesus is encouraging people—even though they are small, they can help." Bible study on Luke 13:18-21, 4 November 1988.

22. Bible study on Luke 11:1-8, 16 December 1988.

23. The Farmers Support Group, affiliated with the University of Natal.

24. Bible study on Matt. 10:26-31, 6 October 1989.

25. Bible study on Matt. 10:1-10, 20 October 1989.

26. Extended discussions around each of these aspects are carried out in Bible studies of 11 November 1988, 12 May 1989, 21 July 1989, 18 September 1989, 16 February 1990, and 20 July 1990.

27. Bible study on Matt. 6:11, 23 February 1990.

28. Michel Foucault, *Power/Knowledge: Selected Interviews and Other Writings, 1972-1977* (New York: Pantheon, 1980).

29. Habermas, *Knowledge and Human Interests.*

30. Raymond Williams, *Keywords: A Vocabulary of Culture and Society* (London: Oxford University Press, 1976).

31. Foucault, *Power/Knowledge,* 142.

32. Ibid., 60.

33. Ibid., 98.

34. Comaroff and Comaroff, *Of Revelation and Revolution,* 22.

35. Ibid., 24.

36. Ibid., 314.

37. We might generally apply the insight in other parts of Africa too, and current dialogues on the tension between inculturation and liberation approaches offer hope of further developments (noting that this dialogue began in the early 1970s, at least, for example, in the essay by Akin J. Omoyajowo, "An African Expression of Christianity," in *Essays in Black Theology,* Mokgethi Motlhabi, ed. (Johannesburg: University Christian Movement, 1972).

38. Glenda Kruss, "Religion, Class and Culture: Indigenous Churches in South Africa, with Special Reference to Zionist-Apostolics" (Ph.D. diss., University of Cape Town, 1985).

39. James Kiernan, "The Healing Community and the Future of the Urban Working Class," in "The Contribution of South Africa's Religions to the Coming South Africa"

(conference proceedings, Department of Religious Studies, Pietermaritzburg: University of Natal, 1993): 2–4.

40. This last aspect, the control of promiscuity, Kiernan believes to be potentially one of the most important weapons available to contemporary South African society in its rapidly spreading battle against AIDS.

41. Kiernan, "Healing Community," 9.

42. James Kiernan, "The Management of a Complex Religious Identity: The Case of Zulu Zionism," *Religion in Southern Africa* 7, 2 (July 1986): 9.

43. Bible study on Rom. 5:12-14 and 1 Cor. 15:21-22, 11 September 1992. On one recorded occasion, a certain African tradition came under fire. In this tradition a woman has to ask her uncle or grandfather to act as intermediary to the ancestors, who in turn acted as intermediaries to God (*Mvelingqangi*). This was described as a "gap" that Jesus had now destroyed, giving everyone (in this case, women) the right to "talk with God" directly.

44. In South Africa, for example, the impact of systematically applied migratory labor policies on rural and semirural communities has been profound and of long duration. Since the early 1910s, at the latest, this system has been widely applied, and it found expression in proposed formal policy as early as in the work of the South African Native Affairs Commission, which sat under the leadership Sir Godfrey Lagden between 1903 and 1905 after the Anglo-Boer War.

45. Jean Comaroff, *Body of Power, Spirit of Resistance: The Culture and History of a South African People* (Chicago: University of Chicago Press, 1985), 154.

46. Ibid., 155. Like Foucault, Comaroff does not think this implies that relations of power are equal; in fact, she describes the articulation between the Tshidi world and the colonial order "profoundly unequal."

47. Ibid., 156.

48. Ibid., 253.

49. Behind this formulation lies a problem not addressed by this essay: that of the reality of overarching social concepts such as systems, cultures, paradigms, the collective unconscious, ideal types, and the like. Stephen Turner (*The Social Theory of Practices: Tradition, Tacit Knowledge, and Presuppositions* [Chicago: University of Chicago Press, 1994]) argues with some force that these concepts are empirically empty in the strict sense that they are theoretical constructs to which no identifiable objects can be attached. Social theories take the effects of consensus as the basis for retrogressively asserting causes, but these causes can never be empirically determined. Moreover, for any effect there may be numerous theoretically possible and plausible causes, each possessing the same empirical indeterminacy. Instead, he proposes that an equally plausible and far less epistemologically flawed interpretation of society would rely on a notion of habits—mental traces—formed in individuals as the identifiable phenomena. The implications of this argument, if Turner is right, are substantial.

50. Comaroff, *Body of Power, Spirit of Resistance,* 253.

51. Foucault, *Power/Knowledge,* 60.

52. Comaroff, *Body of Power, Spirit of Resistance,* 261.

53. Ibid., 263.

54. Some commentators define popular religion as a general mind-set linked to collective behavior which receives some kind of transcendent or anthropological legitimation through symbols, slogans, rituals, and the like, analogous to what happens in an established religion. Thus secular liberal culture may be defined as the popular religion of many developed Western capitalist societies. But perhaps the notion of civil religion implicit here is too general, and certainly I use the term *popular religion* in the more limited sense of distinguishing the religious beliefs, values, and practices of people of a particular faith from the formally taught tenets of that faith.

55. Erhard Kamphausen, *Anfänge der kirchlichen Unabhängigkeitsbewegung in Südafrika: Geschichte und Theologie der Äthiopischen Bewegung, 1872–1912* (Frankfurt: Peter Lang, 1976).

56. In my earlier book *Servants of Power: The Role of English-Speaking Churches in South Africa, 1903–1930* (Johannesburg: Ravan, 1987), this thinking is demonstrated in another way, namely, in my use of then current historiographical models, drawn from a Marxian revisionist interpretation of South African history. Because these models often depended quite heavily on a binary model of consciousness, they made it difficult to account for the complex and nuanced expressions of resistance which are not overtly political or consciously intended as such. Thus my use of archival records of the Anglican and Methodist churches, aimed primarily at structural-functionalist interpretations of the texts I read, did not develop any insight into specific, local, and more nuanced readings of these texts and their originators. (Such insight may be found in Comaroff and Comaroff, *Of Revelation and Revolution.*) My purpose at the time, to be sure, was precisely to confront the English-speaking churches with their own location in structures of power; nevertheless, a more complex analysis of power may have been more helpful in doing so.

57. One of the strongest influences in this direction, in Africa and other parts of the so-called Two-thirds World, came from Albert Memmi's evocative and provocative study of hegemony and ideology in Algeria, *The Colonizer and the Colonized,* expanded ed. (Boston: Beacon, 1991).

58. Comaroff and Comaroff, *Of Revelation and Revolution,* 19ff, 25.

59. Ibid., 20–27.

60. Just such a counterrevolutionary example—the honorary visit of President P. W. Botha to the annual gathering of the Zion Christian Church, by far the largest AIC in South Africa—provides the occasion for delimiting the problem in Petersen's study of the significance for the prophetic church of the AICs (1995). See Robin Petersen, "Time, Resistance and Reconstruction: Rethinking Kairos Theology in South Africa," (Ph.D. diss., University of Chicago, 1995).

61. Petersen's own well-substantiated view is that Itumeleng Mosala's work on the AICs offers us the only developed analysis from theologians of any kind to date, though he takes issue with Mosala in respect of his understanding of power. See Petersen, "Time, Resistance and Reconstruction," 105ff.

62. Takatso Mofokeng, "Black Theology in South Africa: Achievements, Problems and Prospects," in *Christianity in South Africa,* Martin Prozesky, ed. (London: MacMillan, 1990), 41, 49.

63. Comaroff, *Body of Power, Spirit of Resistance,* 261.

64. Comaroff and Comaroff, *Of Revelation and Revolution,* 28.

65. Ibid.

66. Bible study on Luke 18:35-43, 2 June 1989.

67. James C. Scott, *Domination and the Arts of Resistance: Hidden Transcripts* (New Haven, Conn.: Yale University Press, 1990), 20.

68. It should be noted that Scott's approach emphasizes that dominant groups also have their hidden transcripts.

69. Nelson Mandela, *Long Walk to Freedom: The Autobiography of Nelson Mandela* (London: Little, Brown, 1994).

70. Scott's work reflects assessments made in strongly oppressive contexts where domination and subjugation stand out as key features of the social landscape. Where this is not the case, infrapolitical activity and discourse may not be strongly masked, and hidden transcripts may be rarer or easier to access. Even where oppression is a dominant feature, however, some anthropologists would question whether things are really as hidden as Scott suggests. Despite these caveats, Scott's basic insights remain particularly fruitful.

71. Scott, *Domination and the Arts of Resistance,* 103.

72. These three controls correspond to the three "modes of reading" the Bible described by Gerald West (*Biblical Hermeneutics of Liberation: Modes of Reading the Bible.* 2nd ed. [Maryknoll, N.Y.: Orbis, 1995]): reading "behind the text" (historical critical tools aimed at getting to the human and environmental context); reading "in the text" (semantic, philological, and literary structures of the text itself); and reading "in front of the text" (reader response, rhetorical criticism).

73. Itumeleng Mosala's biblical hermeneutics, characteristically defined by a radical suspicion of all biblical texts as texts written by the dominant or ruling classes and therefore unrepresentative of the oppressed or subordinate groups of people, may be said to work with a decision to regard the hidden transcript as the locus of truth. Of course, the hidden transcript resists interpretation precisely because it is hidden, so it is not surprising that Mosala is able to find few scripture verses, if any, he could regard as valid and valuable for the oppressed. See Mosala, *Biblical Hermeneutics and Black Theology in South Africa* (Grand Rapids, Mich.: Eerdmans, 1989).

From Scott's point of view, this would place too much emphasis on the hidden transcript as the only locus of languages or "arts" of resistance, making it impossible to understand the complex and mutually determining nature of power relations between the dominant and the subordinate classes. In other words, it does not match empirical evidence taken from contexts of domination in his anthropological investigations. As Scott puts it, "Power relations are not . . . so straightforward that we can call what is said in power-laden contexts false and what is said offstage true. Nor can we simplistically describe the former as a realm of necessity and the latter as a realm of freedom." Scott, *Domination and the Arts of Resistance,* 5.

74. Comaroff and Comaroff, *Of Revelation and Revolution,* 31.

75. Ibid.

76. Scott, *Domination and the Arts of Resistance,* 138.

77. Ibid., 90.

78. George Herbert Mead, *Mind, Self and Society* (Chicago: University of Chicago Press, 1934). The relationship of the self to the "generalized other," a key feature of Mead's social

theory when linked with other writings of his, allows us to draw the conclusion that the self, in its identity, is powerfully constructed by a changing but also enduring body of other people whose lives function as significant models of the kind of person we would like to be. We internalize our perception of them and draw upon these internalized images in order to orient ourselves.

5. Voices of the Other

1. Paul Ricoeur, *Oneself as Another,* K. Blamey, trans. (Chicago: University of Chicago Press, 1992), 22.

2. By *fiction* here I mean deceit, or something not real but illusory. In a second sense all human life is a fiction insofar as it is made, constructed, shaped in language and behavior. It is not a negative term, but a pointer to the nature of our reality as always interpreted. In fact, I would argue that the narrative this book represents is fiction in the second sense, and is thus good fiction.

3. I am indebted to Theodore Jennings for pointing out the need to make these distinctions.

4. Gerald West prefers to substitute the term *speaking with* for the term *speaking to* in contexts where the encounter between trained and untrained readers of the Bible take place. Where the trained person is organically one of the local community, this seems to make sense. But where this is not so (as is most commonly the case of clergy in many churches, for example), the preposition *with* seems too strong an indication of common identity. I use West's term here because it implies mutuality, but elsewhere I use *speaking to* because it more clearly retains the sense of permanent tension I believe to be present in such encounters. See Gerald O. West, *Biblical Hermeneutics of Liberation: Modes of Reading the Bible,* 2nd ed. (Maryknoll, N.Y.: Orbis, 1995).

5. Bible study on Luke 17:20-21, 11 November 1988.

6. Anselm Min, *Dialectic of Salvation: Issues in Theology of Liberation* (New York: State University of New York Press, 1989), 53–56. My own work approximates the first model, my research assistant moved toward a partial realization of the second model, and the facilitator of the Bible studies exemplifies the third model.

7. Bible study on Matt. 7:24-29, 18 September 1989, and on Matt. 5:13-16, 26 August 1989.

8. Bible study on Matt. 6:11, 23 February 1990.

9. Gayatri Spivak,"Can the Subaltern Speak?" in *Marxism and the Interpretation of Culture,* C. Nelson and L. Grossberg, eds. (London: MacMillan, 1988), 271–73.

10. The poor is a contentious category, seen by Black theologians in South Africa as another theoretical fulcrum whereby white liberal theology may avoid facing racism or the term *black* as the definition of oppression. The poor is a sociologically imprecise category, but so is the term *black,* I believe. Both are polemical in our context. Although I prefer other terms, I use *the poor* as a commonly recognized heuristic device and a more general indicator

to subordinate groups within structures of domination, including such groups as women, the materially poor, and blacks. Sexism, classism, racism—one might add groups such as the aged, gays and lesbians, the physically challenged, and so on, as often subject to significant structures and practices of domination—are key issues in this context.

11. Spivak, "Can the Subaltern Speak?" 275.

12. West, *Biblical Hermeneutics of Liberation*.

13. James R. Cochrane and Gerald O. West, "War, Remembrance and Reconstruction," *Journal of Theology for Southern Africa* 84 (1993): 25–40.

14. Gustavo Gutiérrez, *The Theology of Liberation* (Maryknoll, N.Y.: Orbis, 1973), ix. See also Per Frostin, *Liberation Theology in Tanzania and South Africa: A First World Interpretation* (Lund, Sweden: Lund University Press, 1988), 201.

15. Frostin, *Liberation Theology in Tanzania*, 6.

16. Ibid., 7–8.

17. Ibid., 6.

18. Min, *Dialectic of Salvation*, 70–72.

19. Bible study on Isa. 61:1-2; 35:5-6, 30 August 1991.

20. Bible study on Luke 19:29-44, 3 March 1989.

21. See Schubert M. Ogden, *Faith and Freedom: Toward a Theology of Liberation* (Belfast: Christian Journals, 1979) and Schubert M. Ogden, "The Concept of a Theology of Liberation: Must a Christian Theology Today Be so Conceived?" in *The Challenge of Liberation Theology: A First World Response,* B. Mahan and L. D. Richesin, eds. (Maryknoll, N.Y.: Orbis, 1981).

22. See Sharon D. Welch, *Communities of Resistance and Solidarity: A Feminist Theology of Liberation* (Maryknoll, N.Y.: Orbis, 1985) and Sharon D. Welch, *A Feminist Ethic of Risk* (Minneapolis: Fortress Press, 1990).

23. Welch, *Communities of Resistance and Solidarity.*

24. Elisabeth Schüssler Fiorenza, "Commitment and Critical Inquiry," *Harvard Theological Review,* 82, 1 (1989): 1–11.

25. Ibid., 1.

26. Ibid., 9.

27. Ibid., 5–6.

28. Ibid., 6.

29. Ibid., 9.

30. David Tracy, "Lindbeck's New Programme for Theology," *The Thomist* 49 (1985): 470ff.

31. That fact that Schüssler Fiorenza is speaking to an academic audience at a convocation address of Harvard University goes some way to explaining this, but her position as expressed there nevertheless promotes the idea of the intellectual Spivak questions.

32. It is impossible here to detail Ricoeur's complex argument, but we might note his third step, to root the self in an ontology, which emphasizes Strawson's claim that there are only two primitive "basic particulars": physical bodies and persons (see Ricoeur, *Oneself as Another,* 30ff). They are basic because there is no statement about reality that does not presuppose the prior existence either of bodies or persons.

33. Ricoeur, *Oneself as Another,* 2–3.

34. Ricoeur's studies ground this claim in terms of three sets of investigations: into lan-

guage and pragmatics, into action and narrative, and into moral norms and practical wisdom. See Ricoeur, *Oneself as Another,* for further consideration of his claim.

35. Ibid., 189, 338.

36. Ibid., 6.

37. Ibid., 18.

38. Buber's philosophical framework, strongly existentialist, is somewhat different from Ricoeur's. The meaning of Buber's I-thou relation tends toward a philosophy of subjectivity that easily loses the material significance of the body for the constitution of the self and the other.

39. Ricoeur, *Oneself as Another,* 352.

40. Ibid., 36. Ricoeur develops this point in terms of the identity of ascription to persons in which, uniquely, there is an irreducible double reference of two series of predicates (to the soul or consciousness on the one hand, to the body on the other) for one and the same entity: "It is the same thing that weighs sixty kilograms and that has this or that thought."

41. Ibid., 354, 355.

42. "Do not do unto your neighbor what you would hate him to do to you. This is the entire Law; the rest is commentary."

43. Ricoeur, *Oneself as Another,* 219.

44. Ibid., 20.

45. Ibid., 107.

46. Ibid., 190.

47. It should be clear now why the individual, independent subject, the Cartesian ego, tends to treat suffering as something done to the I. Logically, an ethical system produced on the back of the ego would emphasize as primary the rights of the individual, considered separately from any other, and it would guarantee the rights of the other only on the basis that the other is treated as another individual within a contractual social relationship in which principles dominate over persons. The suffering of the other, in this case, leaving aside guilt or remorse, affects the I only to the extent that the other is referred to the social contract and any institutions it may support. A variety of idioms popular in modern times (though not necessarily original to modernity) have given force to this ethic, among them: To each his own, Charity begins at home, You get what you deserve, and Survival of the fittest. Elsewhere, Ricoeur describes the difference between the ego and the self as follows: "the ego posits itself" and "the self . . . recognizes itself only through" the ways in which the other affects it. Ricoeur, *Oneself as Another,* 329.

48. Ibid., 320.

49. Ibid., 194.

50. This formulation of practical wisdom is very close to what Habermas means by praxis, namely, critically reflective action aimed at the transformation of the conditions of life toward the good.

51. Ricoeur, *Oneself as Another,* 240ff.

52. Ibid., 243.

53. Ibid., 247.

54. Ibid., 266.

55. Ibid., 268. "Availability," says Ricoeur, "is the key that opens self-constancy to the dialogic structure" of the self and the other.

56. A direct example of what I mean here may be found in much of what has happened in my own institution, the University of Natal School of Theology. Our initial involvement with the Amawoti community began with the Bible study facilitator's registration in a master's degree program. After some time, because of the commitment of both the facilitator and the School of Theology to a theological model that takes seriously in terms of reciprocity the interface between the formally trained and the untrained believer, more of our staff and students began to work with the Amawoti community at the request of the BEC.

At the School of Theology, it soon became clear that reciprocity meant that we would have to take into our own programs (teaching, research, and community projects) the challenges and demands being made upon us by the Amawoti BEC. Structures were put in place to enable this, incorporating our activities at every level of our operation, including the advocacy role we play in theological education for the ministry of the churches. The fact that this commitment was structured, that is, embodied in specific kinds of contractually negotiated appointments and processes that bound school staff to its original commitment, has meant that no individual, not even the head of the school, is in a position to isolate the voice of the other without considerable and serious practical implications.

57. We know well that it is usually safer to hold on to actuality, to what one knows and what one has, than to risk something of which one is unsure and by which one might be threatened. A self shattered by the winds of change is not an alternative to a self chained by the bonds of sameness. Freedom and security cannot be treated as if they are simple alternatives to each other. Without the risks of freedom, the self shrinks and ultimately fades away: the condition of apathy, resignation, anomie. Without a sound base upon which it may stand, the self breaks its moorings and ultimately loses itself: the condition of estrangement, alienation, disintegration. The dialectic of freedom and security is internal to the self as another. The focus of the present discussion is on the most basic foundation upon which the self may stand in order to be able to risk fully.

58. (McGaughey 1997:408ff.)

59. (McGaughey 1995:420, where he follows Husserl's thought)

60. Ibid., 414.

61. Ibid., 415.

62. Ibid., 436.

6. Widening the Circle

1. Robert J. Schreiter, *Constructing Local Theologies* (Maryknoll, N.Y.: Orbis, 1985).

2. E. F. Schumacher, *Small Is Beautiful: A Study of Economics as if People Mattered* (London: Blond & Briggs, 1973).

3. Applying this claim to local theologies, my approach would be classified in the scheme of Schreiter (see *Constructing Local Theologies*) as a contextual model of local theology of liberation. His other contextual type he calls "ethnographic," its focus being cultural identity. The present work in fact moves in the direction of a recovery of identity as essential to an adequately redefined understanding of liberation. In Schreiter's typology, the weaknesses of a liberationist approach are (1) a temptation to activism over adequate reflection, (2) a neglect of the biblical foundations of faith, and (3) the undermining of a hermeneutics of reconstruction by an overemphasis on a hermeneutics of suspicion. The weaknesses of the ethnographic approach are complementary: (1) a tendency to overlook conflict and contradictions, (2) an inclination to cultural romanticism, and (3) a bias toward analytical categories defined by anthropological experts. If we are to stick with Schreiter's typology, we may regard the present work to be an attempt to deal simultaneously with the weaknesses of both the liberationist and the ethnographic models.

4. Schreiter, *Constructing Local Theologies*.

5. The appellation *universal* in this context, following our earlier usage, should be read as meaning the church that "endures in history as a tentative approximation of the ideal of the Body of Christ."

6. Bible study on Isa. 9:1-7 and Luke 2:8-15, 22 November 1991.

7. Bible study on Luke 2:4-7 and Luke 1:51–53, 14 October 1988.

8. Theologies along the lines of Hegelian dialectics perhaps have come closest to finding a solution via the thesis-antithesis-synthesis model of dialectics. I myself have moved along this route previously. However, the causal logic of nominalist epistemologies remains the major weakness of such approaches. A grand systemic view of history and world emerges in Hegelian approaches, including those that have been "turned on their head" (Marx). The world and human society is not reducible to systems, even historically sensitive developmental ones. Equally, spirit or its analogues, if understood in terms of a transcendent historical force (either immanently in the motor of productive forces, as in Marx, or ideally in the unfolding of mind, as in Hegel), makes it extremely difficult to take into account what is local, particular, personal. An impersonal force reigns. This is not unlike the Unmoved Mover of Aristotelian metaphysics, and it is equally unsatisfactory in offering an understanding of the ambiguity, multiplicity, and fragility of life. System imperatives should not be forgotten, lest we lose the valuable gains made by system-oriented theories of social life. The same is true of those historical materialist theories that have contributed to our understanding of change. But neither should they override that which is non-systemic. In either case, an impoverished view of social life would appear, with negative practical consequences.

9. David Tracy, *The Analogical Imagination: Christian Theology and the Culture of Pluralism* (London: SCM, 1981), 4.

10. That the plurality of publics is internalized and always implicit in addressing any one public does not mean that every actual theological discourse exhibits clarity about, and congruency between, the three publics. On the contrary, Tracy suggests that one of the malaises of modern theology lies precisely in a widespread confusion at this point.

11. For these comments on gender and power I am indebted to discussions with Denise Ackermann.

12. Tracy, *Analogical Imagination*, 28.

13. For example, in the School of Theology at the university, the key question we faced was how to alter our teaching and research in a way that would more congruently match the

experience and concrete realities of communities such as the one at Amawoti. This includes ways of putting students into such contexts while studying for their degree, as a basis for reconstituting our understanding of theology itself and, in particular, our understanding of how churches might be shaped by such contextualized theological reflection. This in turn was intended to impact upon the way the churches whose ministerial candidates we were training would view the purpose of that training.

14. Here is where Tracy's notion of differing plausibility structures for each public becomes pertinent, for different norms, criteria of validity, and forms of argument are likely to be operative in each.

15. Charles Villa-Vicencio, *A Theology of Reconstruction* (Cambridge: Cambridge University Press, 1992). In this work Villa-Vicencio concentrates primarily on the question of law in relation to constitution making, and human rights as the key to a theology of reconstruction. This would comply with the model developed by Habermas, in which law is the interface between life world and system through which the articulation of life world and system is discursively regulated. My argument goes beyond Villa-Vicencio's position by attempting to systematically understand the significance of national reconstruction in the life world itself via the identity of the proclamation of the church in public life.

16. Kairos Theologians, *The Kairos Document: Challenge to the Church,* rev. 2nd ed. (Johannesburg: Institute for Contextual Theology, 1986). Anonymous, *The Road to Damascus: Kairos and Conversion* (Johannesburg: Skotaville, 1989).

17. Linell E. Cady, "Hermeneutics and Tradition: The Role of the Past in Jurisprudence and Theology," *Harvard Theological Journal* 79 (1986): 463.

18. Jürgen Habermas, *The Theory of Communicative Action: Reason and the Rationalization of Society,* vol. 1 (Boston: Beacon Press, 1984), 8.

19. Ibid., 13.

20. The notion of taken-for-grantedness is used by Habermas to indicate the difference between life world, a largely unconscious framework for thinking, and worldview, a consciously held perspective.

21. Habermas, *Reason and the Rationalization of Society,* 137–38. Habermas defines three primary processes: the "continuation of valid knowledge," the "stabilization of group solidarity," and the "socialization of responsible actors."

22. A fascinating discussion of the link between an African communal ethic and the discourse ethics of Habermas and Karl-Otto Apel may be found in Bénézet Bujo, *Die Ethische Dimension der Gemeinschaft: das afrikanische Modell in Nord-Süd-Dialog* (Vienna: Herder, 1993). Bujo compares their discourse ethics with Charles Taylor's critique of its emphasis on right/wrong rules (rationalist norms that seek universal foundations and thus remain at best cautious about traditions and particular claims) as opposed to good/evil rules (communitarian norms that seek particular foundations and thus emphasize the wisdom of traditions and their plurality against a merely rationalist will). Bujo himself defends an African communitarian ethic that strongly includes the dimension of discourse ethics I stress in my discussion here. He regards such discursive approaches to the construction of ethics, provided they are understood in relation to the wisdom of the past and present members of the community, as essentially African and calls it "Palaver ethics." In this model, a person is a person not by virtue of mind (*cogito*) but in relation to others (*relatio* or *Beziehung*) and through relationship

(*cognatio* or *Verwandtschaft*). Bujo thus seeks an African reinterpretation to account for an ethic that combines the insights of both Habermas/Apel and Taylor.

23. For Habermas, a "*situation* represents a segment of the life world delimited in relation to a theme." Habermas, *Reason and the Rationalization of Society*, 127.

24. Ibid., 17.

25. Jürgen Habermas, *Legitimation Crisis* (London: Heinemann, 1976), 108.

26. Ibid., 111.

27. Habermas, *Reason and the Rationalization of Society*, xi.

28. Ibid., 101. Habermas makes it clear in this context that communicative action is critically related to the coordination of social action, but that it cannot be limited simply to such a function: "In the case of communicative action the interpretive accomplishments on which cooperative processes of interpretation are based represent the mechanism for *coordinating* action; communicative action is *not exhausted* by the act of reaching understanding in an interpretive manner. . . . But communicative action designates a type of interaction that is *coordinated through* speech acts and does *not coincide with* them."

29. Ibid., 18.

30. Ibid., 283.

31. Ibid., 286.

32. Ibid., 341.

33. Jürgen Habermas, *The Theory of Communicative Action: Lifeworld and System: A Critique of Functionalist Reason*, Vol. 2 (Boston: Beacon Press, 1987), 61.

34. Still a penetrating study of this disjunction, but an easy one to grasp, is John Berger's book on which a BBC film series was based, *Ways of Seeing* (Middlesex, U.K.: Pelican, 1972).

35. The best contemporary example may be found in the work of French postmodernist Jean Baudrillard, who doubts that we know anything about what really happened in the Gulf War, for example. Indeed, he even doubts that what we saw on television screens or in newspapers happened at all. A summary of Baudrillard's arguments and a critical perspective on such radical doubt may be found in Christopher Norris, *Uncritical Theory: Postmodernism, Intellectuals and the Gulf War* (London: Lawrence & Wishart, 1992).

36. John Eagleson and Philip Scharper, *Puebla and Beyond* (Maryknoll, N.Y.: Orbis, 1979).

37. South African Black Theology, a counterhegemonic movement like liberation theologies in general (see Lebamang Sebidi, "The Dynamics of the Black Struggle and Its Implications for Black Theology," in *The Unquestionable Right to Be Free*, Itumeleng J. Mosala and Buti Tlhgale, eds. [Maryknoll, N.Y.: Orbis, 1986] and Itumeleng J. Mosala, "Black Theology in South Africa and North America: Prospects for the Future, Building of Alliances," *Journal of Black Theology* 1, 2 [November 1987], is one example of an attempt to establish a new paradigm, with a key foundation of this new paradigm being situatedness—a conscious departure point in the black struggle. See also Allan Boesak, *Farewell to Innocence: A Socio-Ethical Study of Black Theology and Power* (Maryknoll, N.Y.: Orbis, 1977); Simon Maimela, *Proclaim Freedom to My People* (Johannesburg: Skotaville, 1987); and Bonganjalo Goba, *An Agenda for Black Theology: Hermeneutics for Social Change* (Johannesburg: Skotaville, 1988).

38. Per Frostin, *Liberation Theology in Tanzania and South Africa: A First World Interpretation* (Lund, Sweden: Lund University Press, 1988), 94ff.

39. Ibid., 22–23.

40. Richard J. Bernstein, *Beyond Objectivism and Relativism: Science, Hermeneutics and Praxis* (Philadelphia: University of Philadelphia Press, 1988), 18.

41. Ibid., 26.

42. Ibid., 229.

43. A theme most strongly introduced in recent theology by Jürgen Moltmann's classic *A Theology of Hope* (New York: Harper & Row, 1965), usually regarded as representative of European political theology, but also present in Latin American liberation theologies, Black theologies, feminist and womanist theologies, and deconstructionist theologies (beginning with Thomas Altizer's *The Gospel of Christian Atheism* [Philadelphia: Westminster Press, 1966]). The latter two trajectories go furthest in accepting the destabilization of the received tradition, which, in one or other version, orthodoxies try to restabilize.

44. See Alisdair MacIntyre, *After Virtue,* 2nd ed. (Notre Dame: University of Notre Dame Press, 1984); Jeffrey Stout, *Ethics after Babel* (Boston: Beacon Press, 1988); and Stephen Fowl,"Could Horace Talk with the Hebrews? Translatibility and Moral Disagreement in MacIntyre and Stout," *Journal of Religious Ethics* (1991): 19.

45. Bernstein, *Beyond Objectivism and Relativism,* 230.

46. Theodore W. Jennings, *Beyond Theism: A Grammar of God-Language* (New York: Cambridge University Press, 1985), 57.

47. Ibid., 47.

48. T. S. Eliot ("Burnt Norton," *Four Quartets*).

49. Jennings, *Beyond Theism,* 49.

50. Ibid., 57.

51. Paul Ricoeur, *Hermeneutics and the Human Sciences,* J. B. Thompson, ed. (Cambridge: Cambridge University Press, 1981); Paul Ricoeur, *From Text to Action: Essays in Hermeneutics II* (Evanston, Ill.: Northwestern University Press, 1991).

52. Ricoeur, *Hermeneutics and Human Sciences,* 16.

53. Ibid., 220.

54. Ibid., 207.

55. Ibid., 208.

56. Paul Ricoeur, *Time and Narrative,* K. McLaughlin and D. Pellauer, trans. (Chicago: University of Chicago Press, 1984).

57. Ricoeur, *Hermeneutics and Human Sciences,* 213.

58. From the point of view of hermeneutics philosophy, here we reach a conclusion identical to that at which Habermas arrives via his social theory of communicative action.

59. M. Mann, in Averil Cameron, *Christianity and the Rhetoric of Empire: The Development of Christian Discourse* (Berkeley: University of California, 1991), 3.

60. Cameron, *Christianity and the Rhetoric of Empire,* 13.

61. Ibid., 9.

62. Ibid., 23.

63. Ibid., 42, 57-62.

64. Ibid., 155ff.

65. Ibid., 188.

66. One may note that these pairs have become dichotomies that, because they have been split asunder, tend to destroy the social fabric of values today.

67. Compare Pablo Richard, *Death of Christendoms, Birth of the Church* (Maryknoll, N.Y.: Orbis, 1987) and Charles Villa-Vicencio, *Between Christ and Caesar: Classic and Contemporary Texts on Church and State* (Cape Town: David Philip, 1986).

68. Michael Worsnip and Desmond van der Water, eds., *We Shall Overcome: A Spirituality of Liberation* (Pietermaritzburg, South Africa: Cluster Publications, 1991).

69. Bible study on Matt. 6:9-10, 16 February 1990.

70. Cameron, *Christianity and the Rhetoric of Empire,* 89.

71. Ibid., 120ff.

72. Again, see Augustine's monumental *City of God*.

73. An earlier attempt to spell out some of the implications of this approach in relation to the conditions of workers and the meaning of labor may be found in James R. Cochrane, "Already . . . But Not Yet: Programmatic Notes for a Theology of Work," and James R. Cochrane et al, "Workers, the Church, and the Alienation of Religious Life," in *The Three-fold Cord: Theology, Work and Labour,* James R. Cochrane and Gerald O. West, eds. (Pietermaritzburg, South Africa: Cluster Publications, 1991).

74. Megan Walker, "Tradition, Criticism and Popular Religion: A Hermeneutic Investigation of Marian Theology" (M.A. diss, University of Natal, 1992), 85.

75. Closest to defining what I mean here is Hans-Georg Gadamer's philosophical notion of the *wirkungsgeschichtles Bewusstsein* (consciousness exposed to the effects of history) by which we are always born in and out of a culture before we add anything to it.

76. One should note here that strategic considerations will affect the extent to which local wisdom and experience is made public or accessible to a wider audience. As James C. Scott repeatedly reminds us, the greater the oppression, the thicker the mask. Still, strategic considerations are bound by a historical conjuncture of forces and they alter according to shifts in these forces. My point is that these strategic considerations cannot permanently exclude intervention in the public arena without being historically impotent. Moreover, evidence of actual contexts of oppression, even where the threat is high and the mask is thick, suggests that no group or community fails in some way or another to address itself to the larger public sphere at some point in time. See James C. Scott, *Domination and the Arts of Resistance: Hidden Transcripts* (New Haven, Conn.: Yale University Press, 1990).

77. See Anthony O. Balcomb, *Third Way Theology: Reconciliation, Revolution and Reform in the South African Church* (Pietermaritzburg, South Africa: Cluster Publications, 1993).

7. Center and Boundary

1. From this point of view, Habermas himself would have to acknowledge that his own theory depends upon a long tradition—a profound history of theories and their related practices which precede him and shape (predispose) his consciousness, including his choice of theoretical frameworks and categories (that which for him is authoritative).

2. Paul Ricoeur, *Hermeneutics and the Human Sciences,* J. B. Thompson, ed. (Cambridge: Cambridge University Press, 1981), 97, 99.

3. See Edward Farley, *Theologia: The Unity and Fragmentation of Theological Education* (Philadelphia: Fortress Publishers, 1989) and Lewis S. Mudge and James N. Poling, eds., *The Promise of Practical Theology: Formation and Reflection* (Philadelphia: Fortress Publishers, 1987).

4. See James R. Cochrane, "Bridging the Theory-Practice Divide: Lessons from Forty Years of Trying and Not Succeeding," in Megan Walker and James R. Cochrane, *The Contextualisation of Theological Education*, Pietermaritzburg: University of Natal (1996): 36–44; and J. W. Fraser, M. E. Friar, B. A. Radtke, T. J. Savage, and K. Schuth, *Cooperative Ventures in Theological Education* (Lanham, Md.: University Press of America, 1989), 18.

5. Farley, *Theologia.*

6. The detail of Mahler's letter is taken from notes accompanying a compact disc recording of his 2nd ("Ressurection") Symphony (Simon Rattle conducting, EMI), 1994 edition.

7. Stephen Toulmin, *Cosmopolis: The Hidden Agenda of Modernity* (New York: Free Press, 1990), 127.

8. One could read the words of this popular and widely sung chorus more positively, as pointing to an eschatological vision of a desired and hoped-for future that, placing the torments and struggles of the present in the background, allows one to act again with renewed strength in the present through the now foregrounded conviction that one is not overcome by the present. But in my experience, it usually expresses a more pietistic, internal orientation of an individualist kind.

9. That one has a responsibility in and for nature was not rejected. Thus the formula *sola fide* (by faith alone), for example, should not be read as *solitaria fide,* that is, faith which stands alone and does not issue in responsibility. Similarly, the Protestant view did not treat grace and nature—or the supernatural and the natural—as ontologically different. Grace is indeed active within the world, and it works below in this sense. But my point is more nuanced, that nature (or analogously, context) gives nothing of itself except through grace. Such a view matches metaphysical notions of the omniscience and omnipotence of God, an impassive God, which have so negatively affected much of modern theology. Perhaps, then, one is not actually implicating classical Protestantism but modernist variations of its original insights.

10. Eberhard Busch, *Karl Barth: His Life from Letters and Autobiographical Texts* (London: SCM, 1975).

11. My schematic representation of Barth's revelational positivism is something of a caricature, and it is really the conservative followers of Barth I criticize here. Barth, at the end of his life, had the grace and the wisdom to recognize the historically conditioned limits of his own work even as he bemoaned his neo-orthodox disciples for adapting his way instead of finding their own.

12. Paul Ricoeur, *The Symbolism of Evil* (Boston: Beacon Press, 1969).

13. Theodore W. Jennings, *Introduction to Theology: An Invitation to Reflection Upon the Christian Mythos* (London: SPCK and Philadelphia: Fortress, 1976).

14. See Charles Davis, *Theology and Political Society* (Cambridge: Cambridge University Press, 1980) and Alfredo Fierro, *The Militant Gospel* (Maryknoll, N.Y.: Orbis, 1977).

15. One need not make this move, but then one is not dealing with Christian theology as such.

16. See H. Richard Niebuhr, *Christ and Culture* (New York: Harper & Row, 1951), 234–241, where he deals with "the relativism of faith."

17. Jennings, *Introduction to Theology.*

18. Paul Ricoeur, *Oneself as Another*, K. Blamey, trans. (Chicago: University of Chicago Press, 1992), 286.

19. Ibid., 143.

20. Ibid., 162.

21. Some have claimed that single-cell animals such as amoeba will not have this capacity in any sense whatsoever, there being no complexity in their neural makeup which allows for any filtering of the enormous range of data affecting organisms at any one moment. Unless the multitude of sources of data (sound, light, electrical impulses, and so on) are filtered out, there is no possibility of a world as we know it. This filtering activity is one way of describing what Ricouer points toward in using the word *fiction,* itself etymologically derived from the Latin *fictio*, meaning "a fashioning."

22. Ricoeur, *Oneself as Another,* 158.

23. Ibid.

24. At this point one may ask, Who arbitrates? The question suggests that the formulation adopted here needs to be read in conjunction with what has been said earlier about the implication of power in all knowledge, the imbalances in power within in any relation, and the subtle forms of power effected through infrapolitics and in the hidden transcripts of the parties concerned.

25. Ricoeur, *Oneself as Another,* 289.

26. Ibid.

27. Kathleen M. Kirby, "Thinking Through the Boundary: The Politics of Location, Subjects and Space," *Boundary 2* (Summer 1993):174.

28. Ibid., 175.

29. See Elisabeth Schüssler Fiorenza, *But She Said: Feminist Practices of Biblical Interpretation* (Boston: Beacon, 1992) and Elisabeth Schüssler Fiorenza, *Jesus: Miriam's Child, Sophia's Prophet* (New York: Continuum, 1994).

30. Bible study on Rom. 5:12-14, 1 Cor. 15:21-22, and Gen. 2:16-17, 11 September 1992.

31. Bible study on Matt. 6:24-25, 9 August 1991.

32. Kirby, "Thinking Through the Boundary," 176, 182.

33. Ibid., 176.

34. Ibid., 198. For Kirby, the boundary as a spatial trope has the virtue of providing "a medium for articulating specificity and punctuality, but also malleability" (1993:187). I would view my own attempts to discuss the nature of theology, church, texts, and tradition in exactly this light.

35. The process I refer to is more fully defined in the work of Graham Philpott (*Jesus Is Tricky and God Is Undemocratic: The Kin-dom of God in Amawoti* [Pietermaritzburg, South Africa: Cluster Publications, 1993]), who facilitated most of the Bible studies I depend upon, and in that of Gerald O. West (*Biblical Hermeneutics of Liberation: Modes of Reading the Bible,* 2nd ed. Maryknoll, N.Y.: Orbis, 1995), whose biblical hermeneutics investigations have depended

on work in the same local community by several members of the Institute for the Study of the Bible at the University of Natal.

36. The reference back to the beginning of the book, reading it as a journey that must be repeated or reproduced again, by myself and by others, is also an allusion to the deconstructionist strategy which Jacques Derrida outlines in "The Law of Genre," 1981.

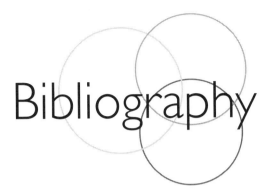

Bibliography

Altizer, Thomas J. J. *The Gospel of Christian Atheism*. Philadelphia: Westminster Press, 1966.

Alves, Rubem A. *Protestantism and Repression: A Brazilian Case Study*. London: SCM, 1985.

Anonymous. *The Road to Damascus: Kairos and Conversion*. Johannesburg: Skotaville, 1989.

Balcomb, Anthony O. *Third Way Theology: Reconciliation, Revolution and Reform in the South African Church*. Pietermaritzburg, South Africa: Cluster Publications, 1993.

Barth, Karl. Introduction to *The Essence of Christianity,* by Ludwig Feuerbach. New York: Harper & Row, 1957.

Bediako, Kwame. *Christianity in Africa: The Renewal of a Non-Western Religion*. Edinburgh: Edinburgh University Press, 1995.

Berger, John. *Ways of Seeing*. Middlesex, U.K.: Pelican, 1972.

Bernstein, Richard. J. *Beyond Objectivism and Relativism: Science, Hermeneutics and Praxis*. Philadelphia: University of Philadelphia Press, 1988.

Boesak, Allan. *Farewell to Innocence: A Socio-Ethical Study of Black Theology and Power*. Maryknoll, N.Y.: Orbis, 1977.

Boff, Clodivus. *Faith on the Edge: Religion and Marginalized Existence*. San Francisco: Harper & Row, 1989.

Bonhoeffer, Dietrich. *Ethics*. New York: Macmillan, 1976.

Bosch, David J. *Transforming Mission: Paradigm Shifts in Theology of Mission*. Maryknoll, N.Y.: Orbis, 1991.

Bria, Ion. "The Liturgy after the Liturgy." In *Martyria Mission: The Witness of the Orthodox Church Today,* edited by Ion Bria, 66–71. Geneva: World Council of Churches, 1980.

Bultmann, Rudolf. "The Primitive Christian Kerygma and the Historical Jesus." In *The Historical Jesus and the Kerygmatic Christ,* edited by Carl Braaten and R. Harrisville. Nashville: Abingdon, 1964.

Bujo, Bénézet. *Die Ethische Dimension der Gemeinschaft: das afrikanische Modell in Nord-Süd-Dialog*. Vienna: Herder, 1993.

Busch, Eberhard. *Karl Barth: His Life from Letters and Autobiographical Texts*. London: SCM, 1975.

Buthelezi, Manas. "An African Theology or a Black Theology?" In *Essays on Black Theology,* edited by Mokgethi Motlhabi. Johannesburg: University Christian Movement, 1972.

Cady, Linell E. "Hermeneutics and Tradition: The Role of the Past in Jurisprudence and Theology." *Harvard Theological Journal* 79 (1986): 439–63.

Cameron, Averil. *Christianity and the Rhetoric of Empire: The Development of Christian Discourse.* Berkeley: University of California, 1991.

Castro, Fidel. *Fidel on Religion: Castro Talks on Revolution and Religion with Frei Betto,* edited by F. Betto. New York: Simon & Schuster, 1987.

Cochrane, James R. *Servants of Power: The Role of English-Speaking Churches in South Africa, 1903–1930.* Johannesburg: Ravan, 1987.

Cochrane, James R. "Nation-Building: A Sociotheological View." In *Building a New Nation,* edited by W. S. Vorster. Pretoria: Unisa, 1991.

Cochrane, James R. "Already . . . But Not Yet: Programmatic Notes for a Theology of Work." In *The Three-fold Cord: Theology, Work and Labour,* edited by James R. Cochrane and Gerald O. West, 177–189. Pietermaritzburg, South Africa: Cluster Publications, 1991.

Cochrane, James R., et al. "Workers, the Church, and the Alienation of Religious Life." In *The Three-fold Cord: Theology, Work and Labour,* edited by James R. Cochrane and Gerald O. West, 253–75. Pietermaritzburg, South Africa: Cluster Publications, 1991.

Cochrane, James R., and Gerald O. West. "War, Remembrance and Reconstruction." *Journal of Theology for Southern Africa* 84 (1993): 25–40.

Cochrane, James R. "God in Context: The Symbolic Construction of a Religious Universe in a Base Christian Community." *Scriptura*, vol. S12 (1993): 35-56.

Cochrane, James R. "Christ from Above, Jesus from Below." *Journal of Theology for Southern Africa* 88 (1994): 3–14.

Cochrane, James R. "Bridging the Theory-Practice Divide: Lessons from Forty Years of Trying and Not Succeeding." Consultation Report in *The Contextualisation of Theological Education,* by Megan Walker and James R. Cochrane. Pietermaritzburg: University of Natal, (1996): 36–44.

Comaroff, Jean. *Body of Power, Spirit of Resistance: The Culture and History of a South African People.* Chicago: University of Chicago Press, 1985.

Comaroff, Jean, & John Comaroff. *Of Revelation and Revolution: Christianity, Colonialism and Consciousness in South Africa.* Chicago: University of Chicago Press, 1991.

Croatto, José Severino. *Biblical Hermeneutics: Toward a Theory of Reading as the Production of Meaning.* Maryknoll, N.Y.: Orbis, 1987.

Davis, Charles. *Theology and Political Society.* Cambridge: Cambridge University Press, 1980.

Denis, Philippe. "The Catholic Church between Monarchy and Democracy." In *A Democratic Vision for South Africa,* edited by Klaus Nürnberger. Pietermaritzburg, South Africa: Encounter, 1991.

Denis, Philippe. "Is Democracy Good for the Church? Reflections of an Historian." *Journal of Theology for Southern Africa* 83 (1993): 46–57.

Derrida, Jacques. "The Law of Genre," translated by A. Ronell. In *On Narrative,* edited by W. J. T. Mitchell. Chicago: University of Chicago Press, 1981.

Draper, Jonathan A. "Jesus and the Renewal of Local Community in Galilee: Challenge to a Communitarian Christology." *Journal of Theology for Southern Africa* 87 (1994): 29–42.

Draper, Jonathan A. "Social Ambiguity and the Production of Text: Prophets, Teachers, Bishops and Deacons, and the Development of the Jesus Tradition in the Context of the Didache." In *The Didache in Context: Essays on its Text, History and Transmission,* edited by C. N. Jefford. Leiden: Brill, 1996.

Eagleson, John, and Philip Scharper. *Puebla and Beyond.* Maryknoll, N.Y.: Orbis, 1979.

Engelsberger, G. "Nachrichten." In *Wir kommen auf Umwegen,* by G. Engelsberger. Karlsruhe: Evangelischen Presseverband, 1991.

Farley, Edward. *Theologia: The Unity and Fragmentation of Theological Education.* Philadelphia: Fortress, 1989.

Fierro, Alfredo. *The Militant Gospel.* Maryknoll, N.Y.: Orbis, 1977.

Foucault, Michel. *Power/Knowledge: Selected Interviews and Other Writings, 1972-1977.* New York: Pantheon, 1980.

Fowl, Stephen. "Could Horace Talk with the Hebrews? Translatability and Moral Disagreement in MacIntyre and Stout." *Journal of Religious Ethics* (1991): 19.

Fraser, J. W., M. E. Friar, B. A. Radtke, T. J. Savage, and K. Schuth. *Cooperative Ventures in Theological Education.* Lanham, Md.: University Press of America, 1989.

Frend, W. H. C. *Martyrdom and Persecution in the Early Church: A Study of Conflict from the Maccabees to Donatus.* Oxford: Blackwell, 1965.

Frend, W. H. C. *The Donatist Church: A Movement of Protest in Roman North Africa.* Oxford: Clarendon, 1985.

Frostin, Per. *Liberation Theology in Tanzania and South Africa: A First World Interpretation.* Lund, Sweden: Lund University Press, 1988.

Gadamer, Hans-Georg. *Truth and Method.* New York: Crossroad, 1982.

Goba, Bonganjalo. *An Agenda for Black Theology: Hermeneutics for Social Change.* Johannesburg: Skotaville, 1988.

Grey, Mary. *Redeeming the Dream: Feminism, Redemption and Christian Tradition.* London: SPCK, 1989.

Gutiérrez, Gustavo. *The Theology of Liberation.* Maryknoll, N.Y.: Orbis, 1973.

Gutiérrez, Gustavo. *The Power of the Poor in History: Selected Writings.* London: SCM, 1983.

Habermas, Jürgen. *Knowledge and Human Interests.* Boston: Beacon, 1971.

Habermas, Jürgen. *Legitimation Crisis.* London: Heinemann, 1976.

Habermas, Jürgen. *The Theory of Communicative Action: Reason and the Rationalization of Society,* Vol. 1. Boston: Beacon Press, 1984.

Habermas, Jürgen. *The Theory of Communicative Action: Lifeworld and System: A Critique of Functionalist Reason,* Vol. 2. Boston: Beacon Press, 1987.

Horsley, Richard with John S. Hanson. *Bandits, Prophets and Messiahs: Popular Movements at the Time of Jesus.* San Francisco: Harper, 1988.

Horsley, Richard. *Sociology of the Jesus Movement.* New York: Continuum, 1994.

Institute for Contextual Theology. *Speaking for Ourselves.* Johannesburg: Institute for Contextual Theology, 1988.

Jay, Martin. *The Dialectical Imagination: A History of the Frankfurt School and the Institute of Social Research 1923–1950.* London: Heinemann, 1973.

Jennings, Theodore W. *Introduction to Theology: An Invitation to Reflection Upon the Christian Mythos.* London: SPCK and Philadelphia: Fortress, 1976.

Jennings, Theodore W. *Beyond Theism: A Grammar of God-Language*. New York: Cambridge University Press, 1985.

Kamphausen, Erhard. *Anfänge der kirchlichen Unabhängigkeitsbewegung in Südafrika: Geschichte und Theologie der Äthiopischen Bewegung, 1872–1912*. Frankfurt: Peter Lang, 1976.

Kairos Theologians. *The Kairos Document: Challenge to the Church*. Rev. 2nd ed. Johannesburg: Institute for Contextual Theology, 1986.

Kiernan, James. "The Management of a Complex Religious Identity: The Case of Zulu Zionism." *Religion in Southern Africa* 7, 2 (July 1986): 3–14.

Kiernan, James. "African and Christian: From Opposition to Mutual Accommodation." In *Christianity in South Africa*, edited by M. Prozesky. London: MacMillan, 1990.

Kiernan, James. "The Healing Community and the Future of the Urban Working Class." In "The Contribution of South Africa's Religions to the Coming South Africa." Conference proceedings, Department of Religious Studies, Pietermaritzburg: University of Natal, 1993.

Kirby, Kathleen M. "Thinking Through the Boundary: The Politics of Location, Subjects and Space." *Boundary* 2 (Summer 1993): 173–89.

Kruss, Glenda. "Religion, Class and Culture: Indigenous Churches in South Africa, with Special Reference to Zionist-Apostolics." Ph.D. diss., University of Cape Town, 1985.

Lamb, Matthew. *Solidarity with the Victims: Towards a Theology of Social Transformation*. New York: Crossroad, 1982.

Lindbeck, George. *The Nature of Doctrine: Religion and Theology in a Postliberal Age*. Philadelphia: Westminster Press, 1984.

MacIntyre, Alisdair. *After Virtue*. 2nd ed. Notre Dame: University of Notre Dame Press, 1984.

Maimela, Simon. *Proclaim Freedom to My People*. Johannesburg: Skotaville, 1987.

Makhubu, P. *Who Are the Independent Churches?* Johannesburg: Skotaville, 1988.

Mamdani, Mahmood. *Citizen and Subject*. Cape Town: David Philip, 1996.

Mandela, Nelson. *Long Walk to Freedom: The Autobiography of Nelson Mandela*. London: Little, Brown, 1994.

Mandew, Martin. "Power and Empowerment: Religious Imagination and the Life of a Local Base Ecclesial Community." Master's thesis, University of Natal, 1993.

Martey, Emmanuel. *African Theology: Inculturation and Liberation*. Maryknoll, N.Y.: Orbis, 1993.

McGaughey, Douglas R. *Strangers and Pilgrims: On the Role of Aporiai in Theology*. New York & Berlin: De Gruyter, 1997.

Mead, George Herbert. *Mind, Self and Society*. Chicago: University of Chicago Press, 1934.

Memmi, Albert. *The Colonizer and the Colonized*. Expanded edition, with the Introduction by Jean-Paul Sartre. Boston: Beacon, 1991.

Min, Anselm. *Dialectic of Salvation: Issues in Theology of Liberation*. New York: State University of New York Press, 1989.

Mofokeng, Takatso. *The Crucified among the Crossbearers*. Kampen: J. H. Kok, 1983.

Mofokeng, Takatso. "Black Theology in South Africa: Achievements, Problems and Prospects." In *Christianity in South Africa*, edited by M. Prozesky. London: MacMillan, 1990.

Mokhtar, G., ed. *Ancient Civilizations of Africa. General History of Africa, II.* Berkeley: University of California Press, 1990.

Moltmann, Jürgen. *A Theology of Hope.* New York: Harper & Row, 1967.

Moltmann, Jürgen. *Hope and Planning.* London: SCM, 1971.

Moltmann, Jürgen. *The Experiment Hope.* Philadelphia: Fortress, 1975.

Moltmann, Jürgen. *The Way of Jesus Christ.* Minneapolis: Fortress, 1993.

Moore, Basil, ed. *The Challenge of Black Theology in South Africa.* Atlanta: John Knox Press, 1973.

Mosala, Itumeleng. "The Relevance of African Independent Churches and Their Challenge to Black Theology." In *The Unquestionable Right to Be Free,* edited by Itumeleng Mosala and Buti Tlhagale. Maryknoll, N.Y.: Orbis, 1986.

Mosala, Itumeleng. *Biblical Hermeneutics and Black Theology in South Africa.* Grand Rapids, Mich.: Eerdmans, 1989.

Mosala, Itumeleng. "Black Theology in South Africa and North America: Prospects for the Future, Building of Alliances." *Journal of Black Theology* 1, 2 (November 1987): 35–41.

Mosala, Itumeleng, and Buti Tlhagale, eds. *The Unquestionable Right to Be Free.* Maryknoll, N.Y.: Orbis, 1986.

Motlhabi, Mokgethi, ed. *Essays on Black Theology.* Johannesburg: University Christian Movement, 1972.

Mudge, Lewis S., and James N. Poling, eds. *The Promise of Practical Theology: Formation and Reflection.* Philadelphia: Fortress, 1987.

Nicolson, Ronald. *A Black Future? Jesus and Salvation in South Africa.* London: SCM, 1990.

Niebuhr, H. Richard. *Christ and Culture.* New York: Harper & Row, 1951.

Nolan, Albert. *Jesus before Christianity.* 2nd ed. Maryknoll, N.Y.: Orbis, 1986.

Nolan, Albert. *God in South Africa: The Challenge of the Gospel.* Grand Rapids, Mich.: Eerdmans, 1988.

Norris, Christopher. *Uncritical Theory: Postmodernism, Intellectuals and the Gulf War.* London: Lawrence & Wishart, 1992.

Nürnberger, Klaus. "The Son Can Do Nothing by Himself: Identification and Authority as Modern Interpretations of the Doctrine of a Divine and Human Nature in the One Person of Christ." *Journal of Theology for Southern Africa* 87 (June 1994): 11–28.

Ogden, Schubert M. *Faith and Freedom: Toward a Theology of Liberation.* Belfast: Christian Journals, 1979.

Ogden, Schubert M. "The Concept of a Theology of Liberation: Must a Christian Theology Today Be so Conceived?" In *The Challenge of Liberation Theology: A First World Response,* edited by B. Mahan and L. D. Richesin. Maryknoll, N.Y.: Orbis, 1981.

Okure, Teresa. "Reflection on Luke 8:40-56." In *The Will to Arise: Women, Tradition and the Church in Africa,* edited by M. A. Oduyoye and M. A. R. Kanyoro. Maryknoll, N.Y.: Orbis, 1992.

Omoyajowo, Akin J. "An African Expression of Christianity." In *Essays in Black Theology,* edited by Mokgethi Motlhabi. Johannesburg: University Christian Movement, 1972.

Oosthuizen, C. G. *Post-Christianity in Africa: A Theological and Anthropological Study.* London: C. Hurst, 1968.

Pelikan, Jaroslav. *The Christian Tradition: A History of the Development of Doctrine, I: The Emergence of the Catholic Tradition (100–600),* Chicago: Chicago University Press, 1971.

Petersen, Robin. "Time, Resistance and Reconstruction: Rethinking Kairos Theology in South Africa." Ph.D. diss., University of Chicago, 1995.

Philpott, Graham. *Jesus Is Tricky and God Is Undemocratic: The Kin-dom of God in Amawoti.* Pietermaritzburg, South Africa: Cluster Publications, 1993.

Pixley, Jorgé, and Clodivus Boff. *The Bible, the Church and the Poor: Biblical, Theological and Pastoral Aspects of the Option for the Poor.* Turnbridge Wells, Kent: Burns & Oates, 1989.

Richard, Paul. *Death of Christendoms, Birth of the Church.* Maryknoll, N.Y.: Orbis, 1987.

Ricoeur, Paul. *The Symbolism of Evil.* Boston: Beacon Press, 1969.

Ricoeur, Paul. *Hermeneutics and the Human Sciences,* edited by J. B. Thompson. Cambridge: Cambridge University Press, 1981.

Ricoeur, Paul. *Time and Narrative,* translated by K. McLaughlin and D. Pellauer. Chicago: University of Chicago Press, 1984.

Ricoeur, Paul. *From Text to Action: Essays in Hermeneutics II.* Evanston, Ill.: Northwestern University Press, 1991.

Ricoeur, Paul. *Oneself as Another,* translated by K. Blamey. Chicago: University of Chicago Press, 1992.

Rückert, Heribert. *Afrikanische Theologie: Darstellung und Dialog.* Innsbruck/Vienna: Tyrolia, 1985.

Schreiter, Robert J. *Constructing Local Theologies.* Maryknoll, N.Y.: Orbis, 1985.

Schumacher, E. F. *Small Is Beautiful: A Study of Economics as if People Mattered.* London: Blond & Briggs, 1973.

Schüssler Fiorenza, Elisabeth. "Commitment and Critical Inquiry." *Harvard Theological Review,* 82, 1 (1989): 1–11.

Schüssler Fiorenza, Elisabeth. *But She Said: Feminist Practices of Biblical Interpretation.* Boston: Beacon, 1992.

Schüssler Fiorenza, Elisabeth. *Jesus: Miriam's Child, Sophia's Prophet.* New York: Continuum, 1994.

Scott, James C. *Domination and the Arts of Resistance: Hidden Transcripts.* New Haven, Conn.: Yale University Press, 1990.

Sebidi, Lebamang. "The Dynamics of the Black Struggle and Its Implications for Black Theology." In *The Unquestionable Right to Be Free,* edited by Itumeleng Mosala and Buti Tlhgale. Maryknoll, N.Y.: Orbis, 1986.

Segundo, Juan Luis. *The Liberation of Theology,* translated by John Drury. Dublin: Gill & Macmillan, 1977.

Segundo, Juan Luis. *The Liberation of Dogma: Faith, Revelation, and Dogmatic Teaching Authority,* translated by Phillip Berryman. Maryknoll, N.Y.: Orbis, 1992.

Sobrino, Jon. *The True Church and the Poor.* London: SCM, 1985.

Soskice, Janet. *Metaphor and Religious Language.* Oxford: Clarendon, 1985.

Spivak, Gayatri. "Can the Subaltern Speak?" In *Marxism and the Interpretation of Culture,* edited by C. Nelson and L. Grossberg. London: MacMillan, 1988, 271–313.

Stendahl, Krister. "Paul and the Introspective Conscience of the West." In *Paul among Jews and Gentiles*. Philadelphia: Fortress, 1976.

Stout, J. *Ethics after Babel*. Boston: Beacon Press, 1988.

Sundkler, Bengt G. M. *Bantu Prophets in South Africa*. London: Oxford University Press, 1961 (2nd Edition).

Tillich, Paul. *Love, Power and Justice*. Oxford: Oxford University Press, 1960.

Toulmin, Stephen. *Cosmopolis: The Hidden Agenda of Modernity*. New York: Free Press, 1990.

Tracy, David. *The Analogical Imagination: Christian Theology and the Culture of Pluralism*. London: SCM, 1981.

Tracy, David. "Lindbeck's New Programme for Theology." *The Thomist* 49 (1985): 470ff.

Turner, Stephen. *The Social Theory of Practices: Tradition, Tacit Knowledge, and Presuppositions*. Chicago: University of Chicago Press, 1994.

Turner, Victor. *The Ritual Process: Structure and Anti-Structure*. New York: Cornell University, 1977.

Verryn, Trevor D. *A History of the Order of Ethiopia*. Johannesburg: Central Mission Press, 1971.

Villa-Vicencio, Charles. *Between Christ and Caesar: Classic and Contemporary Texts on Church and State*. Cape Town: David Philip, 1986.

Villa-Vicencio, Charles. *A Theology of Reconstruction*. Cambridge: Cambridge University Press, 1992.

Walker, Megan. "Tradition, Criticism and Popular Religion: A Hermeneutic Investigation of Marian Theology." M.A. diss., University of Natal, 1992.

Walshe, Peter. *Church Versus State in South Africa: The Case of the Christian Institute*. London: Hurst, 1983.

Welch, Sharon D. *Communities of Resistance and Solidarity: A Feminist Theology of Liberation*. Maryknoll, N.Y.: Orbis, 1985.

Welch, Sharon D. *A Feminist Ethic of Risk*. Minneapolis: Fortress Press, 1990.

West, Gerald O. *Biblical Hermeneutics of Liberation: Modes of Reading the Bible*. 2nd ed. Maryknoll, N.Y.: Orbis, 1995.

West, Martin. *Bishops and Prophets in a Black City*. Cape Town: David Philip, 1975.

Williams, Raymond. *Keywords: A Vocabulary of Culture and Society*. London: Oxford University Press, 1976.

Wittenberg, Gunther. "King Solomon and the Theologians." Inaugural Professorial Lecture presented to the University of Natal, Pietermaritzburg, August 1987, published 1988.

Wittenberg, Gunther. "The Relevance of Historical Geography for Old Testament Theology with Special Reference to Exodus 34:10-26." Paper presented at Society for Historical Geography, Stellenbosch, South Africa, March 1995.

Worsnip, Michael, and Desmond van der Water, eds. *We Shall Overcome: A Spirituality of Liberation*. Pietermaritzburg, South Africa: Cluster Publications, 1991.

Index

Mahler, Gustav, 154-55
Mandela, Nelson, 32, 90-91
Mandew, Martin, 6-7, 72-75
Marginalization, 8, 81, 101, 105, 133, 148, 166, 168
Marx, Karl, 72, 86
Mary, image of, 145
Maslow, Abraham, 34-35
McGaughey, Douglas, 64-69, 116-17, 141, 182 nn. 68, 60, 63
Mead, George Herbert, 189 n. 78
Meaning, 105
    reproduction of, 84
Memmi, Albert, 187 n. 57
Memory, 143
    and the dead, 37
Migratory labor policies, 186 n. 44
Min, Anselm, 55, 97, 101, 107
Mind, 64
Mission, as internal, 149
Modernism/modernity, 2, 82, 134, 154, 157, 163
Mofekeng, Takatso, xvi, 28, 88, 176 n. 13
Mohanty, Chandra, 165-66
Moltmann, Jürgen, 17, 33, 53, 59, 196 n. 43
Mosala, Itumeleng, 43, 50, 172 n. 10, 188 n. 73
Mutuality, 108, 110
Mystery, role of, 141

Narrative identity, 95, 107, 111, 139, 160-61
Nicolson, Ronald, 50
Nolan, Albert, 34, 60, 86, 176 n. 23
Nominalism, 64-65
Nomos, 183 n. 73
Normative agreements, 131
Norms
    Analytical, 87
    in theology, 54, 159-60
    justifiable, 130
Nous, 183 n. 73. See also Mind
Nürnberger, Klaus, 181 n. 46

Objectivism, 134-35
Okure, Teresa, 2, 8
Ontology, 65, 158
    of the self, 106, 110
Ordinary reader/believer, xvii, 15-18, 22, 62, 120, 123, 142, 144, 149, 154, 160, 189 n. 4
Orthodoxy, 61, 85, 145, 158, 196 n. 43
Other, the 95-96, 106-10, 113-14, 169
    as judge, 106-7

Paradigm shift, 103, 133
Paradox, 106, 121, 141

Particularity, 28, 43, 63, 102, 120, 126, 133, 158, 160, 161
Pastoral psychology,
Patriarchy, 159, 163-64
Paul, Saint, 178 n. 1
Pelikan, Jaroslav, 178 n. 4
Personal, and the public, 82, 122, 136, 142
Petersen, Robin, 87, 172 n. 11, 187 nn. 60, 61
Philpott, Graham, 174 n. 42
Place, and space, 165
Plato
    and universals. See Universals
    simile of the line, 65, 182 n. 60
Plurality, 62, 103
Polis, 103, 134
Poor, the, 25
    as category, 190 n. 10
    preferential option for, 38, 56, 98, 101-2, 133, 146, 149, 160
Popular religion, 46, 85, 87, 187 n. 54
Possibility, and actuality, 57, 65-66, 68-69, 116
Postmodernism, 48-49, 102, 104, 171 n.2b
Poverty, reality of, 13
Power, 31-32, 71-88, 110-111, 136, 143, 164
    agentive, 79, 96
    and powerlessness, 106
    and redemption, 29
    as asymmetric, 72, 79, 92, 110
    as diffuse, 50
    as positive, 32, 76, 97-98, 177 n. 30
    binary understanding of, 78-79, 84
    competence as, 81
    decoding of, 87, 92
    distinctions about, 72, 76, 110-111, 114, 184 n. 3
    from below, 75
    networks of, 77-82
Practical reason. See Reason: practical
Pragmatism, 182 n. 63
Praxis, 38, 103, 129, 132, 191 n. 50
    and speech/language, 137, 139
Prejudice, notion of, 152
Privatization, 157
    cult of, 53, 180 n. 37
Protestants, 57, 198 n. 9
Public, meaning of, 90, 123, 134
Public sphere, and theology. See Theology: public character of

Rationality, 125-26, 131
Reason
    critique of pure, 104
    mundane, 127
    practical, 113